ETHICAL LEADERSHIP AND DECISION MAKING IN EDUCATION

The third edition of the best-selling text, *Ethical Leadership and Decision Making in Education*, continues to address the increasing interest in ethics and assists educational leaders with the complex dilemmas in today's challenging and diverse society. Through discussion and analysis of real-life moral dilemmas that educational leaders face in their schools and communities, authors Shapiro and Stefkovich demonstrate the application of the four ethical paradigms—the ethics of justice, care, critique, and profession. After an illustration of how the Multiple Ethical Paradigm approach may be applied to real dilemmas, the authors present a series of cases written by students and academics in the field representing the dilemmas faced by practicing educational leaders in urban, suburban, and rural settings in an era full of complexities and contradictions. Following each case are questions that call for thoughtful, complex thinking and help readers come to grips with their own ethical codes and apply them to practical situations.

New in the Third Edition:

- An entire new chapter on privacy versus safety, including ethical issues such as strip searches, gang membership, cyber-bullying, and sexting.
- New cases infused into chapters on early childhood education, diverse student populations, and technology.
- Updates throughout to reflect contemporary issues and recent scholarship in the field of ethical leadership.

Including teaching notes for the instructor stressing the importance of self-reflection, this text is easily adaptable for a variety of uses with a wide range of audiences. *Ethical Leadership and Decision Making in Education* is a valuable book for both aspiring and practicing administrators, teacher leaders, and educational policy makers.

Joan Poliner Shapiro is Professor of Educational Administration at Temple University and Co-Founder of the New DEEL (Democratic Ethical Educational Leadership) movement.

Jacqueline A. Stefkovich is Professor of Education Law and Ethics at The Pennsylvania State University and Co-Director of the UCEA's D.J. Willower Center for the Study of Ethics and Leadership.

ETHICAL LEADERSHIP AND DECISION MAKING IN EDUCATION

APPLYING THEORETICAL PERSPECTIVES TO COMPLEX DILEMMAS

Third Edition

Joan Poliner Shapiro
Jacqueline A. Stefkovich

Routledge
Taylor & Francis Group

NEW YORK AND LONDON

First edition published 2001
by Lawrence Erlbaum Associates, Inc.

Second edition published 2005
by Lawrence Erlbaum Associates, Inc.

This edition published 2011
by Routledge
711 Third Avenue, New York, NY 10017

Simultaneously published in the UK
by Routledge
2 Park Square, Milton Park, Abingdon, Oxon OX14 4RN

Routledge is an imprint of the Taylor & Francis Group, an informa business

© 2001, 2005 Lawrence Erlbaum Associates, Inc.
© 2011 Taylor & Francis

Typeset in New Baskerville
by Keystroke, Tettenhall, Wolverhampton

Library of Congress Cataloging-in-Publication Data
Shapiro, Joan Poliner.
Ethical leadership and decision making in education : applying theoretical perspectives to complex dilemmas / by Joan Poliner Shapiro and Jacqueline A. Stefkovich. — 3rd ed.
p. cm.
1. Educational leadership—Moral and ethical aspects—United States. 2. School administrators—Professional ethics—United States. 3. School management and organization—Moral and ethical aspects—United States. 4. Ethics—Study and teaching—United States. 5. Decision making—United States. I. Stefkovich, Jacqueline Anne, 1947– II. Title.
LB1779.S416 2010
371.2′011—dc22
2010017579

ISBN 13: 978–0–415–87460–1 (hbk)
ISBN 13: 978–0–415–87459–5 (pbk)
ISBN 13: 978–0–203–84959–0 (ebk)

Contents

Preface

Since the publication of the first edition of this book, the world has become more unstable owing to terrorism, wars, and financial uncertainty. The impact of different cultures and religions as well as the advancement of technology and the emphasis on high stakes testing in many educational systems has also changed our society and the world. To deal with some of these changes, in the second edition of this book we added two new chapters. One chapter emphasized religious differences and presented the contradictions between religion and culture. The other chapter focused on testing, juxtaposing the paradox of accountability with responsibility. We also added several dilemmas focusing on higher education, recognizing that many educational leadership preparation programs include students with this focus.

For the third edition, our editor asked a number of faculty members from the U.S. and abroad, who have used our book, what they felt should be added as we move further into the 21st Century. In response to their valuable comments, we have added a chapter on privacy versus safety that focuses on ethical issues dealing with drug use, strip searches, and gang membership. This chapter also contains, under the rubric of technology, problems of cyber-bullying on the internet, and sexting and sexual orientation made public via cell phones. We have also infused early childhood and special education cases in a number of the chapters. Beyond these new cases, there are modifications, throughout this book, that make it more up-to-date. The revisions include citations that will keep the reader current in the field of ethical leadership.

Initially, the impetus for writing this book came from three developments in the field of educational leadership: (1) a burgeoning interest in the study of ethics among educational leaders, (2) a rising tendency to use case studies as a method of reflection on administrative problems, and (3) the introduction of licensure standards for school leaders that require an understanding of ethical issues.

Keeping these developments in mind, this Preface addresses the purposes of this book, what this book contains, how it is organized, and how the information provided fills a gap in the educational leadership knowledge base. Also included is a brief introduction to the instructor who decides to teach a course using this book and acknowledgments to those who have been helpful in seeing this work through to its publication.

PURPOSE OF THIS BOOK

This book has several purposes. First, it demonstrates the application of different ethical paradigms through the discussion and analysis of real-life moral dilemmas. Second, it addresses some of the practical, pedagogical, and curricular issues related to the teaching of ethics for educational leaders. Third, it emphasizes the importance of ethics instruction from a variety of theoretical approaches. Finally, this book provides a process that instructors might follow to develop their own ethics unit or course.

CONTENTS AND ORGANIZATION

This book discusses how students and practitioners should take into account each of four paradigms presented (i.e., the ethic of justice, the ethic of care, the ethic of critique, and the ethic of the profession) to help solve authentic dilemmas. We have structured these dilemmas with key questions to assist the readers to think in ways that they may not have considered in the past. These questions may also help to open the minds of students, practitioners, or both when introduced to the four paradigms in the book. If they are presented as options, these paradigms may help students and practitioners to better solve complex dilemmas in today's challenging and diverse society.

Part I, comprising the first two chapters of this book, provides an overview of why ethics is so important, especially for today's educational leaders, and describes the Multiple Ethical Paradigms framework that can be essential to practitioners as they grapple with ethical dilemmas.

Part II deals with the dilemmas themselves. After a brief introduction as to how the cases were constructed, an illustration is provided of how the multi-paradigm approach may be applied to a real dilemma. This example is followed by chapters 3 through 10, which contain ethical dilemmas written primarily by graduate students and by some colleagues. These are the kinds of dilemmas faced by practicing educational leaders in urban, suburban, and rural settings in an era full of complexities and contradictions.

Part III focuses on pedagogy. Chapter 11 provides teaching notes to the instructor. To do this, we, as professors and authors,[1] discuss the importance of self-reflection on the part of instructors as well as students. We model how we thought through our own personal and professional ethical codes as well as reflected on the critical incidents in our lives that shaped our teaching and frequently determined what we privileged or emphasized in class.

THE CASE STUDY APPROACH TO TEACHING ETHICS

The case study approach to teaching educators has garnered considerable interest in the past few years. Much of this interest has been stimulated by educational theories focusing on the merits of reflective practice (Dewey, 1902) and prompted by the successful use of cases for the training of business leaders, an effort spearheaded by Harvard University's Business School. Indeed, Nash (1996), in his book on professional ethics, pointed out that "a good case can be a provocative, almost indispensable tool for teaching the relevant moral concepts" (p. 64). In response to this interest, a number of authors have written case books aimed at teaching (Cooper, 1995; Goodlad, Soder, & Sirotnik, 1990; Greenwood & Fillmer, 1997; Strike & Soltis, 1992) and at general aspects of educational administration (Asbaugh & Kasten, 1995; Kirschmann, 1996; Merseth, 1997; Willower & Licata, 1997). A few others have written texts with case studies in ethics focused on higher education (Strike & Moss, 2007) and a general population (e.g., Glaser, 1994).

There are also a number of fine scholarly ethics books aimed at educational administrators (e.g., Beck, 1994; Beckner, 2004; Begley & Johansson, 2003; Fullan, 2003; Rebore, 2001; Starratt, 1994b, 2003, 2004). In 1988, Strike, Haller, and Soltis combined a scholarly approach with cases to present a textbook of ethical dilemmas aimed specifically at the problems faced by educational administrators. Their approach to ethics has been primarily from a justice perspective.

In the past few years, however, there has been a resurgence of interest in and recognition of the importance of ethics for educational leaders. Here, the justice perspective has been joined by other approaches, such as care (Katz, Noddings, & Strike, 1999; Noddings, 1984, 2003; Sernak, 1998); and critique (Apple, 2004, 2006; Purpel, 2004; Starratt, 2003). More recently,

---

[1] The authorship of this book is in alphabetical order. Both authors contributed equally to the writing of this book.

the four ethics of justice, care, critique, and the profession have been combined with the concept of school law (Stefkovich, 2006) and with turbulence theory (Gross & Shapiro, 2004; Shapiro & Gross, 2008; Shapiro, Gross & Shapiro, 2008). In addition, the profession of educational leadership has recognized a need for ethics' competencies or standards. Such developments have exposed gaps in the knowledge base that cry out for a response.

GAPS IN THE KNOWLEDGE BASE

The idea for the first edition of this book germinated over a nine-year period during which we taught ethics to diverse educational leaders. During this time, we came to realize the dearth of materials available for our training. We advocate reflective practice and, thus, saw the benefits of including a case study approach as part of our instruction. However, most of the case books we could find either focused broadly on educators in general and did not consider the unique problems of educational leaders, or centered on educational administrators but not on ethical issues, or did both but only discussed ethics primarily from a justice perspective (Strike et al., 1988).

Viewing ethics through different paradigms is a relatively recent phenomenon. Hence, few texts have been developed that discuss ethical dilemmas from multiple perspectives (i.e., to include the ethics of care and critique as well as justice). When we began our work, scholars and practitioners were concerned with issues of professional ethics, but none had grappled with the concept of professional ethics as a separate paradigm. Ten years later, with the advent of this third edition of our book, many faculty as well as doctoral students throughout the United States and abroad have incorporated this concept of the ethic of the profession into their teaching and doctoral dissertations.

Thus, we see this book as complementing others that have gone before it by filling a real gap in the knowledge base of ethics training for educational leaders. It provides a conceptual model for the analysis of professional ethics and then includes dilemmas and questions designed to stimulate discussion, taking into account the ethics of justice, care, critique, and the profession.

We believe our approach is an authentic one, incorporating the voices of our students and using many dilemmas that they have developed in our classes. We believe that this approach, although somewhat unorthodox, responds to Nash's (1996) concerns and observations when he said, "The difficulty I have with some textbook cases . . . is that they are oftentimes so overly dramatic they make no claim to verisimilitude. . . . I have found over the years that the best provenance for cases is in my students' own work lives" (p. 64).

Finally, we believe there is merit in providing a process by which professors and practitioners alike can come to grips with their own ethical codes and then apply these codes to practical situations. We have both incorporated this approach into our own teaching and have found it most helpful.

TEACHING NOTES TO THE INSTRUCTOR

We have taken considerable time to design this book so that it can be easily used for instructional purposes. In Chapter 2, we give an overview of multiple ethical perspectives that instructors might wish to present to the students. Additionally, in each of the chapters that contain ethical dilemmas, we offer a series of questions to assist the instructor in facilitating the discussion of each dilemma.

In the teaching of ethics, we not only ask instructors to help students reflect on their own personal values and professional beliefs, but we strongly encourage instructors to do the same. We believe it is imperative that we all become reflective practitioners when attempting to solve ethical dilemmas. We do not advocate one best way to accomplish this task, but we do provide some detailed information in Chapter 11 as to how we have taught ethics to our students by engaging in a process of self-reflection. We not only invite instructors to read this chapter but we hope that students will find this section of interest as well.

We have also designed this book so that it is easily adaptable for a variety of uses with a wide range of audiences. It may be used either as a basic or supplementary text for university courses related to the preparation of educational leaders, including, but not limited to, principals, super-intendents, curriculum coordinators, personnel administrators, business administrators, higher education administrators and faculty, teacher leaders, and early childhood directors. It is appropriate for either intro-ductory or advanced levels of educational administration programs and may be infused into almost all of the educational administration curricula or taught in a discrete ethics course in any educational area.

This book may also be used as an excellent professional reference for aspiring and practicing school leaders, central office personnel, educational policy makers, state department personnel, and regional- and federal-level education staff. Others interested in the book as a reference might include school board members, parents' organizations, and professional asso-ciations. Moreover, we do not see this case book as limited to the United States; professionals working in other countries have responded positively to the dilemmas we have presented.

Acknowledgments

We thank Heather Jarrow, Associate Editor in Education from Routledge, as well as Naomi Silverman, formerly from Erlbaum and now from Routledge, for their helpful and insightful suggestions. We also thank the following reviewers who provided worthwhile and useful feedback on our first through third editions: William P. Foster, University of Indiana; William D. Greenfield, Portland State University; Larry W. Hughes, University of Houston; Marla Israel, Loyola University; Sharon D. Kruse, University of Akron; Carl Lashley, University of North Carolina, Greensboro; Nel Noddings, Stanford University; Katarina Norberg, Umea University; Anthony Normore, California State University—Dominguez Hills; Ellen Reames, Auburn University; H. Svi Shapiro, University of North Carolina, Greensboro and Ronald Williamson, Eastern Michigan University. We appreciate the efforts of all our student contributors (but we are especially grateful to the lead authors in each of the dilemma chapters—Patricia A.L. Ehrensal, Kathrine J. Gutierrez, James K. Krause, Hollie J. Mackey, G. Michaele O'Brien, Leon D. Poeske, and Deborah Weaver). Not only did they contribute through their writing, but they spent endless hours coordinating the work of their co-contributors into a coherent chapter.

In addition, we appreciate all the valuable input from the following: Judy Leonard, Staff Assistant at Penn State's Department of Educational Policy Studies, who provided detailed and meticulous assistance in the final editing and formatting stages of the second and third editions; Tom Dodd, Emily Crawford, and Mehnaz Jehan, Penn State graduate assistants who diligently tracked down our contributors and updated their biographical statements; Temple University's Educational Leadership & Policy Studies (ELPS) 1998 and 1999 doctoral cohorts, who piloted earlier drafts of our cases; Robert

D. McCaig and Lynn Cheddar for their preliminary editing of the first edition, and all our students who, throughout the years, have helped us not only to formulate our professional ethical paradigm but also to grow as professors and as human beings.

PRACTICE AND PARADIGMS IN THE STUDY OF ETHICS

Part I sets the stage for exploring and solving the ethical dilemmas that make up a central portion (Part II) of this book. It serves as an introduction and consists of chapters 1 and 2.

Chapter 1 offers a brief overview of the Multiple Ethical Paradigms as a framework. It also deals with the framework's applicability, and its importance in view of the complexities and diversity of this current era. It incorporates the voices of our students, who support our assertion that the study of ethics is needed for all school leaders, particularly in light of changes in society. This chapter explores implications for practice and for programs aimed at the preparation of educational leaders.

Chapter 2 describes the conceptual framework underlying our teaching and scholarship in the area of ethics. Here, we stress the importance of preparation for educational leaders in the ethics of justice, care, and critique. To these we add a fourth ethic: that of the profession. It is in this chapter that we explain our framework for understanding and using ethics. The discussion of the four paradigms is meant to encourage the reader to deal with the ethical dilemmas, which follow in Part II, in a multi-dimensional way.

We believe it is important to try out diverse approaches for the solving of ethical cases even for those of us who usually respond to dilemmas as moral absolutists or as moral relativists, or react to cases using only one or two ethical paradigms. Practice in working through a multiple ethical paradigm process should provide current and future educational leaders with options for dealing with complex and difficult ethical dilemmas that they will face daily.

Chapter 1

Multiple Ethical Paradigms and the Preparation of Educational Leaders in a Diverse and Complex Era

> *Of all the courses I have taken, at all levels, this course has no boundaries. What I mean is all the materials we have read, the discussions we have had and the lessons I have learned, directly impact all I will study and all I will do. . . . Ethics courses should not be only for students who are interested in going on to law school or medical school. [They] should be for students who are interested in becoming citizens. . . . If anyone ever challenges the relevance of a course such as this in an educational leadership curriculum, [he or she is] not an educated individual.* (Graduate student in educational leadership)

Foster (1986) expressed the seriousness and importance of ethics in educational administration when he wrote, "Each administrative decision carries with it a restructuring of human life: that is why administration at its heart is the resolution of moral dilemmas" (p. 33). In this paradoxical, unstable, and ethically polarized era, we began to think that there was a need to offer differing perspectives to help educational leaders solve real-life dilemmas that they frequently face in their schools and in their communities.

In this chapter, we discuss the complexities of this era, particularly as they relate to schools and leadership in an increasingly diverse society. We also discuss why ethical leadership is needed, especially as we deal with this new millennium. We then introduce a multiple ethical paradigm approach to assist educational leaders in grappling with complexities, uncertainty, and diversity.

This section ends with comments relative to the training of practitioners. Throughout this discussion, we emphasize the voices of our numerous and diverse graduate students, many of whom indicate support and provide a basis for our belief that the teaching of ethics is critical in the preparation of educational leaders.

ETHICAL LEADERSHIP IN A COMPLEX AND DIVERSE SOCIETY

In the 21st Century, as society becomes even more demographically diverse, educators will, more than ever, need to be able to develop, foster, and lead tolerant and democratic schools. We believe that, through the study of ethics, educational leaders of tomorrow will be better prepared to recognize, reflect on, and appreciate differences. This need for ethical preparation is perhaps best expressed by our own graduate students, many of whom are practitioners in schools and in colleges and universities.

Consider the words of this woman, who, in her journal, described the essence of this need by writing about some of the scandals of the 1990s involving high-ranking government officials, rock stars, and athletes. Her words captured our imaginations, mainly because of their empowering effect on school leaders, and they appear just as relevant, if not more so, to this new century. She wrote:

> Given this admittedly bleak picture of life in the not-so-moral America of the 90s, it does not seem hyperbolic to say that we, as educators and administrators in our nation's schools, may well be part of an ever-dwindling group of citizens who continue to form a bastion against the growing phenomenon of unethical behavior in our country. How then could a program aimed at preparing men and women to serve as administrators in our nation's educational institutions possibly be considered complete without the inclusion of a course that requires would-be pedagogical leaders to examine both their personal and professional ethics and the impact that their ethical codes will have on their day-to-day administrative decision making?

Likewise, many of our students made direct connections between what was taught in our ethics class and the importance of diversity. Here, we use a broad definition of *diversity* that encompasses the cultural categories of race/ethnicity, religion, social class, gender, disability, and sexual orientation as well as individual differences in learning styles, exceptionalities, and age (Banks, 2001; Banks & Banks, 2006; Cushner, McClelland, & Safford, 1992; Gay, 2000, 2003; Gollnick & Chinn, 1998; Nieto, 2007; Shapiro, Sewell, & DuCette, 2001; Sleeter & Grant, 2003).

As one of our students, a White, male biology professor in a rural setting, pointed out:

> I believe that there is strength in diversity. Diverse biological ecosystems are more stable, might this also be true of social systems? How can we prevent institutions from co-opting women and other minorities and instead cherish the diversity they provide? As educators, we must strive to foster diversity as a source of variability enabling our society to adapt and contribute constructively in a rapidly changing world.

During our teaching of ethics, we also began to recognize that diversity was not only across students, but within each group of students as well. For example, our classes contained a number of students of color; yet, in some instances, race seemed to be their only commonality. Although of the same race, some of these students were male and others were female. Some were in their twenties, whereas others were closer to 50. Some were African American; others were from non-American countries. Some were from urban areas; others lived and worked in suburbia. Some came from poverty, others from affluence. Therefore, many of the perspectives that these particular students of color held were not race-bound, but were influenced just as much or more so by demographics, culture, age, gender, or by a combination of these factors.

Illustrative of this concept is a comment from an African-American female who observed issues relative to age, race, and gender:

> It has been my experience that younger women in my classes think this feminist thing is blown out of proportion because they have not faced any of the glass ceilings society can impose. The historical perspective is essential in order that males and females have some basis for challenging themselves and their assumptions with respect to race and gender. Perhaps the humanistic, caring leader is the answer, or at least the best possibility on the horizon. Politics and social reforms have not solved the problem, so educators—with the eventual help of parents—must.

Similarly, division across gender lines was not always the case. In all of our classes, there were often differences of opinion between women, with some taking a more traditional justice perspective and others favoring feminist approaches such as those of Gilligan (1982) and Noddings (1992, 2003). In addition, there were always men who made sure the class understood that women did not corner the market on caring. A number of men and women alike asserted that caring was not gender-specific, especially in professions such as education. As one such student said, "We are all in the caring business, so how can we not consider what is best for all people concerned in these situations?"

Religion, too, in combination with other factors such as gender and age, influenced students' perceptions. Consider the comments of this White male teacher in his thirties who expressed his reactions on reading Gilligan's abortion dilemmas. He wrote:

> I found myself considering the different feelings that women must go through in considering an issue such as abortion. Even though my own personal belief is one that centers around my religious upbringing, I felt myself struggling with the decisions that had to be made.

Thus, in considering themes of diversity, we found that no one characteristic of students (e.g., race, gender, age, religion, professional experience) resulted in a monolithic view of ethics. Rather, students' views of ethics emanated from a combination of diverse factors and cut across lines of race and gender. A Black, female foreign student in her late fifties summed up the importance of ethics in a diverse society when she presented this global, cross-cultural view:

> I think the effort of finding our voice(s) is going to continue for a long time, and it will also continue along lines of class, race, ethnicity, and other divisiveness; we will in no way speak with almost one voice until the pendulum swings again in the opposite direction. But with each shift, we pick up more and more contentious issues.

However, perhaps this urban-based, African-American male best captured issues related to our complex and diverse society when he made this observation. Reflecting on personal liberty rather than the public good, he asked: "Who is the public? Who is the majority? And how do educational leaders fit into this scheme?" He described his dilemma as follows:

> I work with a colleague who prides himself on being able to treat all of his students the same way. Regardless of race, economic status, or ability, he claims to have the means to maintain a completely unbiased view on all. After working with him for six years, I have noticed that he does not have this ability. On a regular basis, I see him playing favorites, making exceptions, and generally doing the exact thing he claims he does not do. As an administrator, he cannot afford to be so rigid. There must be some room for partiality. And he shows it (though he would not admit to it) daily. It seems to me that this inability to be impartial grows out of his position and, in fact, would evolve from any position of administration when the interests of minorities and the oppressed have to be served. A 21st-Century administrator must be ready to bend, adjust, and, when necessary, show partiality to those he/she serves if equity and justice are to be served.

This is only one illustration of the many types of paradoxes that educators must grapple with in making ethical decisions. To assist in the analysis of such dilemmas, we advocate a multiple paradigm approach that crosses over and combines various approaches to ethics.

THE IMPORTANCE OF THE MULTIPLE ETHICAL PARADIGMS

Throughout this book, the reader is asked to consider current and challenging real-life ethical dilemmas using four paradigms. The four paradigms include the ethics of justice, critique, care, and the profession. Justice, critique, and care are familiar to many in the field of educational leadership. All too often, however, professional ethics is seen as an extension of another paradigm and not thought to stand alone. That is why, in this book, we spend considerable time on the ethic of the profession rather than on the other three forms of ethics. We are convinced that this paradigm deserves to be treated as an independent model. We think that it is extremely important and complements the other paradigms.

We believe that it makes sense, when dealing with the ethic of the profession, for graduate students and practitioners to take the time to locate the formal codes of the profession and the standards of the field. Along with these activities, we strongly recommend that everyone write out personal and professional ethical codes and compare and contrast their two codes. In this way, educators can determine where consistencies exist between the codes and where clashes of codes might appear. These exercises lead to a much better understanding of "self" both as a professional and as a person. The four perspectives or paradigms should help educational leaders solve real-life, complex dilemmas that they frequently face in their institutions and in their communities.

By using the different paradigms, educators should become aware of the perspective or perspectives which they tend to use most often when solving ethical issues. For example, if an individual has a strong religious upbringing, then, depending on the religious persuasion, the ethic of justice with an emphasis on rights and laws may be the favored approach, or perhaps the ethic of care with its emphasis on compassion and empathy may be the paradigm of choice. In addition, as just mentioned, factors such as age, gender, race, or more likely a confluence of factors may influence the paradigm one prefers.

However, despite any inclinations toward one perspective, the intent of this book is to ask students and practitioners to open their minds by taking into account a variety of models, not simply one or two. Dilemmas in educational institutions can be complicated and may naturally lead to the use of two or more paradigms to solve problems. Today, with the complexity of situations and cultures, it seems more important than ever for educational leaders to think more broadly and go beyond "self" in an attempt to understand others.

In Chapter 11, we discuss our own experiences of self-reflection to provide some concrete examples of this process. Learning to be self-reflective is not easy. It requires a concentrated effort on the part of individuals. This can be accomplished in privacy. It can also be encouraged in a staff development program or as part of an educational leadership preparation program.

THE PREPARATION OF ETHICAL EDUCATIONAL LEADERS

In many ways, the teaching of ethics diverges from the traditional paths employed by many educational administration programs. Although we do not necessarily advocate that standard courses be changed, we do believe that the teaching of ethics can be a welcome and important addition to those programs. As one of our students wrote in her class journal:

> This course has been very enlightening. It has been a thought-provoking break from the practical mundane courses of educational administration. . . . My vision has increased and multiplied. Even though I still view the world with racial vision, I am now more in tune with my feminist "ear." I will investigate, read, and learn more and react more critically to my environment.

Others, through our classes, began to recognize the importance of ethics and its contribution to our larger society. This student, in particular, seemed to show a grasp of this bigger picture as it related to the issue of social justice:

> Social justice or equity really seems very obvious as a concept, but it apparently is necessary to make this topic a large part of the doctoral program because it is brought up so often in the readings and discussion. The result is that I am keenly aware of equity as an issue now, and I doubt that I will look at such issues the same as before I started the doctoral program. It is hard to know exactly what my thoughts were about equity before I started the program. I really can't say because the awareness has come so gradually.

Clearly, the majority of students in our courses wanted ethics taught as part of the educational leadership curriculum. In fact, there was no ambivalence in their wish that it be continued and even expanded as a disciplinary area in their program. This student's thoughts illustrate the types of comments that we have heard through the years:

> I feel it imperative for the administrator to be cognizant of . . . the need for institutions of higher learning to maintain a careful balance between those courses that are offered for some instrumental end and those which are offered merely for the sake of obtaining knowledge. I perceive that there is a greater societal pressure on the university for more of the former and less of the latter. We seem to place a much greater focus on acquiring knowledge for the sake of gaining employment than for the sheer joy of knowing. [Yet,] there is a special feeling, indescribable though it may be, in learning something that is new, different, and stimulating.

IN SUMMARY

In this book, we propose that there should not be one best ethical paradigm. Instead, we believe that by using different models, students, and practitioners will be able to work through their own personal and professional ethical codes, try out what they discovered about themselves by reflecting on the solutions they reach as they analyze diverse ethical dilemmas, and gain greater insights into the conceptual underpinnings of the ethical paradigm or paradigms they have chosen.

While analyzing the dilemmas in chapters 3 through 10, educational graduate students and practitioners should consciously reflect on the processes used to find solutions to cases. Along with the analysis related to a case, each individual should be able to do a great deal of reflection and soul-searching about his or her private code and professional code and should be open-minded enough to revise either of them as self-awareness and growth occur.

It is our hope that this book will empower educational leaders, including, but not limited to, principals, superintendents, curriculum coordinators, personnel administrators, business administrators, higher education administrators and faculty, teacher leaders, and early childhood directors to make wise ethical decisions in a complex, chaotic, and contradictory era.

Chapter 2

Viewing Ethical Dilemmas
Through Multiple Paradigms

According to John Dewey (1902), *ethics* is the science that deals with conduct insofar as this is considered to be right or wrong, good or bad. Ethics comes from the Greek word *ethos*, which means customs or usages, especially belonging to one group as distinguished from another. Later, ethics came to mean disposition or character, customs, and approved ways of acting. Looking at this definition from a critical perspective, one might ask: Ethics approved by whom? Right or wrong according to whom?

In this chapter, in an attempt to answer these and other important questions, we turn to three kinds of ethics emanating from diverse traditions that impact on education in general and educational leadership in particular. These paradigms include ethics from three viewpoints: justice, critique, and care. To these we add a fourth model, that of the ethic of the profession. What follows is a broad overview of the ethics of justice, critique, and care, and a more detailed explanation of the ethic of the profession.

Regarding the ethics of justice, critique, and care, we would like you to keep in mind that these are broad descriptions. Our intent for these three kinds of ethics is to provide enough of an introduction to the paradigms or models to enable you to receive a general sense of each of them. In an effort to be brief, we have had to leave out some outstanding scholars whose works are related to each of the paradigms. For in-depth coverage of scholars and their work regarding the ethics of justice, critique, and care, we suggest that you turn to our references in this book, locate other readings related to the models, and move beyond these introductory remarks.

In the case of the ethic of the profession, however, special attention is given to this paradigm. We do this because we believe there has been a gap in the educational leadership literature in using the paradigm of professional ethics to help solve moral dilemmas. All too frequently, the ethic of the profession is seen as simply a part of the justice paradigm. We do not believe this is so, and we want to make the argument that this form of ethics can be used separately as a fourth lens for reflecting on, and then dealing with, dilemmas faced by educational leaders. Therefore, what we present in this chapter is a more involved discussion of the ethic of the profession than of the other three paradigms.

THE ETHIC OF JUSTICE

The ethic of justice focuses on rights and law and is part of a liberal democratic tradition that, according to Delgado (1995), "is characterized by incrementalism, faith in the legal system, and hope for progress" (p. 1). The liberal part of this tradition is defined as a "commitment to human freedom," and the democratiç aspect implies "procedures for making decisions that respect the equal sovereignty of the people" (Strike, 1991, p. 415).

Starratt (1994b) described the ethic of justice as emanating from two schools of thought, one originating in the 17th Century, including the work of Hobbes and Kant and more contemporary scholars such as Rawls and Kohlberg; the other rooted in the works of philosophers such as Aristotle, Rousseau, Hegel, Marx, and Dewey. The former school considers the individual as central and sees social relationships as a type of a social contract where the individual, using human reason, gives up some rights for the good of the whole or for social justice. The latter tends to see society, rather than the individual, as central and seeks to teach individuals how to behave throughout their life within communities. In this tradition, justice emerges from "communal understandings" (p. 50).

Philosophers and writers coming from a justice perspective frequently deal with issues such as the nature of the universe, the nature of God, fate versus free will, good and evil, and the relationship between human beings and their state. Beauchamp and Childress (1984) and Crittenden (1984) describe competitive concepts related to the ethic of justice. Although acknowledging other perspectives and their positive aspects in their writings, Beauchamp and Childress, and Crittenden return to the ethic of justice and argue that educational leaders in societies whose governments are committed to certain fundamental principles, such as tolerance and respect for the fair treatment of all individuals, can and should look to laws and public policies for ethical guidance (Beck & Murphy, 1994b, p. 7).

Educators and ethicists from the ethic of justice have had a profound impact on approaches to education and educational leadership. Contemporary ethical writings in education, using the foundational principle of the ethic of justice, include, among others, works by Beauchamp and

Childress (1984); Goodlad, Soder, and Sirotnik (1990); Kohlberg (1981); Sergiovanni (1992); Strike (2006); and Strike, Haller, and Soltis (1998).

Kohlberg (1981) argued that, within the liberal tradition, "there is a great concern not only to make schools more just—that is, to provide equality of educational opportunity and to allow freedom of belief—but also to educate so that free and just people emerge from schools" (p. 74). For Kohlberg, "justice is not a rule or set of rules, it is a moral principle . . . a mode of choosing that is universal, a rule of choosing that we want all people to adopt always in all situations" (p. 39). From this perspective, education is not "value-free." This model also indicates that schools should teach principles, in particular those of justice, equity, and respect for liberty.

From the late 1960s through the early 1980s, Kohlberg introduced his "just community" approach to the schools. In institutions as diverse as Roosevelt High, a comprehensive school in Manhattan, The Bronx High School of Science, and an alternative high school in Cambridge, Massachusetts, students and teachers handled school discipline and sometimes even the running of the school together. In a civil and thoughtful manner, students were taught to deal with problems within the school, turning to rules, rights, and laws for guidance (Hersh, Paolitto, & Reimer, 1979).

Building on Kohlberg's "just community," Sergiovanni (1992) called for moral leadership and, in particular, the principle of justice in the establishment of "virtuous schools." Sergiovanni viewed educational leadership as a stewardship and asked educational administrators to create institutions that are just and beneficent. By beneficence, Sergiovanni meant that there should be deep concern for the welfare of the school as a community, a concept that extends beyond the school walls and into the local community, taking into account not only students, teachers, and administrators, but families as well.

Unlike a number of educators in the field, Sergiovanni (1992) placed the principle of justice at the center of his concept of school. "Accepting this principle meant that every parent, teacher, student, administrator, and other member of the school community must be treated with the same equality, dignity, and fair play" (pp. 105–106).

The ethic of justice, from either a traditional or contemporary perspective, may take into account a wide variety of issues. Viewing ethical dilemmas from this vantage point, one may ask questions related to the rule of law and the more abstract concepts of fairness, equity, and justice. These may include, but are certainly not limited to, questions related to issues of equity and equality; the fairness of rules, laws, and policies; whether laws are absolute, and if exceptions are to be made, under what circumstances; and the rights of individuals versus the greater good of the community.

Moreover, the ethic of justice frequently serves as a foundation for legal principles and ideals. This important function is evident in laws related to education. In many instances, courts have been reluctant to impose restrictions on school officials, thus allowing them considerable discretion in making important administrative decisions (Board of Education v. Pico, 1981). At the same time, court opinions often reflect the values of the education community and society at large (Stefkovich & Guba, 1998). For example, only in recent years have courts upheld the use of metal detectors in schools to screen for weapons (People v. Dukes, 1992). In addition, what is legal in some places may be considered illegal in others. For instance, corporal punishment is still legal in 20 states and strip searching is legal in all but seven (Center for Effective Discipline, 2010; Hyman & Snook, 1999). In those states, it is left up to school officials, and the community, whether such practices are to be supported or not. Here, ethical issues such as due process and privacy rights are often balanced against the need for civility and the good of the majority.

Finally, what is to be done when a law is wrong, such as earlier Jim Crow laws supporting racial segregation (Starratt, 1994c; Stefkovich, 2006)? Under these circumstances, one must turn to ethics to make fair and just decisions. It is also in such instances that the ethic of justice may overlap with other paradigms such as the ethics of critique (Purpel, 1989, 2004) and care (Katz et al., 1999; Meyers, 1998; Sernak, 1998). Overall, the ethic of justice considers questions such as: Is there a law, right, or policy that relates to a particular case? If there is a law, right, or policy, should it be enforced? And if there is not a law, right, or policy, should there be one?

THE ETHIC OF CRITIQUE

Many writers and activists (e.g., Apple, 1986, 2000, 2001, 2003; Bakhtin, 1981; Bowles & Gintis, 1988; Foucault, 1983; Freire, 1970, 1993, 1998; Giroux, 1994, 2000, 2003; Greene, 1988; Purpel & Shapiro, 1995; Shapiro, 2009; Shapiro & Purpel, 2005) are not convinced by the analytic and rational approach of the justice paradigm. Some of these scholars find a tension between the ethic of justice, rights, and laws and the concept of democracy. In response, they raise difficult questions by critiquing both the laws themselves and the process used to determine if the laws are just.

Rather than accepting the ethic of those in power, these scholars challenge the status quo by seeking an ethic that will deal with inconsistencies, formulate the hard questions, and debate and challenge the issues. Their intent is to awaken us to our own unstated values and make us realize how frequently our own morals may have been modified and possibly even corrupted over time. Not only do they force us to rethink important concepts such as democracy, but they also ask us to redefine and reframe other concepts such as privilege, power, culture, language, and even justice.

The ethic of critique is based on critical theory, which has, at its heart, an analysis of social class and its inequities. According to Foster (1986), "Critical theorists are scholars who have approached social analysis in an investigative and critical manner and who have conducted investigations of social structure from perspectives originating in a modified Marxian analysis" (p. 71). More recently, critical theorists have turned to the intersection of race and gender as well as social class in their analyses.

An example of the work of critical theorists may be found in their arguments, occurring over many decades, that schools reproduce inequities similar to those in society (Bourdieu, 1977, 2001; Lareau, 1987, 2003). Tracking, for example, may be seen as one way to make certain that working-class children know their place (Oakes, 1993). Generally designed so that students are exposed to different knowledge in each track, schools "[make] decisions about the appropriateness of various topics and skills and, in doing so . . . [limit] . . . sharply what some students would learn" (p. 87). Recognizing this inequity, Carnoy and Levin (1985) pointed to an important contradiction in educational institutions, in that schools also represent the major force in the United States for expanding economic opportunity as well as the extension of democratic rights. Herein lies one of many inconsistencies to be addressed through the ethic of critique.

Along with critical theory, the ethic of critique is also frequently linked to critical pedagogy (Freire, 1970, 1993, 1998). Giroux (1991) asked educators to understand that their classrooms are political as well as educational locations and, as such, ethics is not a matter of individual choice or relativism but a "social discourse grounded in struggles that refuse to accept needless human suffering and exploitation" (p. 48). In this respect, the ethic of critique provides "a discourse for expanding basic human rights" (p. 48) and may serve as a vehicle in the struggle against inequality. In this vein, critical theorists are often concerned with making known the voices of those who are silenced, particularly students (Giroux, 1988, 2003; Weis & Fine, 1993).

For Giroux (1991, 2000, 2003, 2006), Welch (1991), and other critical educators, the language of critique is central, but discourse alone will not suffice. These scholars are also activists who believe discourse should be a beginning leading to some kind of action—preferably political. For example, Shapiro and Purpel (1993, 2005) emphasized empowering people through the discussion of options. Such a dialogue would hopefully provide what Giroux and Aronowitz (1985) called a "language of possibility" that, when applied to educational institutions, might enable them to avoid reproducing the "isms" in society (i.e., classism, racism, sexism, heterosexism).

Turning to educational leadership in particular, Parker and Shapiro (1993) argued that one way to rectify some wrongs in school and in society would be to give more attention to the analysis of social class in the preparation of principals and superintendents. They believed that social class analysis "is crucial given the growing divisions of wealth and power in the United States, and their impact on inequitable distribution of resources both within and among school districts" (pp. 39–40). Through the critical analysis of social class, there is the possibility that more knowledgable, moral, and sensitive educational leaders might be prepared.

Capper (1993), in her writings on educational leadership, stressed the need for moral leaders to be concerned with "freedom, equality, and the principles of a democratic society" (p. 14). She provided a useful summary of the roots of, and philosophy supporting, the ethic of critique as it pertains to educational leaders. She spoke of the Frankfurt school in the United States in the 1920s, in which immigrants tried to make sense of the oppression they had endured in Europe. This school provided not only a Marxist critique but took into account psychology and its effect on the individual. Capper (1993, p. 15) wrote:

> Grounded in the work of the Frankfurt school, critical theorists in educational administration are ultimately concerned with suffering and oppression, and critically reflect on current and historical social inequities. They believe in the imperative of leadership and authority and work toward the empowerment and transformation of followers, while grounding decisions in morals and values.

Thus, by demystifying and questioning what is happening in society and in schools, critical theorists may help educators rectify wrongs while identifying key morals and values.

In summary, the ethic of critique, inherent in critical theory, is aimed at awakening educators to inequities in society and, in particular, in the schools. This ethic asks educators to deal with the hard questions regarding social class, race, gender, and other areas of difference, such as: Who makes the laws? Who benefits from the law, rule, or policy? Who has the power? Who are the silenced voices? This approach to ethical dilemmas then asks educators to go beyond questioning and critical analysis to examine and grapple with those possibilities that could enable all children, whatever their social class, race, or gender, to have opportunities to grow, learn, and achieve. Such a process should lead to the development of options related to important concepts such as oppression, power, privilege, authority, voice, language, and empowerment.

THE ETHIC OF CARE

Juxtaposing an ethic of care with an ethic of justice, Roland Martin (1993, p. 144) wrote the following:

> One of the most important findings of contemporary scholarship is that our culture embraces a hierarchy of value that places the productive processes of society and their associated traits above society's reproductive processes and the associated traits of care and nurturance. There is nothing new about this. We are the inheritors of a tradition of Western thought according to which the functions, tasks, and traits associated with females are deemed less valuable than those associated with males.

Some feminist scholars (e.g., Beck, 1994; Belenky, Clinchy, Goldberger, & Tarule, 1986; Gilligan, 1982; Gilligan, Ward, & Taylor, 1988; Ginsberg, Shapiro, & Brown, 2004; Goldberger, Tarule, Clinchy, & Belenky, 1996; Grogan, 1996; Larson & Murtadha, 2002; Marshall, 1995; Marshall & Gerstl-Pepin, 2005; Marshall & Oliva, 2006; Noddings, 1992, 2002, 2003; Noddings, Stengel, & Alan, 2006; Sernak, 1998; Shapiro & Smith-Rosenberg, 1989; Shapiro, Ginsberg, & Brown, 2003) have challenged this dominant, and what they consider to be often patriarchal, ethic of justice in our society by turning to the ethic of care for moral decision making. Attention to this ethic can lead to other discussions of concepts such as loyalty, trust, and empowerment. Similar to critical theorists, these feminist scholars emphasize social responsibility, frequently discussed in the light of injustice, as a pivotal concept related to the ethic of care.

In her classic book *In a Different Voice,* Gilligan (1982) introduced the ethic of care by discussing a definition of justice different from Kohlberg's in the resolution of moral dilemmas (see the ethic of justice section in this chapter). In her research, Gilligan discovered that, unlike the males in Kohlberg's studies who adopted rights and laws for the resolution of moral issues, women and girls frequently turned to another voice, that of care, concern, and connection, in finding answers to their moral dilemmas. Growing out of the ethic of justice, the ethic of care, as it relates to education, has been described well by Noddings (1992), who created a new educational hierarchy placing "care" at the top when she wrote, "The first job of the schools is to care for our children" (p. xiv). To Noddings, and to a number of other ethicists and educators who advocate the use of the ethic of care, students are at the center of the educational process and need to be nurtured and encouraged, a concept that likely goes against the grain of those attempting to make "achievement" the top priority. Noddings believes that holding on to a competitive edge in achievement means that some children may see themselves merely as pawns in a nation of demanding and uncaring adults. In school buildings that more often resemble large, bureaucratic, physical plants, a major complaint of young people with regard to adults is, "They don't care!" (Comer, 1988). For Noddings, "Caring is the very bedrock of all successful education and . . . contemporary schooling can be revitalized in its light" (1992, p. 27).

Noddings and Gilligan are not alone in believing that the ethic of care is essential in education. In relation to the curriculum, Roland Martin (1993) wrote of the three Cs of caring, concern, and connection. Although she did not ask educators to teach "Compassion 101a" or to offer "Objectivity 101a," she did implore them to broaden the curriculum to include the experiences of both sexes, and not just one, and to stop leaving out the ethic of care. For Roland Martin, education is an "integration of reason and emotion, self and other" (p. 144).

Although the ethic of care has been associated with feminists, men and women alike attest to its importance and relevancy. Beck (1994) pointed out that "caring—as a foundational ethic—addresses concerns and needs as expressed by *many* persons; that it, in a sense, transcends ideological boundaries" (p. 3). Male ethicists and educators, such as Buber (1965), Normore (2008), and Sergiovanni (1992), have expressed high regard for this paradigm. These scholars have sought to make education a "human enterprise" (Starratt, 1991, p. 195).

Some scholars have recently associated the ethic of care with the philosophy of utilitarianism. For example, Blackburn (2006) believes that Bentham, Mills, and Hume spoke of the ethic of care as part of the public sphere. The concept of the greatest happiness of the greatest number, according to Blackburn (2001, p. 93), moved care into the civic realm. He wrote:

> An ethic of care and benevolence, which is essentially what utilitarianism is, gives less scope to a kind of moral philosophy modeled on law, with its hidden and complex structures and formulae known only to the initiates.

The ethic of care is important not only to scholars but to educational leaders who are often asked to make moral decisions. If the ethic of care is used to resolve dilemmas, then there is a need to revise how educational leaders are prepared. In the past, educational leaders were trained using military and business models. This meant that they were taught about the importance of the hierarchy and the need to follow those at the top, and, at the same time, to be in command and in charge of subordinates (Guthrie, 1990). They led by developing "rules, policies, standard operating procedures, information systems . . . or a variety of more informal techniques" (Bolman & Deal, 1991, p. 48). These techniques and rules may have worked well when the ethic of justice, rights, and laws was the primary basis for leaders making moral decisions; however, they are inadequate when considering other ethical paradigms, such as the ethic of care, that require leaders to consider multiple voices in the decision-making process.

Beck (1994) stressed that it is essential for educational leaders to move away from a top–down, hierarchical model for making moral and other decisions and, instead, to turn to a leadership style that emphasizes relationships and connections. Administrators need to "encourage collaborative efforts between faculty, staff, and students [which would serve] . . . to promote interpersonal interactions, to deemphasize competition, to facilitate a sense of belonging, and to increase individuals' skills as they learn from one another" (p. 85).

When an ethic of care is valued, educational leaders can become what Barth (1990) called, "head learner(s)" (p. 513). What Barth meant by that term was the making of outstanding leaders and learners who wish to listen to others when facing the need to make important moral decisions. The preparation of these individuals, then, must more heavily focus on the knowledge of cultures and of diversity, with a special emphasis on learning how to listen, observe, and respond to others. For example, Shapiro, Sewell, DuCette, and Myrick (1997), in their study of inner-city youth, identified three different kinds of caring: attention and support; discipline; and "staying on them," or prodding them over time. Although prodding students to complete homework might be viewed as nagging, the students these researchers studied saw prodding as an indication that someone cared about them.

Thus, the ethic of care offers another perspective and other ways to respond to complex moral problems facing educational leaders in their daily work. One aspect of its intricacy is that this lens tends to sometimes deal with emotions. Highlighting this complexity, Paul Begley, an educational ethicist, raised the question: Is the ethic of care an emotional or rational model? Thinking through this important question, it became clear that aspects of this ethic could be considered rational, such as providing discipline and attention to students; however, empathy and compassion toward others are also part of this paradigm and tend to demonstrate emotions. Hence, portions of this model coincide well with the emerging brain research regarding decision making, in general, in which emotions and reason are blended in intricate ways (Lehrer, 2009).

Viewing ethical dilemmas through the ethic of care may prompt questions related to how educators may assist young people in meeting their needs and desires and will reflect solutions that show a concern for others as part of decision making. This ethic asks that individuals consider the consequences of their decisions and actions. It asks them to consider questions such as: Who will benefit from what I decide? Who will be hurt by my actions? What are the long-term effects of a decision I make today? And if I am helped by someone now, what should I do in the future about giving back to this individual or to society in general? This paradigm also asks individuals to grapple with values such as loyalty and trust.

THE ETHIC OF THE PROFESSION

Starratt (1994b) postulated that the ethics of justice, care, and critique are not incompatible, but rather, complementary, the combination of which results in a richer, more complete, ethic. He visualized these ethics as themes, interwoven much like a tapestry:

> An ethical consciousness that is not interpenetrated by each theme can be captured either by sentimentality, by rationalistic simplification, or by social naivete. The blending of each theme encourages a rich human response to the many uncertain ethical situations the school community faces every day, both in the learning tasks as well as in its attempt to govern itself. (p. 57)

We agree with Starratt; but we have also come to believe that, even taken together, the ethics of justice, critique, and care do not provide an adequate picture of the factors that must be taken into consideration as leaders strive to make ethical decisions within the context of educational settings. What is missing—that is, what these paradigms tend to ignore—is a consideration of those moral aspects unique to the profession and the questions that arise as educational leaders become more aware of their own personal and professional codes of ethics. To fill this gap, we add a fourth to the three ethical frameworks described in this chapter: a paradigm of professional ethics.

Although the idea of professional ethics has been with us for some time, identifying the process as we have and presenting it in the form of a paradigm represents an innovative way of conceptualizing this ethic. Because this approach is relatively new—one which we have developed through more than a decade of collaborative research, writing, and teaching ethics—we devote more time to explaining this ethic than was given to others. The remainder of this chapter includes some brief background information on the emergence of professional ethics and the need for a professional ethics paradigm. Following these introductory remarks, we describe our model of professional ethics and how it works. This chapter concludes with a discussion of how the paradigm of professional ethics fits in with the other three ethics of justice, critique, and care.

PROFESSIONAL ETHICS AND THE NEED FOR
A PROFESSIONAL PARADIGM

When discussing ethics in relation to the professionalization of educational leaders, the tendency is to look toward professions such as law, medicine, dentistry, and business, which require their graduate students to take at least one ethics course before graduation as a way of socializing them into the profession. The field of educational administration has no such ethics course requirement.

However, in recent years there has been an interest in ethics in relation to educational decision making. A number of writers in educational administration (Beck, 1994; Beck & Murphy, 1994a, 1994b; Beck, Murphy, & Associates, 1997; Beckner, 2004; Begley, 1999; Begley & Johansson, 1998, 2003; Cambron-McCabe & Foster, 1994; Duke & Grogan, 1997; Greenfield, 2004; Mertz, 1997; Murphy, 2006; O'Keefe, 1997; Starratt, 1994b; Willower, 1999) believe it is important to provide prospective administrators with some training in ethics. As Greenfield (1993) pointed out, this preparation could "enable a prospective principal or superintendent to develop the attitudes, beliefs, knowledge, and skills associated with competence in moral reasoning" (p. 285). Stressing the importance of such preparation, Greenfield left us with a warning of sorts:

> A failure to provide the opportunity for school administrators to develop such competence constitutes a failure to serve the children we are obligated to serve as public educators. As a profession, educational administration thus has a moral obligation to train prospective administrators to be able to apply the principles, rules, ideals, and virtues associated with the development of ethical schools. (p. 285)

Recognizing this need, ethics was identified as one of the competencies necessary for school leaders in the document, *Interstate School Leaders Licensure Consortium: Standards for School Leavers* (NPBEA, 1996). This document, developed by the consortium, under the auspices of the Council of Chief State School Officers and in collaboration with the National Policy Board for Educational Administration (NPBEA), was produced by representatives from 24 states and nine associations related to the educational administration profession.

More recently, in a revised document, *Educational Leadership Policy Standards* (NPBEA, 2008), school leaders again set forth six standards for the profession. Of these, Standard 5 remained: "An education leader promotes the success of every student by acting with integrity, fairness, and in an ethical manner." Slightly modified from its 1996 document, it goes on to add the following functions:

A. Ensure a system of accountability for every student's academic and social success; B. Model principles of self-awareness, reflective practice, transparency, and ethical behavior; C. Safeguard the values of democracy, equity, and diversity; D. Consider and evaluate the potential moral and legal consequences of decision-making; and E. Promote social justice and ensure that individual student needs inform all aspects of schooling. (NPBEA, 2008, pp. 4–5)

Although there are some changes from the 1996 version, this standard, with its functions, officially continues to recognize the importance of ethics in the knowledge base for school administrators. Commensurate with these standards, many states now require principals to pass an exam measuring related competencies, including ethics, and these standards are now incorporated into the National Association for the Accreditation of Teacher Education (NCATE; Murphy, 2005).

In the past, professional ethics has generally been viewed as a subset of the justice paradigm. This is likely the case because professional ethics is often equated with codes, rules, and principles, all of which fit neatly into traditional concepts of justice (Beauchamp & Childress, 1984). For example, many states have established their own sets of standards. The Pennsylvania Code of Professional Practice and Conduct for Educators (1992) is an 11-point code of conduct that was subsequently enacted into state law. Texas has a similar code of ethics, standards, and practices (Texas Administrative Code, 1998) for its educators that, among other things, expects them to deal justly with students and protect them from "disparagement."

In addition, a number of education-related professional organizations have developed their own professional ethical codes. Defined by Beauchamp and Childress (1984) as "an articulated statement of role morality as seen by members of the profession" (p. 41), some of these ethical codes are relatively new and others are long-standing. Examples of these organizations include, but are certainly not limited to, the American Association of School Administrators, the American Association of University Professors, the American Psychological Association, the Association of School Business Officials, the Association for Supervision and Curriculum Development, and the National Education Association.

However, ethical codes set forth by the states and professional associations tend to be limited in their responsiveness in that they are somewhat removed from the day-to-day personal and professional dilemmas which educational leaders face. Nash (1996), in his book on professional ethics for educators and human service professionals, recognized these limitations as he observed his students' lack of interest in such codes:

What are we to make of this almost universal disparagement of professional codes of ethics? What does the nearly total disregard of professional codes mean? For years, I thought it was something in my delivery that evoked such strong, antagonistic responses. For example, whenever I ask students to bring their codes to class, few knew where to locate them, and most get utterly surly when I make such a request. I understand, now, however, that they do not want to be bothered with what they consider a trivial, irrelevant assignment, because they simply do not see a correlation between learning how to make ethical decisions and appealing to a code of ethics. (p. 95)

On the other hand, professional codes of ethics serve as guideposts for the profession, giving statements about its image and character (Lebacqz, 1985). They embody "the highest moral ideals of the profession," thus "presenting an ideal image of the moral character of both the profession and the professional" (Nash, 1996, p. 96). Seen in this light, standardized codes provide a most valuable function. Thus, the problem lies not so much in the codes themselves, but in the fact that we sometimes expect too much from them with regard to moral decision making (Lebacqz, 1985; Nash, 1996).

The University Council of Educational Administration has recognized the need for a code that is developed in a participatory fashion and is not static (UCEA Ethical Code Committee, 2004–2009). This organization is developing a code, using the internet and continual committee meetings over time, which will hopefully provide an ongoing set of principles in response to some of the current criticisms of organizational codes.

Recognizing the importance of standardized codes, the contributions they make, and their limitations, we believe the time has come to view professional ethics from a broader, more inclusive, and more contemporary perspective. This type of approach is reflected in the ISLLC Standards. Focusing on rules, principles, and identification of competencies, these standards are essentially regulatory in nature. At the same time, they acknowledge the importance of knowing different ethical frameworks. In addition, competence for the profession is assessed through an examination based on a case study approach; that is, an analysis of vignettes asking what factors a school leader should consider in making a decision.

A PARADIGM FOR PROFESSIONAL ETHICS

Our concept of professional ethics as an ethical paradigm includes ethical principles and codes of ethics embodied in the justice paradigm, but is much broader, taking into account other paradigms, as well as professional judgment and decision making. We recognize professional ethics as a dynamic process requiring administrators to develop their own personal and professional codes.

We believe this process is important and, like Nash, we observed a dissonance between students' own codes and those set forth by states or professional groups. For the most part, our students were not aware of these codes or, if they were, such formalized professional codes had little impact on them; most found it more valuable to create their own codes. As one of our students, a department chair, pointed out after his involvement in this process:

> Surprisingly to me, I even enjoyed doing the personal and professional ethics statements. I have been in union meetings where professional ethical codes were discussed. They were so bland and general as to be meaningless. Doing these statements forced me to think about what I do and how I live, whereas the previous discussions did not. It was a very positive experience. I also subscribe to the notion that [standardized] professional ethical codes are of limited value. I look to myself to determine what decisions I can live with. Outside attempts at control have little impact on me and what I do.

Through our work, we have come to believe that educational leaders should be given the opportunity to take the time to develop their own personal codes of ethics based on life stories and critical incidents. They should also create their own professional codes based on the experiences and expectations of their working lives as well as a consideration of their personal codes.

Underlying such a process is an understanding of oneself as well as others. These understandings necessitate that administrators reflect on concepts such as what they perceive to be right or wrong and good or bad, who they are as professionals and as human beings, how they make decisions, and why they make the decisions they do. This process recognizes that preparing students to live and work in the 21st Century requires very special leaders who have grappled with their own personal and professional codes of ethics and have reflected on diverse forms of ethics, taking into account the differing backgrounds of the students enrolled in U.S. schools and universities today. By grappling, we mean that these educational leaders have struggled over issues of justice, critique, and care related to the education of children and youth and, through this process, have gained a sense of who they are and what they believe personally and professionally. It means coming to grips with clashes that may arise among ethical codes and making ethical decisions in light of their best professional judgment, a judgment that places the best interests of the student at the center of all ethical decision making.

Thus, actions by school officials are likely to be strongly influenced by personal values (Begley, 1999; Begley & Johansson, 1998; Willower & Licata, 1997), and personal codes of ethics build on these values and experiences (Shapiro & Stefkovich, 1997, 1998). As many of our students found, it is not always easy to separate professional from personal ethical codes. The observations of this superintendent of a large rural district aptly sum up our own experiences and the sentiments of many of our practitioner-students:

> A professional ethical code cannot be established without linkage and reference to one's personal code of ethics and thereby acknowledges such influencing factors. In retrospect, and as a result of . . . [developing my own ethical codes], I can see the influence professional responsibilities have upon my personal values, priorities, and behavior. It seems there is an unmistakable "co-influence" of the two codes. One cannot be completely independent of the other. (Shapiro & Stefkovich, 1998, p. 137)

Other factors that play into the development of professional codes involve consideration of community standards, including both the professional community and the community in which the leader works; formal codes of ethics established by professional associations; and written standards of the profession (ISLLC).

As educational leaders develop their professional (and personal) codes, they consider various ethical models, either focusing on specific paradigms or, optimally, integrating the ethics of justice, care, and critique. This filtering process provides the basis for professional judgments and professional ethical decision making; it may also result in clashes among codes.

Through our work, we have identified four possible clashes, three of which have been discussed earlier (Shapiro & Stefkovich, 1998). First, there may be clashes between an individual's personal and professional codes of ethics. This may occur when an individual's personal ethical code conflicts with an ethical code set forth by the profession. Second, there may be clashes within professional codes. This may happen when the individual has been prepared in two or more professions. Codes of one profession may be different from another. Hence, a code that serves an individual well in one career may not in another. Third, there may be clashes of professional codes among educational leaders; what one administrator sees as ethical, another may not. Fourth, there may be clashes between a leader's personal and professional code of ethics and custom and practices set forth by the community (either the professional community, the school community, or the community where the educational leader works). For example, a number of our students noted that some behavior that may be considered unethical in one community may, in another community, be seen merely as a matter of personal preference.

Furman (2003, 2004), expanding on what she characterizes as a separate "ethic of the community" and defining it as a process, asks leaders to move away from heroic (solo) decision making and to make decisions with the assistance of the community. Her definition of community is broad and all-encompassing, relating to a distributive model of leadership (Spillane, Halverson, & Diamond, 2001) as well as to participatory democracy.

To resolve the four clashes, we hark back to Greenfield's earlier (1993) quote that grounded the "moral dimension" for the preparation of school administrators in the needs of children. Greenfield contended that schools, particularly public schools, should be the central sites for "preparing children to assume the roles and responsibilities of citizenship in a democratic society" (p. 268). To achieve Greenfield's goal, we must also turn to teachers, in leadership positions, and their ethics (Burant, Chubbuck, & Whipp, 2007; Campbell, 2000, 2004; Hansen, 2001; Hostetler, 1997; Strike & Ternasky, 1993). Teacher leaders, such as heads of charter schools and learning communities or teacher coaches, need to be prepared as ethical professionals.

Not all those who write about the importance of the study of ethics in educational leadership discuss the needs of children; however, this focus on students is clearly consistent with the backbone of our profession. Other professions often have one basic principle driving the profession. In medicine, it is "First, do no harm." In law, it is the assertion that all clients deserve "zealous representation." In educational leadership, we believe that if there is a moral imperative for the profession, it is to serve the "best interests of the student." Consequently, this ideal must lie at the heart of any professional paradigm for educational leaders.

This focus is reflected in most professional association codes. For example, the American Association of School Administrators' Statement of Ethics for School Administrators (American Association of School Administrators, 1981) begins with the assertion, "An educational administrator's professional behavior must conform to an ethical code" and has as its first tenet this statement: "The educational administrator . . . *makes the well-being of students the fundamental value of all decision making and actions*" [emphasis added]. It is in concert with Noddings' (2003) ethic of care, which places students at the top of the educational hierarchy, and is reflective of the concerns of many critical theorists who see students' voices as silenced (Giroux, 1988, 2003; Weis & Fine, 1993). In addition, serving the best interests of the student is consistent with the ISLLC's standards for the profession, each of which begins with the words, "An education leader promotes the success of *every* student [emphasis added]" (NPBEA, 2008).

Frequent confrontations with moral dilemmas become even more complex as dilemmas increasingly involve a variety of student populations, parents, and communities comprising diversity in broad terms that extend well beyond categories of race and ethnicity. In this respect, differences encompassing cultural categories of race and ethnicity, religion, social class, gender, disability, and sexual orientation as well as individual differences that may take into account learning styles, exceptionalities, and age often cannot be ignored (Banks, 2001; Banks & Banks, 2006; Cushner,

Figure 2.1 *Diagrammatic representation of the ethic of the profession.*

Notes

The circles indicate major factors that converge to create the professional paradigm. The circles shown are: Standards of the Profession; Professional Code of Ethics; Ethics of the Community; Personal Codes of Ethics; Individual Professional Codes, and Best Interests of the Student. Other factors also play a part in the professional paradigm. They are found surrounding the Best Interests of the Student circle and include: Clashing Codes; Professional Judgment, and Professional Decision Making. The arrows indicate the various ways in which the factors interact and overlap with each other.

McClelland, & Safford, 1992; Gollnick & Chinn, 1998; Shapiro et al., 2001; Sleeter & Grant, 2003).

The literature does not define "best interests of the student" (Stefkovich, 2006; Stefkovich, O'Brien, & Moore, 2002). In the absence of such clarification, school leaders have often referred to a student's best interests to justify adults' interests (Walker, 1998). Recent attempts have been made, however, to fill this gap (Stefkovich, 2006; Stefkovich & O'Brien, 2004; Walker, 1995, 1998). Stefkovich conceptualizes decisions related to a student's best interests as those incorporating individual rights, accepting and teaching students to accept responsibility for their actions, and respecting students. These three Rs—rights, responsibility, and respect—are key to making ethical decisions that are in a student's best interests and, in turn, to fulfilling one's professional obligations as educational leaders.

In sum, we have described a paradigm for the profession that expects its leaders to formulate and examine their own professional codes of ethics in light of individual personal codes of ethics, as well as standards set forth by the profession, and then calls on them to place students at the center of the ethical decision-making process. It also asks them to take into account the wishes of the community. As such, the professional paradigm we are proposing is dynamic—not static—and multidimensional, recognizing the complexities of being an educational leader in today's society. (See Figure 2.1 for a visual representation of this model).

Thus, taking all these factors into consideration, this ethic of the profession would ask questions related to justice, critique, and care posed by the other ethical paradigms but would go beyond these questions to inquire: What would the profession expect me to do? What does the community expect me to do? And what should I do based on the best interests of the students, who may be diverse in their composition and their needs?

PART II

A MULTIPARADIGM APPROACH TO ANALYZING PARADOXICAL DILEMMAS

Chapters 3 to 10 present ethical dilemmas that lend themselves to analysis through a multiparadigm approach. They highlight inherent inconsistencies existing within education in particular, and our communities in general, that tend to give rise to dilemmas. Thus, we have framed each chapter as a paradox, and the cases included illustrate the tensions that surround the concept. The paradoxes highlighted are individual rights versus community standards; the traditional curriculum versus the hidden curriculum; personal codes versus professional codes; the American melting pot versus the Chinese hot pot; religion versus culture; equality versus equity; accountability versus responsibility; and privacy versus safety.

Purpel (1989, 2004), in describing the moral and spiritual crisis in contemporary education, turned to paradoxes to bring out many current problems and tensions. We agree with him that many of today's strains and stresses have occurred owing to the contradictions that exist in our society. When these paradoxes are brought to the reader's attention, through the discussion of real-life dilemmas, we hope that they will not only lead to stimulating conversations, but that they will also encourage reflection and guidance for wise decision making in the future.

Because many of the dilemmas are based on true experiences, there has been a genuine effort to make sure that anonymity and confidentiality have been maintained. The cases are meant to be used in educational administration classes and in other courses related to education or leadership in general. They are intended to make certain that students and other readers are exposed to differing paradigms and diverse voices—of justice, rights, and law; care, concern, and connectedness; critique and possibility; and professionalism. They also reflect the diversity of students and of communities in a complex era.

These cases focus on persons holding a variety of positions in schools and in higher education. In constructing the scenarios, we purposely tried to balance the gender, race, ethnicity, and age of both the persons confronting the dilemmas and those with whom they had to deal. In this respect, we gave these persons names that would reflect this diversity. We feel that in view of our diverse, multicultural school communities, this was the most appropriate approach. We were very conscious of the risks in not giving everyone Anglo-sounding names, as is the usual practice in case studies, and consciously tried to avoid reinforcing or adopting stereotypes. We apologize in advance for any stereotyping that may have occurred inadvertently.

Before we turn to the cases in the next few chapters, we provide a brief illustration of how an ethical dilemma may be viewed by applying the Multiple Ethical Paradigms. We turn to a dilemma that we developed and used toward the beginning of our course called The School Uniform Case. When we first discussed this case, we raised issues associated with the ethic of justice dealing with the legal ramifications of school uniforms. Although our students understood the concepts associated with the justice paradigm and learned much from this analysis, they also seemed frustrated, and we began to think that the discussion was incomplete. Instinctively, we and our students began to bring in other analyses related to the ethics of care, critique, and the profession. These paradigms tended to complement the justice perspective and no longer limited the discussion.

It was by reflecting on this process, and other subsequent similar situations, that we came to realize that dilemmas are best viewed in a multidimensional, or kaleidoscopic fashion, as through a series of lenses. What follows is a brief synopsis of The School Uniform Case, some of the issues presented in this dilemma, and some suggestions for analysis using four paradigms. This is not meant to be a complete analysis of the case, as such an endeavor would take up more time and space than we feel is necessary for the intent of this introduction. Instead, we use this case and the suggested approaches only as an illustration as to how to reflect on an ethical dilemma through the use of multiple paradigms.

The School Uniform Case is about a poor, inner-city teenager named Tom, who came to school wearing a new pair of tennis shoes. The shoes were expensive and he said that he had saved three weeks of his salary from his after-school job to pay for them. Tom was extremely proud of his shoes and showed them off to everyone. The next day, the school was in an uproar when the news came that Tom had been killed. Only a few days later, a 17-year-old classmate of Tom's was seen wearing a new pair of tennis shoes identical to those which Tom had worn.

Prior to the murder, the school's principal, Dr. Smith, had suffered minor irritations regarding students' dress. She became tired of overhearing students complaining that they had nothing new to wear, and she was annoyed at their tardiness due to taking hours to dress for school; but the killing of a student only indicated how severe the problem really had become. There were many issues related to this terrible situation, but, in an effort to do something quickly, Dr. Smith decided to consider a disarmingly simple solution for dealing with the problem of envy over other students' possessions. She decided to take seriously the idea of requiring that each student wear a school uniform.

Although this solution sounded simple and appropriate to Dr. Smith, we recommend that she pause and reflect on this dilemma, taking into account four ethical paradigms or lenses before deciding that school uniforms are the answer. If, for example, Dr. Smith analyzed the case using the ethic of justice, she would have to look closely at laws, rules, and principles regarding dress codes. These reflections have to take into account the laws regarding public schools and students' rights. Dr. Smith would need to consider the First Amendment and the free speech clause within it. A dress code, it may be argued, would come under symbolic free speech. However, despite the law, students might be regulated, particularly if they were indecent or immodest in dress or disrupted the learning process in some way. Under the ethic of justice, then, Dr. Smith might ask the following: In a public school, do students have a right to choose what they want to wear? How far does this right extend, or are there any limits on their dress?

Turning to the ethic of care, it is clear that Dr. Smith is concerned about her students' safety. She believes that school uniforms would be a great equalizer and would protect individual students from future dangers caused by others' envy of their clothes. In addition, aware of the poverty in her area, she cares about her students' finances. School uniforms would no doubt be a great saving for her students and their families. In this regard, using the lens of care and concern, some questions she could raise for reflection and discussion include: Shouldn't the school uniform be required because it will serve as an equalizer and, hence, help to make students safe? Won't the requirement of a school uniform assist students in a poverty area who currently pay too much money for designer clothes and jewelry?

If Dr. Smith focuses on the ethic of critique, questions of a broader nature could be asked, such as: What kind of system encourages young people to compete with each other over clothes and fosters envy to such a degree that a young person would kill over what another student wears? How can this system be made better, enabling students to focus on learning rather than on spending money and effort on clothes and jewelry?

Finally, if Dr. Smith turns to the professional ethical paradigm, she might consider all these questions and then go beyond them to determine if there were inconsistencies. To accomplish this, she might ask: What would the profession expect her to do? According to her personal and professional codes of ethics, what should she do? And what would the school and local communities expect her to decide? Still keeping in mind the professional paradigm, she might also ask this key question: Is it in the best interests of students to require that they be dressed in school uniforms?

Thus, what at the outset appears to be a simple solution to a disturbing problem becomes something quite different and far more complex. This type of questioning, using four different ethical paradigms, would hopefully provide Dr. Smith with in-depth and detailed knowledge and sensitivities regarding school uniforms. Although it might take longer than she originally intended to reach a decision, what Dr. Smith decided to do would no doubt be wiser and more informed owing to the different perspectives she had used, and various questions she had explored.

Now let us turn to Chapter 3, which contains the first of the paradoxes and the cases that illustrate some of the tensions as they relate to schooling. This paradox focuses on individual rights versus community standards.

Individual Rights Versus Community Standards

G. Michaele O'Brien, Kimberly D. Callahan, John A. Schlegel, Loree P. Guthrie, and Jeannette McGill-Harris

In this chapter, dilemmas are presented that focus on community standards. Frequently, in these cases, the standards of the community are pitted against individual rights. In reading and discussing the dilemmas, we expect that the reader must begin to grapple with the differing views of ethics in demographically shifting communities.

One of the paradoxes which American society faces is that of individual rights versus community standards. This dichotomy emanates from individuals' desires to be unique, independent, and hold a strong self-identity. Yet, at the same time, people seek interdependence by developing strong human and symbolic relationships (Purpel, 1989, 2004). This need for a group identity compels communities to develop their own identities, ultimately creating community standards. However, moral dilemmas may arise when community standards conflict with individual rights.

The balance between the needs of both the individual and the greater community goes back to the foundations of the American republic. It is natural that the education of our nation's students has always fueled this debate. The "special position of trust and responsibility" which teachers hold, given their proximity to youth, makes the situation unique (DeMitchell, 1993, p. 217). Educational leaders are a natural buffer of this paradox as it manifests itself especially in the public school settings. Specifically, the view of the teacher as role model for students based on an ethical foundation of different communities contrasts with the principle of individual rights. This tension between the community and individual rights must be faced frequently by those educational leaders working at the very heart of the debate. Since the move away from the common school to the establishment of the school system and profession of teaching, administrators have had to balance community ethics with teacher privacy rights.

Early schooling in America was characterized by teacher conduct as a matter of public concern (Tyack, 1974). Throughout the first half of the nineteenth century, schools fell largely under local community control (DeMitchell, 1993). As such, most details of teachers' lives were placed under the rules, regulations, and scrutiny of local community members. Matters such as marital status, dress, and living arrangements were often direct conditions of employment (Apple, 1986; Hoffman, 1981; Tyack, 1974). However, as reformers after 1850 began to make progress toward the establishment of bureaucratized school systems, the "rise of professionalism" began to "counterbalance community control" (DeMitchell, 1993, p. 217). Certainly, teachers were still responsible to the public for life outside of the classroom. However, the rise of a school bureaucracy often made the scrutiny less intense. The picture of the teacher as role model began to be joined by a vision of the teacher as private individual.

The following discussion took place during proceedings of the Supreme Court of Pennsylvania in 1993:

> Immorality is not essentially confined to deviation from sex morality; it may be such a course of action as offends the morals of the community and is a bad example to the youth whose ideals a teacher is supposed to foster and to elevate. . . . It has always been the recognized duty of the teacher to conduct himself in such a way as to command the respect and good will of the community, though one result of the choice of a teacher's vocation may be to deprive him of the same freedom of action enjoyed by persons in other vocations. (DeMitchell, 1993, p. 221)

Despite the shift away from direct community control, it was not until the 1960s and 1970s that there was any significant movement toward acceptance of greater personal freedom for teachers. Yet, in many cases, the selection and retention of teachers continued to remain intertwined based on community values and expectations. Even into the latter half of the twentieth century, dismissal of teachers for conduct outside of school was practiced by various communities (McBroom v. Board of Education, 1986).

The paradox between community control and individual rights continues to exist. However, there has been a strong move away from communities monitoring teachers' private lives. Along with the courts, many school leaders and boards of education look for a direct relationship between teacher action and adverse effect on students (Morrison v. Board of Education, 1969).

Although court cases may illuminate the issues surrounding the dispute between teacher as exemplar and teacher as private citizen, administrators must continue to fill a unique role. They must frequently deal with the move to objectify criteria that may be used to balance the community view of teachers as role models and the idea of teachers as professionals. In this chapter, individual rights and personal liberties are juxtaposed against the standards of the community. Important questions to be asked include: Are there values and moral standards that are absolute or fixed? Do the ends ever justify the means? In considering these questions, this chapter examines the changing face of ethics in different communities.

The four ethical dilemmas examined in this chapter are: The Adult Fantasy Center, Artificial Insemination, The Trouble with *Daddy's Roommate*, and The School of Hard Knocks.

In The Adult Fantasy Center (Case study 3.1), a male teacher's job is in jeopardy because his principal has found out that he moonlights as a sex shop manager. The principal knows that the parents in her community would find this teacher's other job objectionable.

In Artificial Insemination (Case study 3.2), an unmarried teacher in her late thirties confides to her friend, the district's personnel director, that she wants to be artificially inseminated. In this small, rural community that is largely Christian fundamentalist, the personnel director is concerned about the teacher's personal plan as well as the community's reactions to it.

The Trouble with *Daddy's Roommate* (Case study 3.3) highlights difficulties with community values. Here, a parent complains about a children's book, assigned in a high school classroom, dealing with sexual orientation and other sensitive issues. Initially, the book is banned, but that is not the end of the problem. In this dilemma one might ask: Does it matter whether there is a consensus regarding values within a local community and even within a school community?

The School of Hard Knocks (Case study 3.4) focuses on a school bully and a security guard. It pits the voices of young children against the wishes of a school superintendent. In this case, two communities are affected—the students in the school and the district administration. Do the voices of the student community count or does the superintendent have the last word?

In all of the above cases, the educational administrator must attempt to view each dilemma from the vantage point of the individual and from that of the community, asking questions such as: When do community standards take precedence over individual rights and liberties? Is the ethical character of educators set at a higher level than those of other citizens in the community? Does the community have a right to place educators at a higher ethical level than its other citizens? Should the community have input into matters regarding school employees' individual liberties? These questions are at the heart of the case studies in this chapter.

CASE STUDY 3.1 THE ADULT FANTASY CENTER

Dr. Angela DiNardo was exhausted. Friday afternoons were always filled with emergencies that could never wait until Monday. During her three years as assistant principal at Madison High School, Angela could not remember the last time she left her office before 5 p.m. Angela looked for her "homework folder" to place in her briefcase. This afternoon she would try to leave around 4 p.m. Her thoughts were interrupted when her secretary entered with a typed observation report to be signed.

This particular observation report was one that Dr. DiNardo enjoyed completing because it described and evaluated a lesson taught by Ted Tressler. Ted appeared to be the consummate professional. His students respected him and were extremely attentive in class. He constantly introduced innovative teaching methods into the health and physical education curriculum. The applied concepts taught in the classroom were transferred to real-life situations, motivating the students to do well in health class. The health teacher led his department in a concerted effort to modify teaching styles to increase student learning. For several of Mr. Tressler's students, it was an unhappy time when the bell rang indicating the end of class. This was evident by the sad looks on their faces and the approach of some of them to Mr. Tressler's desk to schedule additional time for tutoring. Interestingly enough, the majority of those students were female.

The administration had approached Ted several times during his five years at Madison, asking him to coach various teams throughout the seasons. Angela always questioned why he declined such opportunities, which could prove to be beneficial if he chose to apply for the athletic director's position, the next logical career step for him. Although she was anxious to mentor her faculty, in this case Angela had never actually approached Ted about his unwillingness to coach. She assumed that his family responsibilities or his frequent tutoring sessions failed to allow him extra time in his schedule to coach. This was unfortunate, Angela thought.

The clock said 4:05 p.m. Dr. DiNardo knew her secretary expected her to have left five minutes ago and would not want to wait a minute longer to photocopy the observation report. Reviewing her suggestions for improvement, Angela recalled an incident that occurred toward the end of the class period she had observed. A female student had asked Mr. Tressler a legitimate question dealing with the curriculum. Immediately following his response, he added an unnecessary compliment that bordered on what Angela construed to be sexual harassment. The class period had gone so well and had been conducted in such a professional manner that she felt, at that time, that the phrase was reflective of the teacher's expressive nature and dismissed any thoughts of mentioning this in written form. She hoped this was a good decision and one that her superintendent would have approved. Dr. DiNardo signed the observation report with little hesitation and handed it to her secretary. Happy Friday!

Angela always tried to plan her weekends so that her activities provided a balance between work and relaxation time. She was pleased that tonight was a fortieth birthday party for a long-time high school friend. It sounded as though it would be fun because Angela and her husband were told that they had to bring an interesting "gag" gift to get in the door, something that would help the friend cope with an anticipated "midlife crisis."

The party was a surprise and would begin promptly at 7 p.m. Angela's husband was away on business and would not be back until just before the party, so it was left up to her, with less than two hours to spare, to purchase a gift, shower, and dress. Where could she go for a quick shopping excursion for a gag gift? Just then, Angela passed the Adult Fantasy Center. "Why not?" she thought. Something really silly from a place like that might just work. After all, her friend was a bit outrageous.

The Adult Fantasy Center was an establishment deemed by many to be offensive, presenting an eyesore to those living in the upscale Madison community. The store was situated just across the border between a squalid borough and the wealthy township of Madison. In fact, when it first opened, the Adult Fantasy Center had been rumored to have in the back of the store a red velvet curtain separating the legal business from unlawful endeavors. Several Madison community members had exhausted all efforts protesting the establishment, fearing that the escort service advertised was really a cover for an illegal prostitution ring. However, they had not succeeded because the store was not within their borders and nothing illegal had developed. Angela had no time to spare. Assuming she would not run into anyone she knew, Angela began her shopping expedition.

Ted Tressler knew that he was about 30 minutes late for work that evening. Friday nights were always busy. Steve would just have to understand. After all, on Wednesday night Ted had closed the store at 2 a.m. Teaching all day Thursday was difficult, but he had somehow coped. Who would have known how lucrative the "adult business" would be? Ted sighed. He initially agreed only to financially support Steve Wilkins in his business venture and serve as a silent partner. Steve really needed help from his old college roommate and, after all, if Ted could make as much money as Steve claimed was possible, how could he resist investing his inheritance from his grandmother's will?

Ted's wife knew the amount of money that the business was accruing and was pleasantly surprised herself. Putting three children through college was extremely expensive. The Adult Fantasy Center had been very busy lately, despite the strong opposition from the neighboring community. Fortunately, no one in Madison High School or that district was aware of

Ted's business venture. Not that he had anything to hide; from Ted's perspective the business was entirely legal. But conservative society members might feel that his part-ownership of an adult center was indecorous, recognizing his position as a public school role model. Ted and his wife preferred that his second profession be kept a secret.

Ted's thoughts stopped as he entered the parking lot of the store. The lot was not filled. This was a relief. As he entered, he noticed that the shipment of new CD-ROMs, which had arrived the previous afternoon, had not been shelved. He would have to speak to the new employee just hired last week and give better directions. He laughed to himself, wondering if a course at Madison High should be implemented stressing job responsibilities. The new employee had graduated from Madison four years before.

The rest of the store looked ready to go for the upcoming weekend. The videos were in place and other paraphernalia was restocked. Ted decided to look for Steve, whom he had somehow missed seeing all week. Ted hoped that Steve's disappearance was not a hint of what might happen in the future. From the initial phases of this business venture, it was made clear that Steve and Ted were partners, but Ted felt as though he had already been doing more than his share.

I will only be a minute, Angela told herself. As she entered the store, she glanced around at the other customers and then at the merchandise. Not seeing any signs for a gift section, she began perusing what appeared to be infinite numbers of sexual paraphernalia. Angela was shopping with such strict focus and intent, wanting to understand the functions of the gadgets she was looking at and anxious to achieve her mission as soon as possible, that she almost did not hear the loud argument coming from the back of the store. As a result of her broken concentration Angela looked up, only to see Ted Tressler coming through the red velvet curtain. He turned and clearly recognized Angela. The embarrassment on both sides was overwhelming. Putting the merchandise back on the shelf, she said, "Hello, Ted. What are you doing here?"

Questions for Discussion

1. Are teachers role models for young people? For their students? Why or why not? If teachers are role models, is it acceptable for a teacher to be part-owner of an adult center? Is a teacher's second profession anyone's concern other than his or her own?

2. If the community became aware of Mr. Tressler's second profession, might it believe that this profession would have an effect on his performance in the classroom? Would the students think of Mr.

Tressler differently and view him in an entirely new light if they knew about his other job?

3. What about Dr. DiNardo's role in finding out about Mr. Tressler's second profession? How could she explain her own behavior with regard to shopping at the Adult Fantasy Center if those in power found out? How might Dr. DiNardo's behavior affect her standing in the local community? Is an administrator exempt from the same kind of scrutiny as teachers?

4. Does the fact that Mr. Tressler has his own children to send to college affect the morality of his decision? Would your answer be different if it were clear that working in the Adult Fantasy Center was the only way that Mr. Tressler could make enough money to support his family? To educate his children?

5. What should Dr. DiNardo do? What would be in the best interests of the students? Would you see this decision differently if the principal were male? If Ted Tressler were female?

CASE STUDY 3.2 ARTIFICIAL INSEMINATION

Sally Fabian is a competent senior high school art teacher with 10 years of teaching experience. She is an advisor to the high school cheerleading squad and volunteers her time to serve on a number of school curriculum committees. She is single and, during the past year, had shared with the district's personnel director the fact that she wanted to be artificially inseminated. Her goal was to parent a child of her own whom she intended to raise as a single mother.

Having thought about being a single parent for several years, Ms. Fabian went through the required process of counseling for a year. Although she did not maintain a steady relationship with any man, she had dated during her 10 years as a teacher at North High. Sally had been raised in New York City. She chose to attend a small rural college located about 30 miles from North High School. She decided on this particular college because of its excellent academic reputation as well as the advice from one of her high school teachers. During her four years in college, Sally fell in love with the area. She felt fortunate when she was hired as a teacher at North High. Sally was a resident of the school district where she taught. In fact, she had recently bought a house directly across from the high school.

Sally's political views could be labeled moderate. She is a registered independent voter. During college, she had done an internship in the local Planned Parenthood Clinic. The community the school district serves is conservative with a small, but unified, group of fundamentalist Christians who are politically active and vitally interested in educational matters. The community as a whole has a rich German heritage along with some traces of ethnic and racial diversity.

As the ethnic and racial composition of the community diversified, the community needed to address the accusation that the lifelong residents were prejudiced and refused to include all community residents in the mainstream of town life. The increase in the diversity of the community was attributed partly to the increase in advertisement in larger urban settings for people to move into the area to take advantage of low-income housing. This was a venture taken on by several local businessmen who sought to make substantial financial gains.

Last year, to meet the demands of this growing, rapidly changing, and often contentious population, the school board approved a new administrative position: director of personnel and community relations. John Edwards was the individual selected to fill this slot. All of Mr. Edwards' teaching experience came from his tenure at a large urban high school where he had taught social studies. Directly before assuming this new position he had been principal at North High, where he had established himself as an effective leader who worked well with students, teachers, and the community.

Mr. Edwards was committed to school reform and believed that all stakeholders should be able to provide input into the change process. As principal, Mr. Edwards had formed an advocacy group of stakeholders to engage in the change process. He was respected by the community, and he sought to conduct himself in a manner that was consistent with community values. Consequently, change did not come about in an abrupt fashion.

Mr. Edwards was friendly with Sally Fabian and knew of her dream, but he had wondered if she were really serious about it. Now, today, Sally had stopped by Mr. Edwards' office to tell him the "good news." She had decided to go forward with the procedure. Mr. Edwards is in a quandary as to how to handle this delicate situation. As an educational leader in this district he is concerned with the growing number of teen pregnancies, especially at North High. Nevertheless, he believes that teachers are entitled to a private life outside of school, and what one does in one's own time is no business of anyone so long as it does not harm others.

Mr. Edwards is concerned that the community will be enraged if Ms. Fabian goes through with her plan. Furthermore, he is uneasy about his own stake in this case if it became known that he had done nothing to prevent Sally from pursuing her goal. The question that Mr. Edwards must answer is whether he should, or even if he has the right to, discuss this issue with Ms. Fabian. Moreover, if Mr. Edwards discusses his concerns with Ms. Fabian, should the discussion be an exchange of ideas or should Mr. Edwards demand that she not follow through with her plan? In addition, does he have an obligation to inform the superintendent or the new principal at North High, both of whom are very conservative in their outlook?

Questions for Discussion

1. Does Mr. Edwards have a right to intercede in Ms. Fabian's decision to have a child as an unmarried person? If so, what are the possible approaches he might take? What is his best course of action?

2. Does the community have a right to challenge Sally's decision to have a child? Does the community have a right to ask that she lose her job if she carries forth her plan? In this case, who is the community, and do you think they are all speaking in one voice?

3. Would Ms. Fabian be a poor teacher simply because she had a baby out of wedlock?

4. Inasmuch as Ms. Fabian is not required to discuss her private life at school, is there any reason that the students would be affected by her actions? Is she setting a poor example for her students? Why or why not? Does it make a difference that she is an adult and her students are minors? Does it make a difference that she is going to be artificially inseminated and not naturally impregnated? Would you see the situation differently if Ms. Fabian had a long-term live-in relationship with a man and decided to get pregnant? If she became pregnant through the usual means but didn't know who the father of her child was?

CASE STUDY 3.3 THE TROUBLE WITH *DADDY'S ROOMMATE*

Did anyone ever say the job was going to be easy? No, of course not, but one hoped the positives would outweigh the negatives. That, however, did not seem to be the case today.

Wedgewood High School's principal, Mary Evans, a former English teacher (and perhaps more comfortable in that role), had just received a briefing regarding the recent action of her new assistant principal, Howard Brill. Brill's action was precipitated by a problem brought to his attention by Mr. Robert Press, a very irate parent.

The parent of a special education child in the school, Mr. Press was incensed that his son was being exposed to some "trash about queers" presented by his teacher that day in class. Mr. Press complained that his son had come home with the news that another English class was reading the children's book *Daddy's Roommate*. This book is about a gay parent and his relationship with a male friend. The assistant principal promised Mr. Press that he would immediately get to the bottom of the situation and see that it was rectified. Mr. Brill's first call was upstairs to the English Department, at which time he demanded that the chairperson inform him of what was going on.

She told him that Elizabeth Bennett, a senior English teacher who had been with the school district for 15 years and who had an excellent reputation, had decided to do a unit on minority groups and the prejudices encountered by them. Censorship was an additional topic in this unit. To let her class know that there are many minority groups that experience prejudice and censorship, Ms. Bennett assigned a variety of literary works, such as *The Diary of Anne Frank, Animal Farm,* and *Inherit the Wind,* and the two children's books, *Little Black Sambo* and *Daddy's Roommate.* Although each member of the class had a copy of all the classics, they did not have copies of the two children's books. These books were presented in class for discussion.

What happened on the day in question was entirely beyond Ms. Bennett's control. Basil Howard, another English teacher (who is considered poor, at best, by his colleagues), saw the book *Daddy's Roommate* on Ms. Bennett's desk and took it. Without stopping to ask why such a book was in a senior-level English class, Howard, enraged, went to his class where he presented the book to his students, making satirical and angry comments about the content of the book. As the remarks became louder, the special education teacher, Paul Jenkins, came by and joined in the book-bashing session. Jenkins then took the book to his special education class and presented it with less than favorable comments; hence, the angry phone call to the assistant principal.

Complaints of parents are taken very seriously by the district's central office administration, and past practice has been to accede to the parents' wishes. Thus, Mr. Brill, the new assistant principal, thought he was taking appropriate action when he banned both *Little Black Sambo* and *Daddy's Roommate* from the curriculum. However, he was hardly prepared for the passionate reaction of Ms. Bennett, who went directly to the principal and stated that Mr. Brill had violated her academic freedom and demanded that the books in question be reinstated.

Principal Evans knew she needed to act quickly before the incident escalated further. She also knew her action had to be fair to all concerned. To complicate matters further, Mary Evans had very strong convictions concerning censorship. She could not ignore these convictions now.

Questions for Discussion

1. Which persons will be affected by Mary Evans' decision? What would each of these persons like to see done? Is there a solution to this problem that would be fair and just to all those concerned? If so, what is it?

2. Is it important to teach students about prejudice and censorship? Why? Is there anything morally wrong with the way Elizabeth Bennett is presenting this issue? Why or why not? Is Principal Evans' decision regarding the book censorship a moral decision? Why or why not?

3. How do you personally feel about censorship? Are your convictions different when applied to a school setting? Why or why not? Do school personnel have a moral obligation to expose students to a multiplicity of ideas? To protect students from knowing about certain issues? Explain your answers.

4. What would you do if you were in Principal Evans' place? Would your decision be different if the issue were strictly political rather than one dealing with sex or sexual orientation?

CASE STUDY 3.4   THE SCHOOL OF HARD KNOCKS

Ricky Johnson was known as a school bully. During the school year several students suffered from his aggressive and mean behavior. Ricky was only in the first grade and had already developed a reputation among his peers and the school community.

This particular day, during lunch, Ricky decided he was going to challenge every boy in his class to a physical battle. He proceeded to run over to several of his classmates and punch them in the stomach. Unfortunately for Ricky, Mr. Washington, the school security guard, witnessed his behavior and was able to stop him before he struck another student.

Mr. Washington brought Ricky kicking and screaming to the main office where he was received by the school nurse and guidance counselor. While in the nurse's office, Ricky continued to scream, stating that Mr. Washington had held him down and allowed another student (John Petterson) to punch him in the stomach. After hearing Ricky's allegation, the guidance counselor immediately located John and questioned him about the incident. John confirmed Ricky's claim and stated that Mr. Washington did give him permission to punch Ricky in the stomach while he held him.

In the midst of this incident, Ms. Henry, the school principal, arrived and immediately the guidance counselor and nurse apprised her of the situation. Not wasting a minute, Ms. Henry spoke to all of the parties involved.

- Mr. Washington denied the allegations and stated that John did punch Ricky in the stomach, but it was while he was holding Ricky and trying to prevent him from punching another student. Mr. Washington also stated that he has worked in this school district for over 25 years and would never do anything to intentionally harm a student.
- Ricky was very adamant about the fact that Mr. Washington had held him and allowed John to punch him in the stomach.
- John Petterson confirmed Ricky's allegation and stated for the second time that Mr. Washington gave him permission to punch Ricky in the stomach while he held him.

Ms. Henry questioned additional student witnesses who were sitting in the area where the alleged incident took place. Each and every witness stated that Mr. Washington held Ricky and gave John permission to punch him in the stomach.

It was extremely difficult for Ms. Henry to imagine that Mr. Washington would ever do anything intentionally to put a child in a harmful situation. She desperately wanted to believe Mr. Washington. Perhaps there was some misunderstanding. However, all the witness statements seemed to support Ricky's allegations.

Later on in this disturbing day, Ms. Henry received a call from Mr. Green, the Millville District Superintendent. Mr. Green called, *off the record*, to inquire about the situation with Mr. Washington. Apparently Mr. Green had worked with Mr. Washington for 10 years. He was the security guard in the school where the superintendent began his career as a principal in the district. Mr. Green went on to further explain that something like this could ruin Mr. Washington's 25-year career and reputation. Mr. Washington had never been involved in this type of incident previously. He was considered to be a pillar in the community. After hearing all the facts of the incident, Mr. Green went on to suggest that perhaps Ms. Henry could reprimand him behind closed doors and have him apologize to the student. After all, said the superintendent, people make mistakes and the student did not sustain any serious injury.

Questions for Discussion

1. Is there a law, policy, or guideline to help Ms. Henry make a wise decision?
2. If there is no law, policy or guideline, should there be one?
3. Was Mr. Green's behavior unethical? Was his call to Ms. Henry, *off the record*, and his suggestion as to how she should handle the situation unethical? Why or why not?

4. Did Mr. Green exercise the ethic of care? If yes, for whom? And why?
5. How might the ethics of the community be applied to this dilemma?
6. What decision would be in the best interest of Ricky? Of Mr. Washington?

Chapter 4

Traditional Curriculum Versus Hidden Curriculum

Leon D. Poeske, Spencer S. Stober, Jane Harstad,
James C. Dyson, and Lynn A. Cheddar

This chapter moves instructional issues beyond the classroom and even the school. It asks educators to consider their own values in relation to their curricular selections and hopefully makes them aware of some unintended outcomes for their students, the school, and the community regarding what they choose to teach or what they must teach.

In American education today, one of the paradoxes that exists has to do with the curriculum. Some writers (e.g., Bennett, 1988; Bennett, Finn, & Cribb, 2000; Hirsch, 1987, 1996; Ravitch, 2003; Ravitch & Finn, 1987) have emphasized the necessity to keep the traditional curriculum of U.S. schools in place. By this, they mean holding on to the classical canon and maintaining meanings and knowledge that have stood the test of time. Above all, these authors focus on the need for shared values and a communal culture.

At the same time, other writers (e.g., Anyon, 1980, 2005; Apple, 1986, 2000, 2001, 2003, 2006; Fine, 1991; Freire, 1970, 1993, 1998; Giroux, 1992, 2000, 2003, 2006; Greene, 1978, 1988, 2000; Weis & Fine, 2005) have stressed the importance of critiquing the traditional curriculum. In their critiques, these scholars have exposed the hidden curriculum of domination (Purpel & Shapiro, 1995). They have drawn people's attention to traditional education that tends to reproduce the inequalities within society. This curriculum of domination teaches many young people to be competitive, individualistic, and authoritarian. It also labels and places a number of students on educational tracks that lead to limited success in adult life.

Although traditionalists may make the claim that their curriculum is value-free and apolitical, this assumption can be challenged. Schools have consistently conveyed the message of "possessive individualism" and "meritocracy." Implicit in the traditional curriculum is the notion that if one doesn't succeed, it is one's own fault. Also implicit is the concept that those who are not middle class, White, male, and Eurocentric are frequently considered to be "others" (i.e., different sex, race, ethnicity, sexual orientation, or culture).

Critical theorists who have exposed the hidden curriculum have done so through the use of inquiry. They have asked specific questions such as: What should be taught about Christopher Columbus? How should the "discovery" of America be presented to students? What are the "facts," and how should they be explored by students? These critics also know that students learn not only from what is taught in school but also from what is *not* being taught. They also ask: Should current controversial topics be discussed in schools? If so, how should the new curriculum be delivered? What is the message sent to students if "hot" topics are ignored in today's schools? And what is the message to students if the school budget is shrinking, and new, important instructional material cannot be added to the curriculum owing to the lack of funds?

By asking difficult and challenging questions, educational leaders can expose the hidden curriculum. Armed with this new knowledge, with the help of teachers, staff, parents, and the community, educational leaders have the possibility of developing a curriculum that is truly in the best interests of their students. Educational leaders can make changes in their schools using a number of lenses and/or approaches. For example, they can turn to the ethic of care and develop, with the help of Noddings (1992, 2002, 2003), a school with a caring curriculum. Noddings has offered educators a framework for a general education curriculum organized around themes of care rather than the traditional disciplines.

Educational leaders can also turn to the work of Starratt (1994b) and build an ethical school with a curriculum that takes into account the lenses of justice, critique, and care. This curriculum gives teachers and students ample time for discussions and projects that "will serve to nurture the basic qualities of autonomy, connectedness and transcendence in developmentally appropriate ways" (p. 68).

In addition, educational leaders can consider the real-world ethics advocated by Nash (1996). This kind of ethics "is a complex admixture of personal, social and professional morality" (p. 1) and is grounded in applied ethics. The study of meaningful and current ethical dilemmas could be of importance not only to students but to teachers, staff, and the community as well.

This chapter contains five cases. In case study 4.1, AIDS and Age-appropriate Education, parents complain about a sixth-grade poster project that is part of a mandated class on AIDS education. State law requires some type of instruction. The posters are very creative, and some have real condoms on them. There are pregnancy problems in the school, but some parents complain to Mr. Thompson, the assistant superintendent for curriculum, that they do not want their children exposed to these posters. Mr. Thompson is in a quandary as to what to do.

Case study 4.2, Vivisection: A Dilemma for the Undergraduate Classroom, addresses first-year college students' problems with the pithing of frogs. Animal rights' issues are pitted against human rights' issues, and the teacher is placed in a difficult situation. Here, the chair of the biology department has to deal with his own beliefs as well as those of the students. He also has to reflect on the traditional curriculum that still provides appropriate training for future scientists and doctors regarding the pithing of frogs, compared with an alternative approach that could take into account students' and society's increasing awareness and support of animal rights.

Case study 4.3, Culturally Responsive Curriculum or an Ethical Dilemma?, involves an administrator who must navigate the fine line between a teacher's attempts to make the curriculum culturally relevant while inadvertently causing problems for a Native American student in her class and a parent's concerns for the welfare of his child and the authenticity of what is being taught. Here, one may consider that even the best of intentions may result in problems if there is cultural insensitivity or a lack of understanding.

Case study 4.4, School Budget Blues and Copyright, focuses on a district with a shrinking school budget where teachers cannot order the materials they need to do their jobs well, and at the same time they are unable to duplicate material because of copyright laws. Recently, the principal had sent out a memo reminding teachers about the copyright legislation. In this case, an outstanding teacher is caught by the principal duplicating materials. The principal is aware of the difficulties placed on the teacher who is desirous of providing her class with current instructional material, and yet he is very concerned about violating the law.

Case study 4.5, There's No Place Like School, illustrates problems that happen when regular classroom teachers are reluctant to be involved in inclusion programs which require that students with disabilities be educated in the same classrooms as all other children. The hard decisions that administrators must make in assigning teachers as well as students are stressed.

CASE STUDY 4.1 AIDS AND AGE-APPROPRIATE EDUCATION

Eugene Thompson, assistant superintendent for curriculum at the Meadow Woods Consolidated School District, was not sure how Dr. Rose Jones, the superintendent, would side on this issue. He knew Dr. Jones was supportive of a K–12 sex education program, but Mr. Thompson also understood her desire to "keep the peace" with the public. Mr. Thompson's concern began when a few parents of sixth-grade students at the district's Forest Middle School objected to posters hanging outside the health room. The parents noticed the posters during the school's Back to School Night. They complained about the posters discussing how to have safe sex. The parents told him how some even had real condoms as part of the poster.

Mr. Thompson knew the posters were in that school's hallway, but he did not actually give it much thought, especially because the health education teacher, Marcus Fine, reminded him of the curriculum for the seventh-grade AIDS unit. It stated, "All students shall understand ways to prevent Acquired Immune Deficiency Syndrome (AIDS) without the instructor placing bias on either abstinence or the use of contraceptive devices." It was Dr. Jones who had pushed for this curriculum unit just three years earlier, and it had been unanimously approved by the district's curriculum committee and supported wholeheartedly by the school's principal, Susan Kaplan. Mr. Fine justified the poster project as a creative approach for students to understand the ways to prevent the transmission of the AIDS virus. He also noted that this project was for the seventh grade and not the sixth grade.

Before Mr. Fine left the Back to School Night event, Mr. Thompson approached him with the parents' concerns. Marcus Fine asked, "Why are the sixth-grade parents complaining to you? This is a project for the seventh-grade students."

"Look, Marcus, the parents feel their sixth-grade students are too young to be exposed to that type of message. They feel their children do not need to be exposed to such graphic representations of how to prevent AIDS. They also believe we are only promoting the use of condoms while not attempting to promote abstinence. They have already called the superintendent's office, and I'm sure we'll both be getting a call from Dr. Jones soon."

"With all due respect, Mr. Thompson," Marcus replied, "I had approached you regarding this project and you gave me the okay. Look, this poster's message is loud and clear: BE SMART, JUST SAY NO. ABSTINENCE IS THE SAFEST WAY TO PREVENT AIDS. I've attempted to be supportive of students who wish to prevent the spread of AIDS—from both sides of this issue."

"Marcus, I understand that, but I am also concerned about Dr. Jones' response to the parents. The parents are going to focus on the posters that blatantly state, USE CONDOMS. This is the type of poster the parents find offensive. They believe their kids are too young to be exposed to condom posters in the school hallways."

Mr. Thompson left the discussion feeling that Mr. Fine was unwilling to understand the other side of the issue. He realized that Marcus Fine had conducted some controversial lessons in the past, but knew that this one could become heated in the community. Even though the state mandated lessons on AIDS education, it was not too long ago that the school board banned some of the library books dealing with sexuality and the human body. The board justified that move by saying they acted on the opinions of the community.

The following day, Mr. Thompson began receiving phone calls from a few parents of current fourth-grade students. They were concerned about this poster project for the following year because their children would be moving into Forest Middle School for fifth grade due to overcrowding at the grade school. Mr. Thompson listened to the parents' complaints. They felt that 10- and 11-year-old children should not be exposed to the explicit message of safe sex. They said it was in "poor taste" and an "obvious decay of moral values in our society." How could the district condone such immorality? Mr. Thompson listened to the parents and mentioned that he also believed it was a little young for fifth graders to be exposed to such sexual messages. He conveyed to the parents the district's policy on the instruction of sex education to all the grades. He emphasized that discussions on the use of condoms was not in the curriculum for the fifth and sixth grades. Even so, the parents made it perfectly clear that their children should not be subjected to such safe-sex posters for the following year.

Mr. Thompson later heard from the superintendent. Dr. Jones wanted to meet with Mr. Thompson and Mr. Fine the following day to discuss the posters. She gave direct orders that Mr. Thompson take the posters down before she arrived at the school. Although she had heard only the parents' side of the issue, Mr. Thompson realized that Dr. Jones was in no mood to debate, and he felt it was best to follow her orders. He knew Mr. Fine would not be pleased with this directive, but understood that it could be considered insubordination if he did not adhere to Dr. Jones' request.

As he walked down to Mr. Fine's room at the end of the day, he passed two seventh-grade girls in the hallway. One was eight months pregnant. He wondered what message was really being sent if the posters came down.

Questions for Discussion

1. Who decides at what age various parts of the curriculum should be introduced? At what age should students be exposed to explicit ways to prevent AIDS and pregnancy?
2. Is there a commonly accepted age when teachers can have students do an assignment such as the one presented? How do teachers or administrators know where to draw the line? Should the community have input into the specifics of the school curriculum? When, if ever,

should the concerns of some community members become school policy?

3. If Dr. Jones had not even seen any of the posters, how could she know that the posters were inappropriate for the middle-school students? Does Dr. Jones have legitimate concerns over the following year's incoming fifth-grade class?

CASE STUDY 4.2 VIVISECTION: A DILEMMA FOR THE UNDERGRADUATE CLASSROOM

Morgan College is an undergraduate private liberal arts institution that is church affiliated. This college takes great pride in its biology department. Many of its students, both male and female, continue with their further education and enter careers in the health and science fields.

In an introductory biology class, several of the laboratory activities require freshly pithed frogs that students use to perform experiments on the functioning frog heart. Frogs are anesthetized prior to pithing to prevent pain and suffering. Biology students take this activity very seriously; experimental success requires careful dissection to expose the frog heart without damaging the surrounding organs and vessels. The first stage of the pithing process renders the frog brain dead, and the second stage reduces skeletal muscle reflex activity.

Specifics of the pithing procedure are not described here; many laboratory manuals include a procedure similar to a classic source-book for biology teachers by Morholt, Brandwein, and Alexander (1966). Several additional experiments that require fresh tissue do not necessitate pithing but do require careful dissection to remove tissue from a freshly killed frog (e.g., a sciatic nerve). For these procedures, most students prefer to use a decapitated frog instead of a pithed (brain-dead) frog.

In general, biology teachers and students are finding it increasingly difficult to justify vivisection, particularly in church-affiliated institutions. Consequently, the chair of the Biology Department, Dr. Hartiz, has decided to not require students to perform or observe the pithing process, but they are encouraged to work through the experimental vivisection procedures with their laboratory group.

Although Dr. Hartiz has made this decision, he has some qualms about the scientific background he is now providing to all of his students. On the one hand, biology students have extensive dissection experience with preserved specimens. On the other hand, the students' experiences of and responses to the procedure are varied. Some students are not willing to observe vivisection whereas others are willing to observe but not perform vivisection. Only a few students are willing to perform the procedure. These students often indicate that they find the experience to be less traumatic if the frog has been treated with an amphibian anesthetic prior to pithing and vivisection.

Students are not in agreement on the vivisection issue, and experimental groupings are usually sufficiently diverse to provide constructive debate among group members. The following dialogue highlights the issues surrounding "live dissection." Ahn contemplates a career in medical technology. She refuses to observe the procedure. Rodney plans to major in premed and eventually become a physician. Rodney is willing to perform the procedure and is attempting to convince Ahn that live dissection is necessary.

Ahn: I refuse to hurt that frog!

Rodney: The anesthetic has knocked him out—won't feel a thing. Besides, pithing renders the frog brain dead.

Ahn: That is not the issue! What gives us the right to take this frog's life, and for what purpose?

Rodney: For months I have been dissecting stinky rubbery preserved specimens. I plan to attend medical school, and I'm going to try my hand at this procedure. If I can't handle it, I better find out now!

Ahn: I'm sure you can handle it . . . you big brute! What makes our species superior to other species?

Rodney: *Think* about it, Ahn. I am sure the frog can't! . . . Or can he? Do you think that doctors never practice?

Ahn: It is not necessary for this frog to be sacrificed so that you can become a doctor or to find out if you have the stomach for medicine. Besides, no medical procedures should be performed unless the result is expected to extend life.

Rodney: Oh! Well, in that case, I'll sew him back up!

Ahn: *You are hopeless!* I'll be back after the procedure.

Rodney: Why should I share my data with you if you don't contribute to the activity?

Ahn: Because the teacher said that I may instead use a new computer program that simulates the effects of acetylcholine and adrenaline on the frog heart.

Rodney: Fine for your purposes, but I plan to use this herbal extract as an additional independent variable—find *that* in your computer simulation!

Ahn: What practical application might your herbal extract have? It is unlikely that *you* would stumble on some amazing substance by accident!

Rodney: If I did, would this frog's death be justified?

Ahn: Depends how amazing the substance is . . . but just experimenting with no practical application in mind is *not* justified.

Rodney: But that is what basic science is all about.

Ahn: Well, Mr. Serendipitous . . . you do your thing and I'll do mine.

Questions for Discussion

1. Do animals have rights? Do we, as human beings, have a responsibility to species other than ourselves?

2. What are the pros and cons of pithing frogs? If you were the chair of the Biology Department, would you permit this procedure? Would your answer be different if the animal were a dog, a cat, a horse? Why or why not? How would you decide where to draw the line?

3. Pithing frogs is legal and sometimes considered to be a good practice. Do these things also make it ethical? Why or why not?

4. If pithing frogs was the only way to improve medical practice and save human lives, would that justify the practice? What if it were not the only way but was clearly the best way, would your answer change? Why or why not?

CASE STUDY 4.3 CULTURALLY RESPONSIVE CURRICULUM OR AN ETHICAL DILEMMA?

Dr. Adams had been repeating her morning ritual of greeting the students in the hallway as they arrive from their various neighborhoods to start their school day. Her administrative assistant, Delta, came rushing up to speak to her, a tormented look on her face. Delta pulled her over to the side of the hallway and spoke in a whispered rush, "You have a student in your office, and he's not alone! This kid brought trouble with him!" Dr. Adams hurried back to her office, determined to resolve whatever issues her visitors had. As she entered the outer office, she heard raised voices coming from her own open doorway.

Dr. Adams had been enjoying a wonderful morning in her urban middle school. Her 425 students came from a variety of neighborhoods in a sprawling Midwestern city. A wide array of children attended her school from many socio-economic and ethnic backgrounds. She prided herself on the fact that her school was normally a smooth-running operation with only a few behavioral issues; the climate of the school was something she had worked at diligently since becoming the administrator four years previously.

When she entered her office she found Jeremy Standing Elk, a normally quiet and shy Lakota student, sitting with his father, Harold. It was obvious that Harold was upset, and Jeremy seemed bewildered. Harold was speaking slowly and surely, yet his tone was heated as he explained the situation.

Jeremy, a student in the core American history block, was in class the previous day studying westward expansion when his teacher, Beth, divided the students into three distinct groups; cowboys, settlers, and Indians. Jeremy was grouped with the Indians. Although he felt apprehensive about it, Jeremy didn't want to speak up and say anything in protest. As the lesson proceeded, the group of five boys who were "Indians" complained that they didn't want to be Indians; they felt that they were all going to get killed off, so they started to talk about scalping some cowboys. The father also explained that the boys in the "cowboys" group were in a different clique in the school and that there was a history of tension between the groups. As the lesson proceeded, each group was asked to write about how they felt about the westward expansion and how it had affected their "group." One person from each group was then asked to "share" these ideas in front of the class.

Teacher Beth was at her desk, on her computer, preparing for the next week's lessons. Although present in the room, she was used to the sound of students chattering and discussing the student ideas so she tuned out the conversations. As the lesson progressed, Jeremy tried to get his group back on track by saying that they needed to write some things down. Unfortunately his words went unheeded; in fact, the boys in his group chided him about being the one who should do the writing because of his Indian heritage. One of the students went so far as to say that Jeremy should get up and do his "war dance" in front of the class.

Teacher Beth didn't see or hear these conversations go on, and the class did not have enough time to share before the bell rang for the end of the period. Jeremy was relieved, and as Beth finished by saying there had been some wonderful conversations going on, Jeremy was feeling rather disheartened about his group situation. As the class filed out of the door, the other boys in his group patted their hands on their mouths and made the "aye yi yi yi" sound prevalent in so many stereotypical old Hollywood movies. Jeremy chuckled at his pals as they left the classroom.

Jeremy's father, Harold, was clearly upset as he told of his son's experience. Dr. Adams respectfully agreed that the purpose of the lesson was good; however, the practices used to achieve the lesson's objectives could be improved. Dr. Adams, knowing she needed to hear the teacher's side of this incident, set up a meeting with Harold and Beth for after school the following day, giving ample time to notify the teacher of the issues the student and his father had brought up.

Meeting to resolve the dilemma

The meeting after school took place in Dr. Adams' office, and as Harold Standing Elk walked in, he was amazed to see five people in the room. Although concerned about the extra people, Harold sat down with Jeremy and placed a book on the table (*Lies My Teacher Told Me* by James Loewen). The meeting started with introductions. Harold was surprised to find two curriculum specialists and a social worker among the group. The teacher then started out emphatically with, "Mr. Standing Elk, I *am* a good teacher, I've been teaching for 17 years now, and I *know* I am a good teacher! But let's talk about Jeremy. He comes to class late maybe two or three times a week, and he hardly ever contributes to class discussions, so frankly, I'm surprised to hear he has anything to say at this point in the year! I have brought in the social worker so maybe we can discuss why Jeremy doesn't really speak up in class, but instead he is telling *you* about what is going on. His grades are mediocre at best, and I'm sure we can all work this out to where Jeremy is going to get a better grade. As a concerned parent, I know you and I can arrive at some agreement."

Dr. Adams was a mildly concerned over the defensive tone of Teacher Beth, and tried to calmly yet assertively interject that Beth was a qualified and professional educator. Harold cut her off abruptly; "Well, I thought I was here to talk about what happened in class yesterday; I am worried about what my son is learning in your class and about how you're teaching about Natives." Harold's voice got louder as he went on. "My boy doesn't like to get up in front of others and say things, and he has few friends as it is. He doesn't want to rock the boat, and he's even mad at me for coming in. I just want to know what you're teaching here in this school, and why my son has to put up with racism in class!" Almost shouting, he added, "And just what in the heck are these folks doing here?" as he gestured at the two curriculum specialists.

Dr. Adams then drew attention to the fact that the curriculum had been recently revised to include ideas other than the Western perspective so prevalent in American history curricula. The specialists told Harold that the lesson was designed to enable Native students to have a say in the history curriculum. They also suggested that if Jeremy was upset by what went on in the classroom, perhaps there was a way that he could speak up during the class rather than deal with it after the incident occurred; this was why the social worker was present. Everyone could see that Harold was very upset by now.

"Doesn't anyone here care about my son? Don't you know what it's like for him trying to get along with kids who make fun of him and his culture every day? All you care about is some silly curriculum that doesn't even teach the *real* history, or that someone's a good teacher even when they don't notice the racism in their own classroom, but you all don't even know my son or what he's about or *how* he thinks!"

Dr. Adams was finding out just how little she knew about how to address this issue.

Questions for Discussion

1. Were the educators in this dilemma caring? Why or why not? How could each of these individuals have worked to resolve this dilemma in a more caring manner?
2. What would be the most just course of action for Jeremy? For the teacher? For the other students in the class?
3. To what extent is the teacher responsible for implementing a culturally responsive curriculum and culturally responsive pedagogy?
4. What is a culturally sensitive curriculum? How might this classroom activity be viewed through a lens of critique?
5. How would the profession expect each of these educators to handle this situation? Did they act in a professional manner? Why or why not?

CASE STUDY 4.4 SCHOOL BUDGET BLUES AND COPYRIGHT

The Pierpoint School District had undergone major changes in the past five years. The student population had more than doubled with no signs of slowing down. A new superintendent had come on board, and construction had begun on three more buildings. The additional students, materials, buildings, and staff needed each year to accommodate the overwhelming growth was staggering. Each year, the budget process grew more tense and territorial as departments fought for the few available dollars. Dr. Sharif, principal of Valley View High School, knew this year's budget would again be tough and bare-bones. What the board and superintendent were demanding seemed impossible.

In compliance with the central administration's request, the following year's school budget was originally submitted without any allowances for inflation, additional students, or the expenses that accompany them. Now central administration was mandating further cuts from every school. The faculty had been complaining about the concessions they were already forced to make. Dr. Sharif knew he would bear the brunt of the teachers' anger and criticism for this new round of cuts. As far as the cuts for his school were concerned, the only fair thing to do would be to take an equal amount from each department.

Throughout the past few years, cost-cutting measures had been put in place in all of the district's operations, presumably to ease the need for additional funds. One major and highly controversial cost-cutting measure was the introduction of a central copying center to be used by the entire district. Although there would still be a copier housed in each building, the large, multiple classroom copying needs were to be sent to the central copying center. Teachers were reminded that even though there had been cuts in instructional materials, they were not to make copies of copyrighted material.

Dr. Sharif was continuing to agonize over which items to cut from each department's budget request when he began to hear noises in the outer office. It had been hours since the office staff had gone home, and the custodians had already cleaned the offices. Dr. Sharif immediately went to investigate and found Jane Tharp, one of the school's most dedicated and well-respected teachers, in the outer office. An instructor of instrumental music, Ms. Tharp had stopped in after a band rehearsal to use the office copier. She was startled by Dr. Sharif's sudden appearance. As Dr. Sharif drew closer, Ms. Tharp appeared to be trying to hide what she was doing. When he was close enough, Dr. Sharif could see that Ms. Tharp was copying music for one of her bands. Dr. Sharif was dumbfounded. Not only was this against district policy, it was illegal. The superintendent had recently sent a memo to all district employees reminding them about the legalities and liabilities of making photocopies of copyrighted materials.

Ms. Tharp immediately began to try to rationalize her deed by pointing to the rising cost of music, the number of students in her bands, and the declining budget money.

Questions for Discussion

1. Is anything truly wrong with what Ms. Tharp is doing? Is she being dishonest? Is she stealing? Explain your answer.

2. Do you think Dr. Sharif is concerned because the superintendent might uncover what is happening? Because the publishing company might possibly find out and he would be held personally liable? What other reasons might there be for Dr. Sharif to be concerned? Would your answer as to what Dr. Sharif should do change depending on his motivations? How would it change?

3. What do you see as the reasoning behind copyright laws? Who do they protect? What are the consequences of violating them? Are they just laws?

4. What action do you think Dr. Sharif should take? What is your reasoning? What would be the fairest decision Dr. Sharif could make? Fairest for whom? What would be the most caring decision? What parties should Dr. Sharif consider in making a caring decision? Explain your logic.

5. Do you think Ms. Tharp's actions would be easier, or harder, to justify if she made multiple copies of music for personal use, to give to her friends? If she were not a good teacher? Why?

CASE STUDY 4.5 THERE'S NO PLACE LIKE SCHOOL

It was that time of year again. Mrs. Stell sighed as she considered her task. As supervisor of special education, she needed to guide the assignment of students receiving special education services to regular education class lists for the upcoming year. Her task was made considerably more difficult at Kessler Elementary due to the number of children with special academic, emotional, and behavioral difficulties moving from third grade to fourth grade. Further complicating her task was the number of teachers less than eager to take on these added responsibilities without the benefit of direct help from learning support teachers. She had only one special education teacher per grade available. She considered the recent history of the district, specifically the past five years. She knew that although momentum was building to move past the difficulties, the district still had many changes to make.

Simonsville and Kessler Township are considered to be part of Hailysburg, one of the fastest growing areas of the state. Until recently, a large steel mill in nearby Blairsville employed many of the area's residents. With the mill's decline, employment lies mainly with smaller factories, companies, and small businesses in the area. The Kessler School District enrollment numbers approximately 2,100 students housed in four buildings sorely in need of renovation. The school district's student population is 96.99% White and very poor.

During the past 13 years, the district has had seven different superintendents during eight periods of leadership. One period in particular sparked great contention. While assistant superintendent in another district, the superintendent had been instrumental in implementing inclusive practices. At Kessler he decreed that all children, to the maximum extent possible, would be taught in the regular education classroom. In the past, the district had an unusually high proportion of identified students with individual education plans (IEPs), suggesting a pointed belief in the "placement" of students with special needs. Previously, personnel of the intermediate unit (IU) provided special education services in pull-out programs. Beginning in the 1993 to 1994 school year, the district assumed responsibility for its learning support students, and immediately many of these began to be included in regular classrooms.

This sudden move to inclusive practices caused substantial dissension in the district. This was a radical departure in philosophy for a district whose special education population exceeded that of the national average. Indeed, during the past four years, Kessler Elementary had special education populations double that of the national average. As a result of the superintendent's mandate, most students labeled as students in need of learning support were placed in regular education classrooms. Learning support teachers ran from classroom to classroom trying to deliver one-on-one instruction to all of the students.

In addition, some members of the school board locked this superintendent out of his office in response to an alleged directive by him that principals attend a meeting where a speaker with a political agenda would be presiding. This action resulted in a court case, much publicity, and growing distrust among the board members, community, teachers, and administration. The upheaval had far-reaching after-effects. The current and assistant superintendents, respectively, both in the district for less than 18 months, were still picking up the pieces. Indeed, they were hired for the express purpose of getting Kessler School District back on track. They have begun the slow process of developing mission statements and goals and reforming instructional and curricular practices with the entire staff. As a result of this lack of continuity of leadership, each school within the district has been handling special education services in differing ways. There is little congruency of practices among the schools.

Mrs. Stell has been a faculty member for 30 years. Due possibly to the existing bad feelings concerning inclusion, she has done little to advocate for the philosophy. Rather than mandating the practice, she has allowed it to develop naturally. Truth be told, she had doubts about its appropriateness. However, she has seen inclusive practices and co-teaching allow more students, including those with IEPs, to attain greater achievements.

Following its initial impact, progress toward the implementation of an inclusive philosophy at Kessler Elementary was slow. For the past several years, all children with learning or emotional disabilities were placed with the two most agreeable and cooperative teachers at each grade level. Thus, the same two teachers at each grade level had a disproportionate number of labeled students each year. A special education teacher provided these two grade-level teachers support. Children in need of more extensive services were placed outside the district.

This move toward inclusive practices was only partially successful. Certainly, the teachers involved felt that students with special education labels belonged in the regular education classroom, but there was still little co-teaching and much pull-out. Generally, students were pulled out of the regular classroom and instructed in small groups in a separate room for a large proportion of the major subjects, such as reading and math. At first, teachers were less inclined to make modifications and adaptations in the classroom; yet, as a few teachers became more comfortable with the practices, their use became rather more frequent. Unfortunately, this practice did not spread through the entire faculty. However, many teachers, when planning for the following year, worked to ensure that their "kids" were placed with those teachers who did make accommodations and modifications and had the support of a special education teacher. As a result, two teachers at each grade level had a preponderance of children who were at risk of failure.

Mrs. Stell recalled conversations she had had with Mrs. Mitchell, a fourth-grade teacher: "I love working with a co-teacher. With two of us in the room, we're able to generate more ideas, observe more about each student, and provide more remediation and enrichment." Mrs. Stell sighed again. Mrs. Mitchell and her co-teacher Mrs. Freed clicked. They both felt that the "specially designed instruction" mandated on their students' IEPs could occur in the classroom. Not so for the third- and fifth-grade teachers. Mrs. Chase expressed those teachers' sentiments well when she said, "Sure, these students get a lot by just being in the regular education class–room, but they can't do the work the regular education students are doing. They need their own materials and instruction at their own levels. And they're so easily distracted, we have to go to another room." Mrs. Stell wondered when these teachers would think about a systematic process of achieving IEP goals within the context of typical classroom instruction and understand that not all students had to do the same thing at the same time.

This year, the situation became intolerable for two third-grade teachers. One, Mrs. Brandle, had five children with IEPs in addition to several other children who were at risk. The other teacher, Mrs. Carou, had seven children, out of 25, with IEPs. Both teachers found that not only did these children have special academic needs, but they had behavioral and emotional difficulties as well.

Mrs. Carou had begun her teaching career as an emotional support teacher. She was devoted to her students and enthusiastically strived to ensure their success. She could very ably articulate what each student was capable of achieving. In addition, she was quite capable of providing differentiated instruction in her classroom, ensuring that all the children would succeed. Despite the difficulties of meeting the needs of her students, it was obvious that each child had made progress.

For Mrs. Carou, this year had been exhausting. She began early in the year to make faculty aware that although all of her students were making progress, keeping the students with IEPs in just two classrooms the following year would do them and the other students a disservice. She was clear and emphatic about these beliefs.

At Kessler Elementary, Mrs. Stell, the guidance counselor, the instructional support (IS) teacher, and the principal met with the learning support teachers, the regular education teachers who worked with the students with IEPs. The discussion revolved around how best to serve the needs of all students the following year. It was evident from the start that the fourth-grade teachers did not agree with Mrs. Carou's recommendation. Most felt that centralizing the children with IEPs was more desirable because it allowed the special education teacher to more effectively deliver direct instruction. It would enable her to work with the students, plan, and co-teach with both of the regular education teachers.

When Ms. Marco, the new IS teacher, questioned why spreading the students among all of the classrooms was not considered, Mrs. Chemsky exclaimed, "We did that before and it didn't work. Because the students were all at different levels, it was a nightmare for the learning support teacher to try and get to all of them and teach them reading and math. She simply couldn't get around to all the students."

Ms. Marco seemed puzzled. "When you look at the instructional techniques, activities, materials, or assessment, modifications can be made in a methodical manner allowing most of our students to have their educational needs met within the context of regular classroom instruction." Most of the teachers greeted her statement with a blank stare. She tried again: "When you plan for instruction with your co-teacher, don't you look at using the least intrusive modifications first?" Many in the group started talking at once. "There was no time to co-teach." . . . "Planning . . . when could we plan?" . . . "The kids couldn't read, in the first place, how could they do any of the worksheets?" . . . "The kids need one-on-one instruction."

At this point, Mrs. Stell tried to engender a conversation about the idea that students receiving special education services did not necessarily need one-on-one instruction from the learning support teacher. Rather, whenever appropriate, instruction should be immersed in the instruction for the entire class. Co-teaching allowed, even encouraged, this to occur. Mrs. Stell could see that most of the teachers agreed emphatically with Mrs. Chemsky. However, it was certainly clear that they all felt that there was not enough support. More teachers and aides were needed to meet the needs of the students with IEPs.

Although the group clearly articulated the need for additional staff, the reality was that there was not enough money to hire more teachers or aides. When discussion focused on placement in two classes versus more classes, Mrs. Stell's comment to the faculty was that placement should be based on students' needs.

Mrs. Stell, the guidance counselor, Mrs. Carou, Mrs. Brandle, the learning support teacher, and the instructional support teacher studied options to optimize placement of students at risk and with IEPs for the following year. After much discussion and debate, it was clear that to best increase achievement for all, the students should be spread among the six fourth-grade classes. The classrooms had been separated into two groups. Three classes would contain the children with IEPs who had more intensive needs and would receive direct service from the special education teacher. The other three would contain the children whose IEP goals could be met by the regular education teacher in consultation with the special education teacher.

There remained a problem: Mrs. Clay. She had been teaching fourth grade for 27 years. She felt that students should be held to a high standard of expectation and that those students who could not meet the standards should be placed elsewhere. She felt that inclusion perpetrated a grave disservice to both regular education students and students with IEPs, placing undue pressure on the latter and also slowing instruction for the other students. She disagreed vehemently with the inclusive philosophy, stating vociferously that those children did not belong in her classroom.

Mrs. Stell considered her options. She could place the students in all fourth-grade classrooms and tell Mrs. Clay that she was responsible for teaching all children. Remembering an article she had recently read and agreed with, indicating that one bad year can affect a student's academic career long afterward, could she possibly consign a child to that possibility? If she did place children with IEPs with Mrs. Clay, she had two options. She could give her the children who would need more intensive adaptations and the part-time help of the learning support teacher. Alternatively, she could give her a class where the children's needs were not as intensive, but in which case she would receive very little direct support. Otherwise, she could choose not to give her any children who were at risk or had IEPs. This last option would probably ensure that students who were at risk would have good fourth-grade experiences. It would also make the other teachers' jobs more difficult. In addition, it did nothing to move the school toward the philosophy by which all children can learn and all children belong.

Questions for Discussion

1. What are the benefits and drawbacks of placing students in need of learning support in Mrs. Clay's classroom? What are the benefits or drawbacks of placing them in classrooms other than hers? Does Mrs. Stell need to consider Mrs. Clay's professional beliefs before placing students in her classroom? Why or why not?

2. If Mrs. Stell refrains from placing students receiving learning support in Mrs. Clay's classroom, how might that affect the school community? How do the students' and parents' wishes play into this problem?

3. If Mrs. Clay is assigned students with learning support, what support should the principal and Mrs. Stell offer? If Mrs. Clay is not assigned students with learning support, what role will she play to effect change toward a more inclusive philosophy?

4. What does the law say about placing students receiving special education services in regular classrooms?

Chapter 5

Personal Codes Versus Professional Codes

Deborah Weaver, William W. Watts, Angela Duncan, Patricia A. Maloney, and Susan Hope Shapiro

In this chapter, we explore the thorny problem of what happens when an individual's personal code of ethics differs from her or his professional code and/or the standards of the profession. This chapter raises personnel issues that go well beyond the people involved in the dilemmas. In these dilemmas, educational leaders are forced into positions in which they may have to draw the line between an individual's personal and professional life.

In chapter 2 of this book, the ethic of the profession was introduced as a paradigm and described in some detail. This ethic was discussed as a fourth paradigm for viewing and solving ethical dilemmas. Whereas the ethics of justice, critique, and/or care have been emphasized as paradigms by different scholars in educational leadership, rarely has the ethic of the profession been treated as a separate and discrete model. In this book, however, an argument has been made for professional ethics to be defined as a paradigm that includes ethical principles, codes of ethics, the ethics of the community, professional judgment, and professional decision making.

Shapiro and Stefkovich (1998) stressed the importance of asking educational leadership faculty and students to formulate and examine their professional codes in light of their personal codes, the codes of professional practice, and the codes of national, state, and local organizations. They are not alone in this emphasis. Duke and Grogan (1997), Mertz (1997), and O'Keefe (1997), to name but a few, have also encouraged a similar process.

The professional paradigm is based on the integration of personal and professional codes. However, an individual's personal and professional codes frequently collide. This makes it difficult for an educational leader to make the appropriate decisions. Shapiro and Stefkovich (1998), in their research of doctoral students in an educational leadership program, found that there were many conflicts both between and among students based on their professional and personal ethics. Not only were the conflicts among students, but they were within oneself. In analyzing codes, Shapiro and Stefkovich and their students thought it was important for educational leaders to look for consistencies and inconsistencies between and within their own personal and professional codes. Clashes were also discovered when an individual had been prepared in two or more professions. In this case, codes of one profession might be different from another; thus, what serves an individual well in one career may not help him or her well in another.

The five cases presented in this chapter offer the reader an opportunity to think through the decision-making process involving dilemmas that arise when an individual's personal ethics conflict with the professional ethics associated with public education. The cases highlight the paradoxes between personal and professional codes. In addition, the questions posed at the end of the cases encourage the discussion of other paradigms in relationship to personal and professional codes. The ethics of justice, critique, and care may be applied to the dilemmas described in this chapter. Educational leaders sometimes cross paradigms in their personal and professional codes but are not aware of this until they spend the time developing and reflecting on their beliefs.

In the first ethical dilemma, Drunkenness or Disease? (Case study 5.1), a director of special education has been convicted of drink driving. He is an alcoholic and the community wants him fired. Legally, the school district can do this because the state law says that school personnel may be fired for criminal convictions. However, the assistant superintendent for personnel is ambivalent because the individual is very effective in his work and has been so for a long time. In addition, the assistant superintendent believes this individual is suffering from a disease requiring support and assistance.

Case study, 5.2, Rising Star or Wife Beater?, focuses on a health and physical education teacher and coach of high school football, wrestling, and baseball who is well regarded by the school superintendent and is in line for a new and important position. The administrator finds that the teacher has been brought up on charges of domestic abuse. Although he has had the greatest respect for the teacher professionally, the superintendent is now beginning to feel differently about the teacher on a personal level. Many angry parents have heard about the teacher's domestic behavior and ask for his dismissal at a school board meeting. The superintendent is faced with a difficult decision that he is asked to make in a public forum.

In case study 5.3, After-school Antics, the leader of a small elementary school attempts to build a cooperative spirit among her staff through professional development. Unfortunately, the new positive relationship extends into "happy hour." On Facebook, a parent in this tight-knit community sees photos of her child's teacher having far too good a time at a local bar. How does the principal deal with a team spirit that moves beyond her teachers' professional codes and into their personal lives?

The fourth ethical dilemma, Job Sharing: Some Real Benefits (Case study 5.4), introduces us to an administrator who must balance the needs of employees and the guidelines of her board of education. This case involves a pilot job-sharing program in a district in which the teachers' union now demands full-time benefits for a year of part-time work. The union makes the case that currently only married people can afford to job share without a proper benefits package. This case resonates with the assistant superintendent for personnel on a personal level because she is single and would like to support benefits for unmarried people. However, professionally, she is aware that the job-sharing arrangement could establish a precedent enabling all part-time workers to request benefits. For the assistant superintendent, any decision made in this case may have repercussions that will affect her at the personal level and especially at the professional level in her relatively young career.

In Case study 5.5, When Teachers Fight, the administrator, in a preschool setting, has to grapple with teachers disrupting the school owing to personal disputes. Despite what most would consider to be highly unprofessional behavior, the director cannot help but feel some sympathy toward a teacher who has worked hard to save her family from homelessness. For this administrator, the ethic of care conflicts with the ethic of the profession.

CASE STUDY 5.1 DRUNKENNESS OR DISEASE?

Dr. Mari Wang sat in her office long after the school day had ended, contemplating the most recent problem that had occurred in the Harrison City School District. Since becoming an assistant superintendent for personnel five years earlier, she had had her share of problems, but never one involving a key administrator, especially one whom she had supported for the position.

Mr. Kidder currently held the central office position of Director of Special Education and had done so for the past four years. He had been a superstar special education teacher and had earned a Master's degree and a supervisory certificate some years previously that qualified him for the position when it fell vacant through a retirement. Mr. Kidder not only interviewed well but was also the teachers' first choice, having earned their respect and support during his 20-year service to the district as a classroom teacher as well as chairperson of several special assignments. In addition to his ability, Mr. Kidder possessed a charming and gregarious personality that often made it easy for him to develop an instant rapport with staff as well as parents. Dr. Wang had to admit that Mr. Kidder often brightened up her day with his stories, jokes, and optimistic attitude about life in general.

How sad that this was not the case today. In fact, just two hours previously, Mr. Kidder looked like the world had come to an end, and Dr. Wang was the only link saving him from a fate worse than death. Mr. Kidder's career was in jeopardy; he was about to go to jail because he had been arrested a few weeks earlier for drunk driving. To make matters worse, it was his third conviction, punishable by a three-month imprisonment in the local county jail.

The court decided that due to his position in the School District, his character witnesses during the trial, and the lack of any other illegal convictions, he would be eligible for the work-release program, pending approval from his place of employment. Mr. Kidder explained that he would arrange to have someone pick him up at the prison in the morning and bring him to work. He would be able to work until 5:30 p.m. each day, when someone would take him back to the prison by the required curfew of 6 p.m. This would be the arrangement for the next three months, which would take him to the end of May.

After the specifics of the court's recommendations and subsequent plans of Mr. Kidder, Dr. Wang felt it necessary to question him about his actions and why he would allow himself to be put in such a situation in the first place. Obviously embarrassed and ashamed, Mr. Kidder revealed that he had finally admitted to himself that he was an alcoholic. He was not sure when it had all started, but the pressures of the job and an unstable marriage had been a lot to handle on a daily basis, so he had gotten into the habit of stopping at a local tavern for a drink or two after work. After the first two arrests, he sloughed it off as just being unlucky that he was caught and paid the fine. He had had a couple of drinks but was certainly able to drive safely. He really felt that he was not doing anything wrong and that the law was unfair, too strict, and the result of political pressure groups.

The third arrest, coupled with the seriousness of the consequences, made him take a hard look at what he was doing to himself. He went on to say that he had taken the first step to recovery by attending an AA meeting and had recently stood up and admitted that he had an alcohol problem. It was his intention to sign himself into an alcohol recovery program, through the district's employee assistance benefit program, after the school year ended. This would involve six weeks during the summer, which also happened to be his vacation allotment.

Mr. Kidder was confident that he would be able to return to work, well on his way to recovery, and that this type of incident would never reoccur. He was extremely apologetic for his actions and any embarrassment it might cause the school administration, and was hopeful that the district would support his plans for recovery from this disease. Dr. Wang thanked Mr. Kidder for his candidness and told him she would get back to him with the decision of what action she would recommend to the superintendent and board of school directors the following day.

Dr. Wang realized that this problem had many facets to review before she could come to a decision. She knew she was in for a long night.

Questions for Discussion

1. Do you see Mr. Kidder's problem mainly as a disease or a lack of moral fiber? Explain your answer. Do you believe that as a teacher Mr. Kidder should be held to a higher moral standard than ordinary citizens? Why or why not? Should what Mr. Kidder does in his private life make a difference in his job status? Why or why not? Does it make a difference that he is a good teacher? A good administrator? A good colleague? Where would you draw the line between what is of public concern and what is strictly private when considering school employees?

2. Suppose that the law was politically motivated. Does that make a difference as to what Dr. Wang should do? Do you believe the law is unjust? Too strict? Why or why not? Who does the law benefit? If the law were unjust, should that make a difference as to Dr. Wang's decision?

3. What would a caring person do in Dr. Wang's place? To whom should care be directed? Are there others who should be considered in addition to Mr. Kidder? Who?

CASE STUDY 5.2 RISING STAR OR WIFE BEATER?

Alex teaches health and physical education in Maple Grove, an affluent school district. He is also a very successful high school football, wrestling, and baseball coach for the district and is recognized by many coaches throughout the state as an exceptional coach. Many of Alex's teams have won conference and state titles during his tenure. His athletes admire and respect him, and revere him as a father figure and role model. A large percentage of his athletes earn athletic scholarships to attend major colleges and universities. Some have gone on to careers as professional athletes. Many people—parents and students alike—feel a great deal of gratitude toward Alex for all of his time and effort in coaching, particularly Superintendent Brown.

Alex began his career as a substitute teacher in Maple Grove, making himself available to the school district at all times. He substituted in all subject areas as well as in physical education classes. He worked with all grades, and even volunteered his services to chaperone school activities such as dances, class trips, and any athletic event he was not coaching. He gave up his evenings and weekends to do what he could for the district in the hope of earning a permanent teaching position that provided him with a contract and stability in his chosen profession. He was motivated and determined to earn a teaching position as soon as possible. After three years of substitute teaching, Alex began to experience frustration and depression because he had not attained a full-time teaching position. However, a position was soon to open, and a contract would be awarded as well. In the interim, Alex continued to substitute as well as to coach football, wrestling, and baseball. Alex was particularly fond of coaching football and was considered an expert. Not only was Alex a talented coach, but he was very committed to coaching a winning program.

At the end of the school term, the teaching position Alex desired would be advertised, and applicants would start interviewing for the position. All of Alex's hard work and effort would soon pay off. A permanent teaching position and head coaching job were imminent. Even the assistant principal of the high school phoned him and offered his endorsement for the position. The interview process proceeded as scheduled. Alex's interview was nearly flawless. The following day, Alex received a phone call from the high school principal, Mr. Young, and was offered the position. Alex was ecstatic. Alex thought Monica, his wife, would be pleased as well. The couple had two children. They lived in a lovely home in the district and both children attended the district's schools. Their older child attended the high school and was actively involved in many activities, and their younger child attended one of the elementary schools. Monica had a teaching degree in special education and also worked for the district as a substitute teacher. There had been days when both Alex and Monica taught together in the same building and had their older daughter in class. On these days, both Alex and Monica acted very professionally and went about their responsibilities as usual.

By all appearances, Alex and Monica seemed to be the ideal couple and consummate professionals. Alex continued to excel at coaching, and the students in his classes all liked him very much. Superintendent Brown and Principal Young were very pleased with his recent evaluation and considered making plans to train and groom him for a future administrative position.

Monica seemed content to substitute regularly and was willing to start coaching a sport if the opportunity presented itself. Administrators were beginning to take notice of her positive teaching style and her ability to work well with students. However, although Alex and Monica's professional lives appeared stable and happy, their private life, especially their marital relationship, was undergoing serious difficulties.

In the ensuing weeks, Alex and Monica had many fights and arguments at home. Their marital problems continued to escalate, and the stress began to have an effect on Alex's professional obligations and responsibilities. Alex was exhibiting a short temper with his students, colleagues, and even some parents. His physical appearance was disheveled, and rumors that alcohol could be smelled on his breath were circulating. Colleagues noticed that he often arrived late to school and late to some of his classes. His athletes also saw a change in his behavior at practices and were very concerned.

Principal Young also noticed these changes and immediately requested a conference with Alex. In their meeting, Alex confided to Principal Young that he and his wife had separated. He said it was a temporary situation and he felt a reconciliation was soon to occur. Alex apologized for his lack of professionalism over the past few weeks and assured Principal Young that it would not happen again. Superintendent Brown was informed of the matter but was not overly concerned.

The following week, Superintendent Brown received a phone call from the school district solicitor, who informed him that Alex had been arrested the previous night for assault and battery of his wife. She was not seriously injured during this incident and, therefore, decided not to press charges against her husband. Because the school year was coming to an end, Principal Young and Superintendent Brown decided not to make an issue of the incident. They also felt that the summer break would ease any community concerns about what had happened. Besides, Alex's reputation in the district was very positive, and he was the football coach. He did not need any bad publicity.

During the summer break, Alex had another altercation with his wife and was again arrested for assault and battery. This time his wife decided to file and press criminal charges against Alex. She even contacted her attorney to begin divorce proceedings. Her decision to press charges resulted in headlines in the local newspaper, thus alerting the community, school board members, and school officials to the situation.

The news of Alex's arrest spread quickly throughout the school district. Many parents were angry and very concerned about the situation. A group of parents organized to discuss their concerns and agreed to go to the school board to demand the resignation or firing of Alex. Reports indicated that more than 100 parents signed a petition supporting Alex's dismissal and that they planned to storm the next school board meeting in protest.

Shortly after Alex's arrest, his wife once again decided to drop the charges. District officials took the news at face value. They did not think about the cycle of battering as it affected this case. They even put aside their concerns about the community discord over the matter. School officials felt that at the upcoming board meeting a few parents would voice their opinions over this incident and then the meeting would proceed as scheduled. School officials, however, underestimated the outrage which community members were experiencing.

More than 100 parents attended the board meeting. There was standing room only, and the line of people outside the door continued to grow longer. A feeling of tension permeated the room as parents discussed their anger about the situation. School officials and board members were getting nervous and were quite concerned with what would take place at the meeting.

As the meeting got under way, one parent blurted out, "Get rid of Coach Alex; we don't want this type of person teaching our children." The other parents in the room started to cheer and yell their concerns. The president of the school board quickly hammered his gavel on the desk in an effort to bring the meeting back to order.

As the voices of angry parents lowered and the meeting came to order, the president of the Parent–Teachers Association, Mrs. Lewis, stood up and spoke on behalf of the concerned parents. In a calm, soft, articulate manner, she praised the accomplishments of Coach Alex. She was careful to address all the positive things he contributed to the success of the school, students, and the athletic program. She even mentioned how he had helped her son earn an athletic scholarship to college, but she stated firmly, "Regardless of his past record, we cannot tolerate such acts of violence from any of our teachers." She continued by saying that teachers are role models to students, and parents entrust their children to people who are believed to be of high moral character. She concluded by saying, "It is very clear that Coach Alex has violated our trust, and therefore, we ask for his dismissal." With that, she turned toward Superintendent Brown and asked, "What are you going to do about this?" The people in the auditorium instantly became silent. Superintendent Brown knew that these people were very upset and wanted a response. It was obvious that Superintendent Brown had an extremely difficult decision to make.

Questions for Discussion

1. What is the fairest choice Superintendent Brown could make? The most caring choice?

2. One might decide to allow Alex to keep his job based on a "greater good for the greater number" reasoning in that he has helped so many young athletes. What are the strengths and weaknesses of this argument? Do you agree with it? Why or why not? What course of action

would be in the best interests of all students? Of the student athletes at Maple Grove High? As a coach, does Alex have a special responsibility to be a role model for his students? Is this responsibility more than that of a teacher who does not coach?

3. Compare Superintendent Brown's dilemma with that of Dr. Wang in the previous scenario. Could it be argued that spousal abuse is a disease as alcoholism is a disease? Why or why not?

4. Alex has yet to strike a student. Is firing him a good preventive strategy? Why or why not? Do you see any ethical problems to this reasoning? If not, why not? If so, what are they? Should a person's private life be just that, private? Why or why not?

5. What questions might a critical theorist ask in this situation? On what concerns might she or he focus?

6. What would you do if you were Superintendent Brown? Explain the reasoning behind your answer.

CASE STUDY 5.3 AFTER-SCHOOL ANTICS

Dana Hajjar smiled as she left her teachers' lounge. The joys of working in a small school again, she thought to herself as she took the long way back to her office. She enjoyed the happy hum of the hallways on a Monday morning. She had been the principal at several much larger schools in recent years, and was starting to remember why she liked leading small schools so much. The people and camaraderie just felt different than at a bigger school. This kind of family atmosphere made it so much easier for everyone to work together as a team. Dana had realized long ago that the key to a happy school often rested in the ability of the staff to get along with one another and to work as a cohesive unit. She prided herself in her ability to always work hard at creating those relationships.

When she started as the new principal of Phelps Elementary at the beginning of the school year, she had gone about the task of implementing numerous social activities and team-building exercises. At first, the staff seemed resistant. Most of them had worked there for several years together and thought that all these "getting to know one another," touchy-feely activities were ridiculous, especially coming from an "outsider from the big city." But slowly, spearheaded by the cooperation and extra efforts of veteran teacher Mr. Kang, the staff was starting to come around. Dana was thankful that Mr. Kang was on board. It was making her job much easier.

One Friday each month, Dana had implemented a professional development work day, in which students had the day off and the staff could spend the day grading, planning units as teams, and working together on projects. Afterward, it seemed that Mr. Kang had instituted a Friday night happy hour at a local restaurant and bar. These evenings were starting to become big staff events, and for that Dana could not have been happier. Even on Fridays without professional development days, members of staff were going out together regularly, enjoying their off-time and beginning to truly become friends. These friendships were starting to be reflected in the school day. The curriculum was getting stronger and the teachers were beginning to depend on one another for advice, critique, and collaboration. Dana knew that with so few employees at the school, it was very easy for the staff dynamic to go one of two ways: not getting along at all, or being very tight-knit. As Dana left the teachers' lounge that morning, watching teachers work together on lesson plans and laugh about Friday night's happy hour antics, she realized that it had become the latter—she had a tight-knit staff who were getting along quite well and whose work was reflecting this new-found sense of teamwork. She couldn't have been more satisfied.

The smile slowly faded from her face as Dana reached the office and heard the parent of one of her second graders yelling at the office secretary. "What kind of school is she running here? That kind of stuff might fly in her big city, but it is not going to happen in this community!" Slowly, anxiously, Dana entered the office.

"Mrs. Sampson. Hello there. What can I help you with this morning?"

"It's about time you showed up! What do you intend to do about my Jimmy's teacher's ridiculous behavior this weekend?"

Dana was dumbfounded. "Why don't you come into my office Mrs. Sampson and we can talk about this."

Mrs. Sampson was one of the most active parents in the community. She had four children come through this elementary school. Her two oldest children had been in Mr. Kang's class, as was her current fifth grader Frankie. Her youngest son, Jimmy, was in Gertrude Voortmann's second-grade class. She had been supportive of the school, and Dana had always had positive interactions with her. This behavior was very uncharacteristic. Visibly angry, Mrs. Sampson stormed into Dana's office.

"Do you know what your teachers did this weekend, Ms. Hajjar? Because I do."

"I'm afraid you've lost me. I know that some of them went out to dinner on Friday night, but I wasn't there for that. I heard they had a nice time."

"Ha! It was a little more than dinner don't you think? So I assume you haven't seen the photos they took?"

Dana shook her head: "No."

"You really should keep better track of your teachers," mumbled Mrs. Sampson under her breath, as she shook her head incredulously.

Dana was trying to keep up, but couldn't figure out where Mrs. Sampson was going, and she didn't like any of the implications of Mrs. Sampson's questions. True, she didn't typically know what her teachers did on the weekends and, quite frankly, Dana didn't really feel like it was her business. They needed their downtime, and they were entitled to it. But then, thought Dana, if their behaviors were causing this kind of parental uproar, maybe she should be better connected to what was going on.

The longer she sat there, the more frustrated Dana became with Mrs. Sampson's questions and tone. She didn't appreciate Mrs. Sampson's assumption that she was in the dark about issues with her staff. "I'm close to my staff, right?" Dana asked herself. She had a growing sense of unease and suddenly felt completely out of the loop. Starting to become irritated, she replied, "Photos? Of what? Where did you see photos, Mrs. Sampson?"

Mrs. Sampson smirked. "You obviously don't have a Facebook account, do you Ms. Hajjar? May I use your computer for a moment?"

Dana stepped away from the desk long enough to let Mrs. Sampson log on to her Facebook account. Mrs. Sampson was right; Dana had never gotten around to joining this "Facebook." She had heard plenty of things about it, including both positive and negative stories in the news and from friends. It seemed mostly like a student yearbook program that she wasn't really interested in being a part of. She was starting to wonder if she should be. She watched as Mrs. Sampson pulled up her Facebook homepage and then her "friend list." To Dana's surprise, Mr. Kang was on Mrs. Sampson's friend list. It sort of made sense, she supposed. They lived on the same side of town. He had had Mrs. Sampson's two oldest children in class and now had Frankie. She guessed that they could be considered "friends."

Mrs. Sampson clicked on to Mr. Kang's homepage. There, on his page, was posted a brand-new photo album entitled "After-school Antics: Ms. Hajjar's Mandatory Fun." Dana exhaled and the blood rushed to her cheeks. This was not right: mandatory fun? Was that what he really thought of it? Dana considered Mr. Kang to be an ally. Now it seemed he was making fun of her.

As Mrs. Sampson scrolled through the pictures in Mr. Kang's photo album, Dana saw that many of them seemed harmless enough, friendly teachers smiling together, having dinner, laughing . . . possibly karaoke? And then, as the evening progressed, so did the photos in the album, until finally Mrs. Sampson rested on the picture that had put her in such a state. There, in the background of a picture of Mr. Kang and his wife, was Ms. Voortmann, her son's second-grade teacher, sitting on top of a table, drinking a shot of what looked like tequila.

"And what do you plan to do about that? My son's second-grade teacher is an alcoholic. And doing this in public?! Is this how you promote together-ness in your staff? Mandatory drunkenness? Maybe that was fine when you were in your big city schools, but here, we take our teachers a little more seriously. They are supposed to be role models for our children, aren't they?"

Dana was speechless. This was not the kind of team building that she was supporting, was it? She guessed she never really asked questions, and happy hour does imply alcohol, doesn't it? But no, this is not what she meant, and they knew better. "I appreciate you bringing this to my attention Mrs. Sampson. I will . . . get on it."

"I should hope so. This is not acceptable behavior, Ms. Hajjar. And I will not let my son be in a class with a woman like this. She obviously has very little control over herself, so I can imagine how irresponsible she must be with a room full of second graders."

Dana seemed finally to calm Mrs. Sampson down with her promise to take care of things, but as she escorted the parent from her office, Dana realized that she had no idea how to fulfill that promise. Gertrude Voortmann was an outstanding educator and an asset to the school. From the little she could tell, Ms. Voortmann didn't even have a Facebook page of her own, and certainly didn't post this picture herself. She wondered if Ms. Voortmann even knew the picture had been posted or, for that matter, had been taken. And Mr. Kang . . . how surprising this was from him! She would have thought he would have known better. As the bell rang signaling the end of the first period of study, she knew she would have to do something, and do something quickly. Ms. Hajjar suddenly remembered the double-edged sword of working in a small community school. Just as she had been lauding it early that morning, she now realized that the power of the small, close-knit community was going to work against her. This information would make its way through the parent circuit within hours, and the school community even quicker. Time was of the essence.

Questions for Discussion

1. If you were Ms. Hajjar, what would be your first move? Analyze this first move based on the paradigms of justice, care, critique, and the profession for each of the players.

2. Does Ms. Hajjar have the right to talk to Mr. Kang about the pictures he posted on his private Facebook page? Does Ms. Hajjar have the right to ask Mr. Kang to remove pictures from his private website? Does Ms. Hajjar have the right to ask Mr. Kang not to be a "friend" of parents of current students? What recourse does Ms. Hajjar have if Mr. Kang refuses? What happens to allegiances and staff morale if Mr. Kang complies, but then suddenly becomes a vocal opponent of Ms. Hajjar?

3. What are the implications for Gertrude Voortmann? What happens if she didn't realize the picture was being taken and is horrified? Or

conversely if she knows and doesn't care—claims that she was at a restaurant on her off-time away from children having a drink and sees nothing wrong with her behavior, the picture, or the posting?

4. Consider the ethic of community as it pertains to this scenario. Can you see the scenario playing out differently in a large city school? If you were Ms. Hajjar, would you handle it differently based on your location? How?

5. Ms. Hajjar stated that she didn't see it as her responsibility to monitor her teachers' behaviors in their off-time. Do you agree or disagree with this statement?

CASE STUDY 5.4 JOB SHARING: SOME REAL BENEFITS

Dr. Marisa Garcia is a single, 35-year-old assistant superintendent for personnel in the Birchwood School District. She has been in her current position for less than a year. Prior to her appointment as assistant superintendent, she was an assistant principal and a classroom teacher in the same district. Dr. Garcia is happy in her current position and usually enjoys the daily challenge of her work. However, today was an exception. As she drove home from a school board meeting, she had to admit that it was difficult to find enjoyment in solving her current dilemma.

The teachers' union had requested a meeting with the school board to negotiate several changes to the school district's employee job-sharing benefit. Before the meeting with the union, Dr. Garcia met with the school board. Bob Johnson, head of the board's personnel committee, made it quite clear that the school board was not interested in any changes at this time. He then noted that Dr. Garcia was expected to make a recommendation to the board following her meeting with the union to enable the district to prepare for negotiations.

Mr. Johnson owned a small business that had not been very profitable, but it had been successful enough to put food on the table. He was always complaining about the cost of insurance and other benefits he had to provide for his own employees. He often voiced his opinion about teachers being "spoiled," especially when he compared education to the business world. He had been known to say, "This is a small town and the taxpayers are getting real angry about how much the teachers get, compared to other workers."

Because contract negotiation was one of Dr. Garcia's responsibilities, she was the administrator who would be meeting with the teachers' union. Although she had never been involved in a contract negotiation from the administrative side of the table, she knew the teachers had no bargaining power. The job-sharing benefit had been presented by the union the previous year. The board adopted it as a one-year pilot program; therefore, it was not officially negotiated into the contract, and the current contract was still in effect for another year.

The meeting began with a review of the current guidelines for job sharing. Although James Jacobs, the union president, was extremely intelligent and an excellent teacher, he often argued for the sake of a good argument, especially with Marisa Garcia. Mr. Jacobs had a problem with Dr. Garcia's quick ascendancy through the hierarchy. It had been rumored that Mr. Jacobs had informed a few union members that this would be an easy sell, insinuating that Dr. Garcia would not be able to hold her ground against him.

After reading the guidelines, Mr. Jacobs requested the first modification. Two other union representatives in attendance remained silent for most of the meeting except to talk among themselves or echo Mr. Jacobs' sentiments. Dr. Garcia agreed to the first modification, as it was merely a change in the wording of a sentence. The second request was not so easy.

Under the current guidelines, a full-time teacher interested in job sharing gives up full-time status for one year. The current teachers' contract states that part-time employees do not receive medical benefits. Therefore, any teacher involved in a job-sharing situation is not eligible for benefits. The union was requesting a revision of this provision. The union felt strongly that the provision was not fair and did not provide equal opportunity to all teachers. The union felt the district was discriminating against teachers based on marital status because only teachers with spouses who were employed and receiving medical coverage would be able to take advantage of the benefit.

Dr. Garcia did not respond to the claim of violating equal opportunity; however, she informed the union representatives that the board would not support the revision of the job-sharing benefit that maintained medical benefits. Part-time employees did not receive benefits in this district. If the district provided benefits for the job-share employees, then all of the part-time employees would expect benefits. The district could not afford to extend benefits to all part-time employees. The union countered by saying that the difference is that the job sharers are full-time, tenured employees and deserve to maintain their benefits: "We don't believe the union can accept it any other way; we represent the entire faculty— not just those who are married with two incomes."

Dr. Garcia then asked, "Are you saying you are rejecting the current proposal?" Although she cared deeply about this issue on a personal level, she knew what her professional strategy should be for this meeting. Thus, she began by explaining that there were three teachers requesting job sharing for the following year.

Absorbing this new piece of information, Mr. Jacobs replied by saying, "Rejecting it would not be fair to those teachers. We will accept it. However, the language should read that the district agrees to extend the pilot for a second year." Despite their personal differences, in Dr. Garcia's opinion, Mr. Jacobs had raised a few valid arguments. Dr. Garcia knew that, on the one hand, she had really wanted to advocate for single people being able to take advantage of this opportunity; on the other hand, she wanted to uphold the guidelines as directed by the school board. Upholding these guidelines would also show Mr. Jacobs who was in charge.

Dr. Garcia knew how important this decision was to her young career as assistant superintendent. What if her recommendation forced a teachers' strike? Or what if her recommendation made the board think she was just another woman who was indecisive and willing to extend job sharing indefinitely under the guise of a pilot program? In order for Marisa Garcia to clearly understand her own position and make a recommendation to the board, she knew that she had to determine if equal opportunity as well as care and concern were afforded to all teachers in the district.

Questions for Discussion

1. What are the possible courses of action which Dr. Garcia might take? Of these, which is the most just? Why? Which is the most caring? Why? In this situation, must there be a conflict between what is just and what is caring? Explain.

2. Dr. Garcia is a single woman with her own personal convictions regarding this matter. What would you expect these convictions to be? Should they enter into Dr. Garcia's judgment of the situation? Why or why not?

3. If benefits are extended to job-sharing individuals, should they then also be extended to other part-time employees? Why or why not? Who do you suppose initiated the job-sharing program? Who benefits from it? Who is left out?

4. From a caring perspective, how should Dr. Garcia address Mr. Jacobs' concerns? Mr. Johnson's concerns? How would you answer this question from a justice perspective? Must these answers be different? Why or why not? If you were Dr. Garcia, what would you do to resolve this dilemma?

CASE STUDY 5.5 WHEN TEACHERS FIGHT

Carol Johnson is the director of a daycare center in a large metropolis. She has just promoted Tanya, a former assistant teacher, to headteacher of the two-year-old classroom. Although she is not the most highly trained person, the children and parents love her.

Tanya is a single mother with a 3-year-old child. She also cares for her sick elderly mother who suffers from multiple sclerosis. Her family had spent several years living in a shelter which has been very hard on everyone. Currently, the money Tanya brings home is the family's major income. The headteaching promotion has given her the ability to move her child and her mother out of the shelter. Ms. Johnson is aware of this situation and has seen the pride Tanya has felt as she was finally able to move her family into a small but safe place that they can call home. Tanya is now able to provide for her family on her own without relying solely on the use of food stamps and welfare which was so impossibly hard to get by on.

Tanya has tried valiantly to get everyone in her family back on their feet. Because of this, Tanya's little sister, Delta, also works at the school as an assistant teacher. She was hired due to Ms. Tanya's high praise of her little sister's work with children. Delta always has a smile on her face each morning and has proved to be a hard-working and caring assistant.

Unfortunately, situations change. Thursday started out like any other day at work. It was a warm spring day and the children were playing outside. They had a good lunch and began to have their rest time. During the children's break, the teachers took their lunch in shifts. One teacher went to lunch while the other watched the sleeping class. Normally it is important for a teacher to eat her lunch within a limited period, and then return to enable the other teacher to eat within the time span of rest time.

On this particular day, Ms. Delta took the first shift for lunch in her room. After a long period of time, she did not return. The other teacher in the room became annoyed because she was hungry and needed a break. Tanya heard about her little sister's lateness and volunteered to miss her own lunch and watch the room so that the other teacher could take a break. As time went by, Tanya became more and more upset. When Delta finally arrived back from lunch, an hour late, Tanya was furious. She told her sister that her lateness was a bad reflection of her own standing within the school. She told her she had missed her own lunch. Despite the reprimand, Delta did not seem to care. In fact, she responded by indicating that Tanya should mind her own business and not tell her how to handle her professional life.

Although the children were still sleeping during rest time, the two sisters began shouting at one another in the classroom. Tanya was furious and

Delta egged her sister on by telling her to punch her if she was so mad. Their shouting grew so loud that Ms. Johnson could hear it in her office at the other end of the school.

Ms. Johnson ran out of her office to discover the cause of the shouting. But by the time she arrived, Tanya had pushed Delta into a stack of chairs and both teachers were screaming. In fact, Tanya was being held back physically by two other teachers who were trying to prevent the fight from escalating.

In the other classrooms, the teachers were doing their best to shield the children from the altercation but, due to the volume of the shouting, the youngsters in this small school were aware of the fight. Some even witnessed the pushing and shoving.

Ms. Johnson's presence quickly ended the altercation but the damage had been done. She separated both teachers and made them take independent walks outside to cool down. Children and teachers saw and heard the altercation. All of the teachers were upset and worried. Some of the children seemed to be fine, as many of them had slept through the fight, but others looked a little anxious and confused.

Ms. Johnson's immediate reaction was that she should fire Tanya and Delta on the spot. However, it did not seem to be such an easy decision when it came to Tanya. Ms. Johnson knew that if she did this, Tanya, her child, and her ailing mother would end up back in the shelter. Ms. Johnson returned to her office and closed the door while she decided what to do.

Questions for Discussion

1. Can Ms. Johnson justify keeping Tanya in her position? What does the law say regarding this kind of behavior in a preschool situation?

2. If there is no law, should there be one? Why?

3. Should Ms. Johnson take into account the problems that Tanya and her family will face if she loses her employment? Should she take into account Delta's difficulties?

4. As a professional, if you were in Ms. Johnson's shoes, what would you do in this case? How would you explain your decision? Discuss.

Chapter 6

The American Melting Pot Versus the Chinese Hot Pot

Patricia A.L. Ehrensal, Robert L. Crawford, Joseph A. Castellucci, Monica N. Villafuerte, and Gregory Allen

In this chapter, administrators and teachers face challenges that extend well beyond the school and move into the home. These dilemmas ask educational leaders to not only think through their own responsibilities and behaviors but also take into account students' and parents' behaviors and especially their backgrounds.

In this chapter, the paradox between the American melting pot and the Chinese hot pot is highlighted. Many of us are familiar with the metaphor of the melting pot. It emerged as an aftermath of the popular play written by Zangwill (1910). The play, *The Melting Pot*, presented an acculturation model molding immigrants into a "predetermined standard of desirability" (Wong, 1993). Along with this concept, the national motto of *e pluribus unum*—from many, one—also conveyed this desire to create Americans from a "dizzying array of peoples, cultures, and races" (Sewell, DuCette, & Shapiro, 1998). The metaphor of the melting pot left it to the schools to educate students from many cultures through a common language, a common history, and common goals, principles, and values. The schools bore the burden of producing the social and cultural integration required to create "real Americans."

But what is meant by real Americans? What is the ideal American who should emerge from the melting pot? Judging by the writings of Cushner et al. (1992), this concept seems not to have changed for more than 100 years. They wrote:

> Real Americans are white and they are adults: they are middle-class (or trying very hard to be); they go to church (often Protestant, but sometimes Catholic as well, although that is a bit suspicious); they are married (or aim to be) and they live in single-family houses (which they own, or are trying to); they work

hard and stand on "their own two feet"; they wash themselves a good deal, and generally try to "smell good"; they are patriotic and honor the flag; they are heterosexual; they are often charitable, only expecting a certain amount of gratitude and a serious effort to "shape up" from those who are the objects of their charity; they eat well; they see that their children behave themselves. (p. 216)

Despite the emphasis on acculturation through the schools and other institutions, there have also existed other forces in America such as the distinct languages, histories, goals, principles, and values of different ethnic groups that emerged from the community, the home, and the individuals themselves. For many minority groups, then, in this age of diversity, the melting pot metaphor no longer seems viable. Instead, the concept of the Chinese hot pot (Tek Lum, 1987, p. 105) may be a better fit for their view of American culture. In the hot pot, although all the food ingredients are cooked together, each maintains its unique flavor and texture. The transition from the metaphor of the melting pot to the hot pot has not been easy or smooth. Tensions and inconsistencies exist that can lead to paradoxes or dilemmas. For example, schools, on the one hand, want students to understand and appreciate other cultures while, on the other hand, they want to socialize young people to develop them into American citizens.

The cases presented in this chapter illustrate paradoxes between the dominant culture of the melting pot and the different ways of life of the hot pot. They challenge the reader to examine the conflicts that occur when the dominant culture in U.S. schools comes in contact with subcultures and "other" backgrounds. Two questions worth considering are: Which party has the greater share of social capital? What are the assumptions the school leaders have about the "other" and their customs/social classes in each case?

After reading the case studies that follow, it is important to take the time to consider the questions at the end of each case. Hopefully, these questions will challenge the reader to reflect on the dilemmas from the perspectives of the ethics of justice, care, critique, and the profession.

Case study 6.1, A Home for Marlon: The Foster-child Case, serves to demonstrate how difficult it can be to determine where the language of rights is rejected and a dialect of care is embraced. Here, a school's director of pupil personnel services must choose between laws, responsibilities, and relationships as he determines whether to pass on to his friend, a teacher, harmful information about a foster-child's background for whom the teacher is providing a home.

In Parents' Rights Versus School Imperatives (Case study 6.2), a principal from a school in an upper-middle-class community witnesses a father spanking his son at school. The father is working class and well meaning, and the son has many behavioral problems. The parents are divorced, and the father has custody of the son to save him from a bad situation with his mother. The principal is legally bound to report this incident as child abuse to the proper authorities, and yet he questions making the report.

Turning to the ethical dilemma, Case study 6.3, Lost in Translation, a special needs English language learner, new to the U.S., although born in that country, has accused his parent of hitting him. The father, who is from South America and illegally living in the U.S., appears to be a caring parent, but he is clearly having trouble managing a challenging child. In this dilemma, the Spanish teacher, who serves as a translator, has to decide whether to provide an accurate translation of the youngster's words which might lead to a child abuse charge for the father or try to deal with the problem in her own way. Interestingly enough, although this dilemma is very different from the previous case, the possible mistreatment of a child is the issue in both instances.

The final dilemma, Case study 6.4, Responsibility and the Organization, involves George, a Jamaican student who attends a music magnet school and is quite talented. However, he is receiving mediocre grades because he has many family commitments related to music, as this is how the family supports itself. The student's father is angry because George has received Cs in music due primarily to absences. The father wants the teacher to change his son's grades because he feels it is unfair to penalize him because he is performing. Yet, would this be fair to the other students?

CASE STUDY 6.1 A HOME FOR MARLON: THE FOSTER-CHILD CASE

Marlon, a 16-year-old-male classified as emotionally disturbed, enrolled at the Benjamin Franklin High School in September and was assigned to a self-contained special education classroom. Marlon had been relocated into the district to be placed in a new foster-care home. He had been in various residential placements and foster-care homes since the age of 10. Marlon was removed from his biological parents after it was discovered that he was the victim of their sexual and physical abuse. Marlon's student file contained reports documenting three years of increasingly disturbing behaviors. He was demonstrating an escalating pattern of frequent fire-setting behaviors, and had reportedly sexually molested two young children with whom he shared a foster-care placement.

Jim Campbell, the school's director of pupil personnel services, is concerned because Marlon's new foster parents are Mr. and Mrs. Kearns, a well-respected, kind couple who fit in well with this conservative, church-going community. Mrs. Kearns is a part-time art aide at the high school. Mr. Kearns is a businessman who travels frequently and works long hours.

They have two young children: a 6-year-old girl and a 3-year-old boy. Mr. Campbell has frequently socialized at the Kearns' home for birthday parties, dinners, and other family activities. He has young children like the Kearns family. As per foster-care state law and policy in this state, Mr. and Mrs. Kearns have not been informed of Marlon's past history and behaviors.

Resolving to put things right, Mr. Campbell quickly left school the day he first read Marlon's student file, firmly convinced that he knew the right thing—the only thing—to do. Although sure in his conviction, Jim also knew he should not act immediately. He needed time to evaluate the situation in order to make a reasoned decision. Walking through the school parking lot that afternoon, he was clear on one thing. No way was he going to permit the Kearns family's two children, children just like his own, to be potential victims of a sexually aggressive, emotionally disturbed youth. Although he felt a need to wait until the following day to make a decision, he felt certain that his desire to protect the Kearns family would primarily inform his decision.

Later that evening, with his children tucked up in bed and his wife asleep early with the flu, Mr. Campbell decided to give the issue deeper consideration. As he settled under the covers, he thought about his own children safely tucked up in their beds. He also hoped for the safety of the Kearns children. Before turning off the bedside lamp, Jim read over the Personal and Professional Code of Ethics he had written down some time ago, now kept as a bookmark in his Bible. What caught his attention was a particular line. It read: "Always be a voice, a presence for the comfort and protection of the weak, the innocent, the defenseless . . . because there but for the grace of God go I." And there but for the grace of God so went his children. However, unlike the Kearns family, they did not have this threat of a stranger in their home as they slept.

Mr. Campbell knew he had to tell Mrs. Kearns about Marlon's past, about the potential danger now posed to her children. Mr. Campbell was a deeply religious family man who valued his children, and all children, immensely. He began his career as a teacher because of his desire to help children. The care and protection of students was central to his moral code.

As he lay thinking of the Kearns' children, Mr. Campbell was confronted with the image of Mrs. Kearns crying in his office, telling him the details of how Marlon one night had done the unspeakable to one of her children. He then saw himself confessing that he was sorry, that he had known about Marlon all along. Perhaps, if he had revealed to her the truth, her tragedy could have been avoided. Jim saw a tearful Mrs. Kearns challenge him: "You knew, you knew about this all along and you did not tell me! How could you let this happen to my children?"

Then something else began to creep into his thoughts. Even as he imagined Mrs. Kearns condemning him, he remembered that, in addition to being a concerned father, he was also a man with a very serious professional responsibility. In his current role as director of pupil personnel services he began to feel a certain uneasiness. In one sense, this was not an unfamiliar position for Mr. Campbell. He had certainly been aware of other situations in the past that were similar or worse, involving issues such as sexual abuse, incest, drugs, and domestic violence. Although he had been disturbed, he had never before been tempted to violate students' privacy and confidentiality, even though some of the situations had actually been much worse than the Kearns family's current situation. His thoughts about confidentiality led him to consider the consequences. "And what about the consequences of my actions?" thought Mr. Campbell. "I've never violated a student's confidentiality before. Credibility demands honesty. If word got out that I told the Kearns about Marlon, how would my teachers and the other students feel? Would they feel confident that they could talk with me confidentially? Would I still be credible in their eyes?"

"Beyond credibility," his thoughts continued, "are there any legal ramifications if I violate the laws governing student privacy? Would this jeopardize my current position? Would I be passed over if I ever wanted to become superintendent?" "Foolish!" he screamed inside. "We're talking about children here. Maybe all these confidentiality laws protecting juvenile criminals weren't good laws in the first place!"

Mr. Campbell was growing increasingly concerned and physically upset at this seemingly unsolvable dilemma. He did not even want to look at the clock, knowing all too well that it was much too late to claim a good night's sleep. He again recalled his Personal and Professional Code of Ethics: "Always be a voice." But for whom was he supposed to be a voice? Who was supposed to receive the charity, mercy, forbearance, and benevolence that he mentioned in his Code? What did these words really mean anyway? Mr. Campbell began to wonder about Marlon. Was he asleep, or was it a sleepless night for him also? Mr. Campbell wondered how many sleepless nights—nights of turmoil and fear—Marlon had suffered in his young 16 years. Wasn't Marlon a victim too? Perhaps it was Marlon who really was the weakest, most defenseless voice in this whole mess. The Kearns' children, like Mr. Campbell's own children, had warm, stable, loving homes, but what was it like to be moved from home to home as a child? The reality of the situation, beyond all the worries, was that only one child had been repeatedly victimized. That child was Marlon.

Mr. Campbell, under his warm covers, felt thankful for the security and comforts of his own home. "If I told Mrs. Kearns, she would immediately have Marlon removed from her house." So where would Marlon go next: another move, another school, another strange room during another sleepless night? A sinking feeling hit Jim; a deeper sadness, not anger, just sadness for Marlon. The youngster did not seem such a monster now. In fact, he did not really know Marlon at all, just what Marlon's records said and what his own fears had portrayed him to be.

Mr. Campbell imagined Marlon reporting to his office prior to leaving the school due to another move, another transfer into another foster home. He saw himself seated at his desk in his office. Before him stood Marlon, who with tired eyes simply said, "You told them about my past. They weren't supposed to know. I wanted to start all over again. I just wanted what every other kid has, a home. I've already been hurt too many times by adults I trusted. How could you do this to me?" As he continued to reflect, Jim did not know what bothered him the most, his own anger or his own tears.

Despite the difficulty, Mr. Campbell knew he must view the current dilemma from a more objective perspective. Thus, a fundamental question remained: Did Marlon's presence in the Kearns' home pose a grave danger to the Kearns family? First and foremost, he considered that although Marlon may have a past history of dangerous behaviors, including fire setting and sexual molestation, he had not yet demonstrated harmful behavior or expressed intent to engage in harmful conduct. Marlon had not yet crossed the line to suggest that he posed a grave risk to the Kearns family.

The dilemma for Mr. Campbell was based partly on emotional identification and affinity for the Kearns family and the projection of his own fears concerning Marlon. The situation that objectively confronted him at this juncture involved only the potential of dangerous behavior and his own fears. Marlon had not shown any indications to warrant concern for the Kearns family.

Mr. Campbell clearly agonized over this decision. Neither course of action relieved him of responsibility for potential adverse consequences. All night, he tossed and turned, and as he did so he constantly asked: What would be the best way to resolve this dilemma? How could I reach a decision that would be in harmony both professionally and personally?

When the morning dawned, Mr. Campbell finally made his decision. He decided not to tell Mrs. Kearns about Marlon's past. His reward was simply a sense of relief stemming from the feeling that his decision was in harmony with who he knew himself to be, as both an administrator and a person.

Questions for Discussion

1. Do you think Mr. Campbell made the best decision? Why or why not? If you were in his place, what would you have done?
2. Assume that Mr. Campbell did not personally know the Kearns family. Would that factor make a difference, in your opinion, as to the best

course of action? Why or why not? What if Mr. Campbell did not know the Kearns family but knew Marlon very well? Should that factor make a difference in his decision?

3. Consider this case from the point of view espoused by Kohlberg (1981), Gilligan (1982), and Noddings (1992, 2002, 2003). How might the decision have played out considering each of these theorists?

4. Mr. Campbell chose not to break his state's law regarding the confidentiality of foster-children's records. Do you agree with his decision? Is it ever justifiable to break a law when making an administrative decision? When? Do you see any way that breaking the law might have been justifiable in this case?

5. Was Mr. Campbell's decision in Marlon's best interests? In the best interests of the other students? In the best interests of the community? What community? Do you see any conflict between what appear to be Mr. Campbell's personal and professional codes of ethics? Between his codes of ethics and his actions? Explain.

CASE STUDY 6.2 PARENTS' RIGHTS VERSUS SCHOOL IMPERATIVES

It was 4 p.m. on Friday afternoon, and Ned Parker was still at his desk. In front of him was the pamphlet distributed by the state's Division of Youth and Family Services that detailed the school's role in preventing child abuse. Among other things, the pamphlet was very specific with regard to school officials' responsibilities. Any school official or teacher who fails to report suspected child abuse, the pamphlet read, could be held criminally liable.

Of course, Ned Parker was well aware of the legal responsibilities of school officials with regard to suspected child abuse cases. Indeed, he had presented in-service training to his teaching staff on just that subject. As principal at Sandalwood Elementary School, Ned had reported dozens of suspected child abuse cases over his eight-year tenure despite the fact that the school was situated in a mostly upper-middle-class community. He understood his responsibilities all too well. Yet, on this particular Thursday afternoon, he felt very unsure of himself. Earlier that day, he had witnessed a parent beating his child but was hesitant to report this incident as child abuse.

The child in this case was Robert Buck, a sixth grader who was both small in stature and emotionally immature for his age. He had transferred to Sandalwood earlier in the school year from a district in another state, following the bitter divorce of his parents. Robert's father, Frank Buck, had been awarded full custody, and the transition was anything but smooth.

Robert was a discipline problem from almost the first day he arrived. He was constantly disrupting his classes, disrespectful to his teachers, and both physically and verbally abusive to his classmates. Needless to say, his academic achievements were few. Robert had been a frequent visitor to Ned Parker's office and had been rapidly progressing through the various levels of the school discipline policy.

Frank had also been a frequent visitor to the school. He was a rough and relatively uneducated working-class man who had dropped out of high school to marry his pregnant girlfriend. He lived on one of the few streets in the community that had escaped gentrification, a street very close to the school district's boundary line. However, he was glad to live in this district, hoping that a good education might make up for all the problems in his son's life. When his marriage went sour, Mr. Buck made every effort to gain full custody of his only child to remove him from what he called the "unhealthy influence of his mother." In his dealings with Frank, Ned had believed him to be a concerned parent who was doing his best with the child under very difficult circumstances. He had personally come to the school each time there was a problem with his son. His meetings with the principal and each of Robert's teachers had always been cordial, and he had often expressed support for the school's efforts toward his son. He regularly attended parent back-to-school nights and was one of the few fathers who was active in the PTA.

It was becoming apparent that Robert was not responding to the typical disciplinary practices of the school. After a series of disruptive behavior reports from teachers, Mr. Parker suggested to Frank that he implement a behavior remediating program suggested by the school psychologist. All indications were that Frank was dutifully following this program.

The final straw came early on Thursday when Robert was sent to the principal's office for what his teacher described as behavior that was out of control. Ned called Frank to inform him of the problem. Angry, Frank said, "This has gone too far. That boy needs to be taught once and for all how to behave." With that, he abruptly hung up the phone.

Ned did not quite know what to make of that phone conversation until Frank appeared at his office door no more than 20 minutes later. With a facial expression clearly displaying anger and frustration, he apologized to Ned for the trouble his son had caused. "Now I'm going to do what I promised if I had to come out to this school again," he said to the boy. With that he grabbed his son's arm and jerked him out of the office and down the corridor. Ned followed him out and was horrified at what followed.

When they got to the end of the corridor, Frank threw his son up against the wall and began thrusting a pointed finger in his chest. Ned could barely make out what was being said, but it sounded angry and threatening. Then Frank forcefully turned his son around and began spanking the boy across the backside no fewer than eight times. Pain and embarrassment were evident on Robert's face as tears streaked down his cheeks. Ned shouted down the hall, "Please, sir. That is not necessary." Frank bellowed back, "I'll decide what is necessary for my son." With that, he grabbed Robert by his shirt collar and marched him out of the door.

Now, Ned Parker sat in his office contemplating whether he should report the incident as child abuse. On the one hand, he thought, he had clearly witnessed behavior he himself would never condone in himself or any of his teachers. The brutal nature of the spanking was also disconcerting and clearly painful to the boy, and who knows what kind of beating Robert might receive in the privacy of his father's home.

On the other hand, it was only a spanking. As a boy, Ned himself had been spanked by his father for misbehavior; yet he would never consider his father to be a child abuser. Many parents spank their children routinely and would be appalled at any suggestion that they were committing child abuse. Anyway, what business does the school have interfering with parents' rights to discipline their own children as they see fit?

Ned knew what the consequences would be if he reported this incident to his state's Division of Youth and Family Services. The division routinely filed child abuse charges against parents for cases with less evidence than this one. The children were typically placed in a foster home until the case was resolved in court. Parents were usually fined and forced to undergo counseling and parenting classes. In the most extreme cases, the child could be removed from the home permanently.

Ned also knew the consequences of not reporting a suspected child abuse case. He remembered an incident from a few years before in a neighboring school district where a man mercilessly beat his 10-year-old daughter to death for accidentally breaking a dish. School officials were accused of neglecting to report suspicions of abuse that they held for months before the child's death. Ned did not want to be held responsible for another such atrocity.

Nevertheless, Ned believed that Robert's father was a concerned and loving parent who had given in to personal frustration over the continued misbehavior of his son. After all the other disciplinary alternatives had failed, he probably resorted to carrying out a standing threat. Was it really child abuse or merely a thorough and well-deserved spanking? Is it right to make this father answer for his actions in a court of law and possibly face losing his son? Is it ethical to ignore this incident and possibly enable this father to severely hurt his son? Ned stared at the phone on his desk and wondered whether he should make that call.

Questions for Discussion

1. Do schools have the right to determine how parents may discipline their children? Do you believe that Mr. Buck's actions constitute child abuse? Why or why not? How do your state laws define child abuse? Should Mr. Parker report this incident to the authorities? Why or why not? If Ned thought Mr. Buck's actions were not child abuse, but feared that Mr. Buck was, or could become, more violent at home, should he report the incident to the authorities? Discuss the pros and cons of taking action against an anticipated wrongdoing.

2. What do you suppose was the purpose of states instituting child abuse laws? Who likely supported or rallied for such laws? Who do these laws benefit? Do you believe that such laws are fair? Why or why not? If there was a class difference between those who fought for the law and those whom the law affected, would that change your opinion of the laws? Why or why not? Should exceptions be made in these types of cases, or should the law be followed literally? Explain your answer. Should professional judgment be a consideration in reporting such incidents? Why or why not? How would this work? Whose professional judgment should be taken into account and why those persons as opposed to others?

3. What is the most caring solution to this problem? Would it be caring to report Mr. Buck? What solution would be in Robert's best interests? The best interests of all students?

4. Some 30 states have passed laws forbidding corporal punishment in schools (Center for Effective Discipline, 2010), and many, if not most, school districts have policies opposing this type of discipline. Discuss the pros and cons of corporal punishment in schools. Is there a difference between corporal punishment in schools and similar types of discipline at home? Explain. Is there a difference between corporal punishment and child abuse? How are they the same? How are they different?

CASE STUDY 6.3 LOST IN TRANSLATION

It was 8:25 a.m. and the day was just beginning at the primary school. Each teacher met her students outside to escort them to the classroom. From the onset of the day, the co-teachers of one of the second-grade classrooms knew this wasn't going to be an ordinary day when Pablo walked into the school sobbing. The young boy could barely utter a few Spanish words when he was warmly greeted by his English-speaking teachers. Both the general education teacher and the special education teacher looked at each other with bewilderment, not knowing how to begin to assist the upset 8-year-old boy.

The child in this case is Pablo Guzman, a new English language learner (ELL) recently arrived from Ecuador. Pablo, born in the United States, has lived with his mother and older brother in South America since the parents' deportation four years ago. Currently the boy and his father rent a room from a neighborhood family as the two adjust to their new living arrangements, getting to know each other on a daily basis. The parents agreed that it was in the child's best interest to return to the U.S. because his schoolteachers were physically abusing Pablo due to his inappropriate behavior at the Ecuadorian public school. The father recounted that he could no longer afford to send his wife enough money to cover his son's medical expenses, since the boy was seeing therapists regularly. On several occasions Pablo had also mentioned that his older brother didn't love him and would often beat him when their mother wasn't home.

Needless to say, Pablo's transition has been anything but smooth, particularly because he has difficulty communicating in his native language, doesn't speak any English, has trouble following directions, trusting others, and socializing with his peers. Pablo disrupts his class several times a day, is disrespectful to his teachers, has pulled down his pants in class, and has shown aggressive behavior towards his classmates. While many of the Spanish-speaking children in class are eager to translate for Pablo and his teachers, the amount of off-task time for all the students is immense.

In an effort to assist the classroom teachers, both the English as a Second Language (ESL) and Spanish teachers have been serving as translators/ guidance counselors/deans on a daily basis. At the teachers' requests, the father has been extremely cooperative in providing previous school records, medical documentation, and demonstrating complete willingness to work collaboratively with the school to assess the child's educational and neurological needs. Within the few short months Pablo has been at the primary school, the young boy is showing willingness to learn English and has shown some academic and social progress in small groups.

Early that Monday morning, the special education teacher shuffled Pablo into the building, and coincidentally ran into the Spanish teacher in the stairwell. She kindly requested a translation to understand her student. Pablo told the Spanish teacher that his father had hit him with a belt the night before and again that morning because he wouldn't eat his meals. Although the boy's speech wasn't very clear, the teacher could decipher the child's accusation. The Spanish teacher knew for a fact that Pablo had never expressed this concern since his arrival at the primary school. As a Latina and mother, she understood the Hispanic culture's acceptance of spanking, empathized with the father's frustrations, and recognized that this could be an isolated incident. Based on her encounters with the father, she strongly believed that this was not a suspected case of child abuse. However, she also acknowledged that her colleague was expecting to hear a true translation of what the boy had stated.

The Spanish teacher knew what the consequences would be upon translating the boy's accusation and she feared what the father's reaction would be if this case was reported to the Department of Youth and Family Services (DYFS). She immediately recalled that during a previous meeting, Mr. Guzman had appeared defeated by the challenges of raising a special needs child alone in this country. He was so distraught that he had mentioned the possibility of sending Pablo back to live with his mother in Ecuador. Fearing for the boy's ultimate safety, she hesitated before translating her conversation with the little boy.

The Spanish teacher wondered if the father's illegal immigrant status might indeed cause him to send the boy back to Ecuador if he felt threatened after the school reported the case to the DYFS. Besides, what constituted "real" child abuse—an occasional spanking from his concerned father or the daily abuse at the hands of his Ecuadorian schoolteachers and older brother? She was sure that if she addressed this concern with the father herself, it could be handled without reporting it to the DYFS.

Questions for Discussion

1. How might this dilemma be viewed through the lens of justice? Are there laws, policies, guidelines, or issues of fairness that the teacher might consider?

2. How might this dilemma be viewed through the lens of critique? Consider the student, the Latina teacher, and the father.

3. Taking into account school/family relations, has the family been treated in a caring manner?

4. What would the education profession expect of the teachers and the principal? How could an understanding of the Latino culture serve to meet the student's best interests?

5. What would you have done in this situation if you were the Spanish-speaking teacher?

CASE STUDY 6.4 RESPONSIBILITY AND THE ORGANIZATION

George Woodley and his musical family had recently arrived in the United States from the island of Jamaica. His father, John, took very seriously the process of finding a high school for George to attend. Owing to George's keen interest in music and piano skills, it was important to Mr. Woodley that his son be placed in a high school with a worthwhile music program. George auditioned for the Westfield High School Music Magnet Program and was accepted. He was asked to give performances in both piano and voice.

George's vocal selection was acceptable but could be described as throaty with a nasal quality. This was partially due to the reggae style of singing that his family had performed for many years. Nevertheless, it was decided that George be placed in the vocal component of the Music Magnet Program at Westfield High. At the time of his son's audition, John Woodley had made it clear that his son would have to miss certain performances owing to the family's professional obligations. This was a major concern because the grades of vocal students are based on their participation in class as well as performances.

As the year progressed, George's effort in class was minimal. He was beginning to miss performances consecutively and would announce that he would not be participating in a performance the very day of the engagement—which Mr. Henderson, the choir director, saw as unfair, especially to the other students. As a result of George's minimal participation in class and lack of attendance at concerts, Mr. Henderson calculated his grade to be C.

John Woodley became furious on discovering that his son had received such a mediocre grade. Consequently, he made an unannounced visit to the school to voice his displeasure. He stated, "My son could have gone to virtually any school, and this school really is beneath him."

Mr. Henderson told Mr. Woodley that George was at Westfield High by choice, and the music program was certainly not inferior by any means. Mr. Woodley felt very strongly that his son should have received a grade A simply because of his advanced music skills and performance experiences. Mr. Henderson made it clear to John Woodley that the criteria he deemed appropriate for assessing George's music grade would not suffice.

George's performance and participation in choir during his second year at Westfield High did not improve significantly from the first year. Mr. Henderson felt he had been more than fair in determining George's grade. Could he continue to allow George to neglect his academic responsibility owing to family musical commitments that John Woodley claimed were a major source of income for the immigrant family? Just how was Mr. Henderson to handle this situation without being unfair to the students who seemed to expend much more effort than George?

Several students overheard Mr. Henderson and George in discussion immediately following choir class one day, at which time the latter attempted to plead his case for a grade A. The students became incensed by what they heard and began to voice their opinions on the matter. Mr. Henderson controlled the situation by discontinuing the conversation and sending the perplexed students to their classes.

Questions for Discussion

1. To what extent should George be responsible to his family? To his school? Where do his greater responsibilities lie? How might George's dilemma be interpreted through Kohlberg's (1981) ethic of justice theory? Through Gilligan's (1982) ethic of care? Through the ethics of other theorists?

2. Who made the rule that all students should be judged on class participation? Where would the basis for such a criterion lie? Is this a fair rule? Fair to whom? Who does the rule benefit?

3. George knew the rules regarding grading up front. Was he then not obligated to abide by them? Why or why not? Would your answer be different if George had not been told the rules ahead of time? George's father had informed Mr. Henderson of George's family obligations from the beginning. Should this knowledge require or expect Mr. Henderson to treat George differently from other students? Should some students be treated differently from others? Why or why not? Discuss the pros and cons of such individualized treatment. From an ethical perspective, how does one know where to draw the line?

4. What are George's rights? His parents' rights? Should a school alter the rules because one parent objects?

5. What do you personally believe should happen in this situation? What do you as a professional in a school believe should happen? Are these answers the same or different? Why?

6. What solution to this dilemma would be in George's best interests? In the best interests of the other students? Do these answers have to be different, or is there a solution that would satisfy both? All parties concerned?

Chapter 7

Religion Versus Culture

Kathrine J. Gutierrez, Susan C. Faircloth, Tamarah Pfeiffer,
Aisha Al-Harthi, and Kuan-Pei Lin

In this chapter, we explore situations in which students' and teachers' religious values and beliefs contradict the practices of the school culture and/or the curriculum being taught in the classroom. This chapter raises ethical concerns related to individual beliefs juxtaposed against traditional school policies and practices. These dilemmas ask educational leaders to consider the best interests of each student as related to the practice of the profession.

Since the origins of the public school movement, the issue of religion in public schools has been a concern for public education (Yudof, Kirp, Levin, & Moran, 2002). From a legal perspective, the U.S. Supreme Court has ruled that certain practices in public schools are clearly illegal. For example, we know that teachers or other school officials may not begin the day with school prayer or biblical readings, as was past practice. They may not lead prayers at school athletic events or have a religious speaker at graduation ceremonies. These practices all violate the Establishment Clause of the First Amendment to the U.S. Constitution.

Not only are school officials prohibited from endorsing one religion over another, they also may not endorse religion over non-religion. As far as the curriculum is concerned, teachers may teach *about* religion (as in a comparative religion class), but they may not teach religion or proselytize in public schools. On the other hand, while public school officials may not endorse religion, neither can they be hostile toward it. It is legal for public schools to provide transportation, books, and other materials and support services to religious schools. It is also generally legal but not usually mandatory (depending on various state laws and school policies) for schools to provide "opt-outs" for students who have religious conflicts with different aspects of the curriculum or for students or teachers who require time off for religious holidays. Finally, if the school runs non-curricular clubs or opens its facilities to non-religious groups, then it must treat religious groups in the same manner. Parents may also take advantage of state voucher systems, when available, to help support their children's education in non-public schools.

At the same time, there are lower court decisions that disagree on a number of issues including the legality of student-led prayer and whether students may use their in-class or homework assignments as a vehicle for proselytizing about their religion. In addition, in some states, laws permitting moments of silence in schools have been declared unconstitutional when it was found that their intent was for prayer. These sometimes conflicting aspects of the law combined with larger issues of cultural diversity and what we expect our public schools to look like give rise to serious ethical dilemmas on the part of educational leaders.

As mentioned in Chapter 6, we contend that diversity strengthens public schools, and exposure to different views better prepares all students to take their place in our increasingly diverse and pluralistic society. David Tyack (1974), a noted educational historian, has pointed out that our public schools were established as common schools with a goal of educating *all* students. Therefore, while we respect the rights of parents to send their children to religious schools (with the possible help of vouchers) or to home school, as a rising number of parents have done, we recognize the importance of all types of difference, including cultural and religious diversity, to our public schools. At the same time, diversity brings challenges, and it is these challenges that represent the focus of this chapter. Oftentimes, ethical dilemmas occur when religion and respect for diverse cultures are pitted against the values and norms of the school and, sometimes, the curriculum being taught in the classroom. Strike and his colleagues (1998) caution us that "schools would need to be careful to help students understand that they need to tolerate views and lifestyles even if they disapprove of them. But they [the schools] would also have to respect students' right to disapproval" (p. 127).

This chapter includes four ethical dilemmas. The first three take place in K–12 school settings. The fourth comes from higher education, but its underlying concepts could well fit a K–12 situation. Although the characters and situations presented in this chapter are fictitious, the content of each dilemma is based in part on a practice or belief characterized by particular cultures, religions, or both.

In these dilemmas, we have purposely focused on situations where religion and culture are so intertwined that they are difficult to separate. We have also chosen a few of the many important racial, ethnic, and religious groups who are either an emerging part of the culture of 21st-Century schools, have previously been ignored as part of this culture, or both. We have done this not only in an effort to illustrate the breadth of perspectives that school officials may confront in an increasingly diverse society but also to show possible connections with how we have historically treated more "traditional" religions. We were fortunate to have been able to work with students who represent these diverse cultures/religions and who were willing to give generously of their time in writing about these dilemmas.

Case study 7.1, Buddhism and the Caring of Animals, shows an ethical conflict between teaching an approved curriculum and respecting the religious beliefs of students. In this dilemma, a third-grade student disagrees with the science curriculum that allows students to keep pets in class and feed them live animals. The teacher and school principal must decide how to adhere to the school's science curriculum while caring for and considering a student's religious beliefs. This dilemma provides an interesting contrast to a case described in Chapter 4. In that scenario, Vivisection: A Dilemma for the Undergraduate Classroom (p. 51), a student expresses ethical, but not religious, concerns about pithing frogs.

In Case study 7.2, Ceremonial Rights, an American-Indian principal is planning to open the new school library with a local ceremonial celebration. The principal is challenged by one of her teachers as to the appropriateness of this celebration in a public school. Here, we urge our readers to grapple with ethical problems related to cultural traditions and religious beliefs as well as to examine possible ethical implications related to the beliefs of the majority and the rights of individuals. One might ask whether this situation is comparable to student-led prayers in school communities that are predominately Christian and if it is not, why it is different.

Case study 7.3, Time Off for Religious Services, involves two relatively new teachers who are troubled by the school's leave policy concerning attendance at religious services. The school principal is confronted with honoring the cultural tradition of the school and its community members and agreeing with the merits of the school's leave policy. Although this dilemma is set in Guam, a U.S. territory with a predominately Catholic population, we ask our readers to compare and contrast other instances where religious holidays have been integrated into "vacations" when large segments of the school community would otherwise be absent or when students, teachers, or both have been given "opt-outs" to attend religious functions.

In Case study 7.4, Religion and Social/Personal Contradictions, a professor faces the dilemma of whether to continue teaching course content about homosexuality that some students find offensive on religious grounds. The professor grapples with the situation of how best to teach what is important content for the course while still respecting issues of diversity. This situation involves a female Muslim student, but a similar situation might occur with other religions, such as fundamentalist Christians or certain sects of Orthodox Jews.

In such situations, Strike et al. (1988) have suggested that "schools might explain to students whose religion teaches that homosexuality is a sin that homosexuals are entitled to equal rights regardless of whether homosexuality is a sin. But schools need not insist that these students view homosexuality as merely an alternative lifestyle" (p. 127). We ask our readers to consider this viewpoint as well as to examine the scenario through other ethical paradigms, such as care, critique, and the profession.

CASE STUDY 7.1 BUDDHISM AND THE CARING OF ANIMALS

Green Hill Elementary School is an urban school in the Brighton School District. Green Hill houses grades K–6 and has 600 students. The socioeconomic status of most students is middle class. Brighton School District has a diverse community representing a mixture of ethnicities, which include White (non-Hispanic), Hispanic, and several immigrants from China, Taiwan, Japan, and Korea. Hence, the community also represents various religious beliefs and cultural backgrounds.

The school's mission statement reads as follows:

> Green Hill Elementary School, in partnership with parents and the community, encourages each student to develop individual abilities to become a life-long learner. Green Hill has several goals: (1) to increase every student's reading and writing proficiency, (2) to increase every student's math reasoning and problem-solving skills, (3) to increase student interest in science and math, (4) to encourage all students to learn to respect each other and value diversity, (5) to offer curricula that help students progress through developmental learning stages and develop appropriate social skills, and (6) to foster student understanding of different worldviews and to encourage life-long learning.

Sophia Shin Liang is an 8-year-old female student of Taiwanese descent enrolled in Green Hill Elementary School. Her family relocated to the Brighton School District from Taiwan before Sophia was born. Sophia was born and raised in the town of Brighton. Although Sophia is a U.S. citizen, her family values their heritage and religious beliefs. Buddhism is the religious belief and practice of the Liang family. A central tenet to the practice of Buddhism is the caring and welfare of all creatures of the Earth. The belief discourages any human being from harming any living creature.

In the fall of August 2003, Sophia Shin Liang became a third-grade student in Mrs. Cullen's science class. All science classes at Green Hill Elementary keep frogs in an aquarium as part of their curriculum to teach the life cycle of prey and predator. As such, live bugs are fed to the frogs. Frogs have been part of the third-grade science curriculum at Green Hill

Elementary School for the past five years, under the supervision of Principal Gary Goodman. The school board approved the science curriculum that supports keeping live animals to aid in the learning and development of elementary science.

On the first day of class, Mrs. Cullen introduced the curriculum for the semester that involved showing and talking about the class frog and the live bugs for its food. Each student had been assigned one week to care for and feed the frog the live bugs. Sophia Shin Liang grimaced at the fact that she would have to feed the frog live bugs because this goes against her Buddhist belief of not harming any living creature. Thankfully, Sophia was not scheduled to feed the class frog until the first week of October. This, in her mind, was sufficient time to talk with both her teacher and parents about the situation and to see if she could be excused from her class obligation to feed the frog.

However, after three weeks into the school year, Sophia witnessed several of her classmates feeding live bugs to the frog. She was appalled, disgusted, hurt, and discouraged that such an awful act was being committed in her presence. On Friday, the third week in September, Sophia set both the frog and the bugs free by carrying the animals outside during recess when no one was in the classroom. She thought no one had witnessed her act of kindness. However, two of her classmates saw her setting the animals free and confronted her about the situation.

Raul: Hey Sophia, what did you do? I saw you set the bugs and frog free.

Stacey: Yes, I saw it too. You are a thief. . . . You stole them from our class and now they are gone! I am going to tell Mrs. Cullen.

Sophia: No! I am not a thief. I just set them free to go where they belong. It is not right to feed the bugs to the frog. We are killing the bugs, protected creatures of the Earth. It is not right and against my religious beliefs! I felt sorry for them. I needed to set them free.

After recess had ended, Raul and Stacey reported the incident to Mrs. Cullen. Mrs. Cullen asked Sophia to talk with her outside the classroom about what happened.

Mrs. Cullen: Sophia, could you please tell me what happened during recess? Is it true you set the class animals free?

Sophia: I am sorry Mrs. Cullen. I did set the animals free because my Buddhist belief does not allow any harm to any living creature. It is not right to feed bugs to the frog because this is killing creatures of the Earth. My belief does not allow killing or harming any living thing.

Mrs. Cullen: I understand your concern for not wanting to harm any animal, but the frog and bugs belong to everyone in the class and are for learning purposes. Now the class is without these animals, and it is highly unlikely that we will be able to purchase another set for our class. I am very disappointed in you. You are a good student and should have talked with me before taking action on your own. I have no other choice but to send you to see Principal Goodman.

Sophia was sent to Principal Goodman's office. Principal Goodman was upset that Sophia had let the animals go and decided to call her parents to speak with him and to take Sophia home for the day. Both Mr. and Mrs. Kuan Lee Liang were upset and confused at the phone call from Mr. Goodman.

"How could our Sophia be in trouble?" they asked one another. "She is such an obedient child and a good student," Sophia's mother told her husband. Within 20 minutes of Principal Goodman's phone call, Sophia's parents arrived at Green Hill Elementary School.

Principal Goodman: Thank you both for coming in so quickly. Sophia explained to me why she set the science class animals free, but I still need to have you talk to her about what she did wrong.

Mr. and Mrs. Kuan Lee Liang: Sophia is just a child and she is just following our religious beliefs without thinking about the big picture of the purpose of these animals in the classroom. We believe that all creatures should be unharmed and even a small bug has the right to survive. Yes, the frog needs to eat food, but if humans get involved in the process to feed the bugs to the frog, we are aiding in the killing of these bugs, rather than the frog surviving and seeking food on its own in a natural habitat.

Principal Goodman: I understand your devotion to your religious beliefs, Mr. and Mrs. Liang. But these animals are an important part of the science curriculum, and I doubt that this situation will be taken lightly by the other parents and the school board.

Mr. and Mrs. Kuan Lee Liang: We understand the importance of the science curriculum. But we will not punish Sophia for embracing the tenets of Buddhism. The school and you, Principal Goodman, should support the school's mission, especially its focus "*to encourage all students to learn to respect each other and value diversity.*" You should respect our belief and value our family's diversity. We ask that Sophia not be punished for what she did and that her classmates are told the truth about why Sophia set the animals free.

Principal Goodman: I empathize with you both. But the school board approved keeping animals in the classroom as part of the science curriculum five years ago, and I have not had any complaints until now. On the contrary, several parents have spoken highly of their children's enthusiasm and increased interest in science because of their experiences with the animals in the classroom. Given my position as principal, I will explain to the school board that this incident is a rare case and that I still encourage the use of animals for the science curriculum. After all, it is in the best interests of the majority of students to foster their learning in science. However, as a resident of this community, I am torn between my own personal beliefs of embracing diversity and respecting and valuing different religious beliefs. I will take a couple of days to think about this situation and then determine the best decision. Until then, I will ask Mrs. Cullen not to have Sophia watch the other students feeding the frog. Sophia will not be punished in any way, but I feel you should take her home for the rest of the day.

Questions for Discussion

1. What are the benefits of students feeding the frog as part of the science curriculum? Does the science curriculum consider the greater good for all students over individual rights? Should it? Why or why not? What would a caring principal do in this situation?

2. Who is determining the curriculum? What do you think other parents with different religious beliefs would say against not having the students feed the frog live bugs?

3. How does the ethic of the profession factor into Principal Goodman's decision? What in this scenario leads you to your decision?

4. Do you see any conflict between Principal Goodman's professional beliefs, the ethic of care, and the community's interests?

5. Considering all the ethical frameworks, is there a resolution that could support both sides, that is, Principal Goodman backing the current science curriculum and the Liang family's Buddhist belief of not harming any living creature? Explain your answer.

CASE STUDY 7.2 CEREMONIAL RIGHTS

Diné High School (DHS) sits at the bottom of a mesa surrounded by native vegetation of yucca and sagebrush. It is a public high school on a Navajo reservation and is one of 35 public schools within a 160-mile radius. The closest school to Diné is a Bureau of Indian Affairs school serving grades K–8.

The student population at DHS is approximately 90% Navajo and Hopi; the other 10% of the students are Anglo. The community is made up of a post office, a church, a chapter house (a community center where tribal council officials hold meetings and gatherings such as dinners and special elections), a hospital, and a tribal housing authority funded by the U.S. Department of Housing and Urban Development.

On August 7, with a new school year scheduled to begin in less than a week, Ms. Tsosie, the principal, was working on the agenda and pre-service schedule for the returning staff. Teachers were returning to the building daily, and the rest of the staff would be in full force within the week. As with most other schools, the beginning of the school year was quite hectic.

On this day, Mr. Bia, a graduate of the school, came to register his ninth-grade son. On entering the school, he saw that the new library had been completed and wanted to take a tour. Seeing that the principal, Ms. Tsosie, was in her office and had just hung up the phone, he knocked on her door and introduced himself. "Ya'ateeh Abini [good morning], Ms. Tsosie. Shei ei Ted Bia Yinishye. Shi ei Todichinii nishili, Tohtsoni bashichiin [My name is Ted Bia; I'm of the Bitterwater clan born for the Redhouse people]." After his formal introduction, he told Ms. Tsosie that he was very happy to see her. He then complemented her on the new library.

"As a graduate of Diné High School I am so pleased to see the library addition. I know that a lot of hard work went into making the high school library a place for the kids here and also a special place for the entire community. I especially hope you were able to add some new technology into the library. I was wondering if I might take a look inside while I'm here?"

Mr. Bia stepped into the hallway and Ms. Tsosie unlocked the library so that he could sneak a peek. Ms. Tsosie was happy to visit and show Mr. Bia around, since this was not the first time he had shown interest in the school. She remembered that on several occasions he had made a point to attend meetings in which community participation was sought. In fact, Mr. Bia, as a parent, was an important advocate in promoting the idea of a community library initiative.

On exiting the library, Mr. Bia addressed Ms. Tsosie and asked in a very low, deliberate tone, "So, Ms. Tsosie, when will a Blessing Way Ceremony[1] be held for the library?" Ms. Tsosie stopped, looked around, and replied, "The day before the students arrive next week." Mr. Bia walked down the hall with Ms. Tsosie and then stopped and said, "That's nice, I hope it is at a time that both my son and I can attend."

Mr. Bia then picked up his son and headed out of the door. Ms. Tsosie returned to her office thinking about her conversation with Mr. Bia. Sitting at her desk she looked down and saw a sticky note. She had placed the note there to remind her to be at school at dawn on August 11 to greet the medicine man and his wife along with all other invited community members who would be attending the Blessing Way Ceremony.

---

[1] Blessing Way is a traditional Navajo ceremony that is most often observed to bring about goodness and harmony to an individual and extended families.

She remembered that early morning was the time of day the medicine man, a Navajo elder who would be traveling some distance to perform the ceremony, had set for the Blessing Way Ceremony. Ms. Tsosie was eager to meet the requests of those who would be participating in the ceremony. Although the Blessing Way is traditionally a four-day event, she was pleased that the medicine man, the superintendent, and the community members had agreed to participate in a shortened version of the ceremony. She was excited to know that the school year would begin with a blessing of the new library and good feelings for the upcoming school year.

After going home for the evening, Ms. Tsosie thought again about her conversation with Mr. Bia. Feeling a little anxious about the ceremony, she called the superintendent, Dr. Begay, and requested to meet with him the following morning.

The next morning, Ms. Tsosie waited patiently to meet with Dr. Begay at his office. When they were finally together, Ms. Tsosie began with a simple question to the superintendent: "We did decide to have a Blessing Way Ceremony for the new library and the beginning of the new year, right?"

Dr. Begay flipped open his calendar, looked at it very seriously, and replied, "I have it right here, August 11 in the library. Correct?"

"Well, that's what I have on my calendar, but I wanted to make sure that I had the right day scheduled," Ms. Tsosie replied.

Ms. Tsosie then asked, "Has the medicine man been contacted?"

The superintendent said in his low, deliberate voice, "Yes, in fact I'll be going out to get him and his wife early that morning. When they arrive, will you and some of your staff members please be at the high school with coffee and food ready for the medicine man and a few guests? We will probably need enough food to feed maybe 50 people."

Ms. Tsosie quietly responded with a "Yes."

Following the meeting with the superintendent, Ms. Tsosie returned to her office. Less than 10 minutes later, her phone rang. "Good morning. This is Ms. Tsosie. What can I do for you?"

"Ms. Tsosie, this is Ms. Dee." (Ms. Dee is a teacher who was at the district office getting a signature on a trip when she saw the notice about the Blessing Way Ceremony.) "I just wanted to ask you a question. I'm at the district office and saw that you are going to have a Blessing Way Ceremony for the new library. I want you to know that I don't think what you are doing is right."

Ms. Tsosie waited for Ms. Dee to pause and then asked, "Why?"

Ms. Dee continued, "I believe that the Blessing Way Ceremonies should not be conducted in schools. I don't believe in this type of practice, and I don't understand why you are having this ceremony at school. My child goes to school here too, and this is not what we believe in at home. Why are you making the students go to this?"

Ms. Tsosie clarified: "There are community members and other district staff who will attend. Invitations have also gone out to all high school personnel and the student council. But, no one has to come if they don't feel like it."

Ms. Dee, sounding a little flustered, continued: "Well, this is not something I believe in and I'm not alone in my beliefs. I think you know, Ms. Tsosie, that there are a lot of staff and faculty who attend local churches of different faiths and don't believe in traditional ceremonies like the Blessing Way Ceremony. And, many of the younger people here don't believe that traditional practices should be part of the school. If people want their children to learn about this type of thing, or participate in these ceremonies, then they should do this stuff at home or in the community—but not in the school."

Thinking that it would be more appropriate to discuss this matter in person rather than over the phone, Ms. Tsosie waited for Ms. Dee to pause before suggesting that they meet in person to discuss this matter further.

"I've told you how I feel, and I don't think there is a need to discuss this further." Without saying goodbye or waiting for Ms. Tsosie to respond, Ms. Dee slammed down the receiver.

Feeling that she had done her best to resolve this dilemma, Ms. Tsosie turned to her desk calendar and wrote in big letters, BLESSING WAY CEREMONY, in the box marked August 11. She then drew a smiley face on the calendar and retired for the night.

Questions for Discussion

1. Does the Blessing Way Ceremony violate the principle of separation of church and state? If so, how and why? If not, why not? What impact should culture have upon decisions to include or exclude religious activities from school?

2. Do you agree with the principal's decision to proceed with the Blessing Way Ceremony? If you were the principal, how would you have handled this dilemma? Explain your reasoning.

3. What would be the most caring resolution to this dilemma?

4. Who is making the rules here? Whose values do these rules represent? Would this situation be different if the school community was predominately Christian? If students initiated and led the ceremony?

5. To what extent should student voice/perspective influence the selection and scheduling of activities and ceremonies in school? To what extent should faculty/staff voice/perspective influence the selection and scheduling of activities and ceremonies in school?

6. How do you distinguish between cultural and religious activities in a school setting?

7. Given the ethical frameworks discussed in this text, are there one or more elements or constructs of ethics that would be most applicable in resolving this dilemma? If so, which one(s) would you suggest? Why?

CASE STUDY 7.3 TIME OFF FOR RELIGIOUS SERVICES

Guam is a small U.S. island community with a population of approximately 140,000. Residents comprise a melting-pot of ethnicities, consisting mostly of Guamanians (natives of the island) as well as Hispanics, Japanese, Koreans, Filipinos, Vietnamese, White Americans (non-Hispanic), African Americans, Puerto Ricans, and Indians. The local elementary public schools house grades K–5 and there are only three schools: Central, Northern, and Southern. The elementary teachers in each of the schools are as diverse as the community residents, but, like the community, the majority of the teachers are Guamanian and devout Catholics. In any given week of the year, Catholic rosary services are held in cathedrals, residents' homes, or both.

On May 30, the day after the Memorial Day weekend and just two weeks shy of the end of the school year, teachers and administrators in the Central School were busily preparing for year-end testing and budget review. At Central Elementary School, teachers had just been notified that one of their recent retiree colleagues, Mrs. Maria Cruz, had passed away over the weekend. A well-liked teacher, Mrs. Cruz had worked at Central Elementary for 30 years. On this Tuesday, Catholic rosary services for Mrs. Cruz were to take place at noon and 6 p.m. at the town cathedral.

Principal Robert Perez circulated a written notice to all teachers regarding the rosary services for Mrs. Cruz. The notice read:

> One of our former teachers, Mrs. Maria Cruz, sadly passed away over the weekend. Noon rosary services for Mrs. Cruz will be held at the cathedral. Any teachers wishing to attend the noon rosary service for Maria may do so as long as their classes are covered by other teachers for the time they are away. No official leave form is required to attend the rosary services. Kindly inform my secretary, Ms. Anita Baza, of your intentions and who will be covering your class.

Later that morning, Principal Perez saw first-grade teacher Ms. Rose Torres in the hallway. "Hi Rose! Are you planning to attend the rosary for Maria anytime this week?" Ms. Torres replied, "Yes, I am. Tina Mafnas [another first-grade teacher] and I are combining our classes and will take turns covering for the hour."

Principal Perez responded, "Great. As always, you do not have to sign a leave form if you stagger the coverage of your classes. Just be sure the kids are working on the set curriculum for that time period and let my secretary, Ms. Baza, know your schedule."

On receipt of the notice, fourth-grade teachers Mrs. Sashi Takagumi (a Japanese resident in the community) and Ms. Brindha Yatar (an Indian resident, originally from Pakistan) fumed over the notice in the teachers' lounge. "The fact is that Principal Perez has practiced a no-leave deduction policy during our entire five years of employment here," Mrs. Takagumi complained. "Just last week, my church celebrated the annual 'harvest moon ceremony', and I signed annual leave to attend the ceremony—in which I returned back to work within one hour." She continued, "Brindha, this is really unfair! Maybe I should say that I am going to attend a rosary service next time so that I do not have to sign annual leave."

"Yeah, but what can we do? We are in the minority when it comes to religious beliefs in this community. And the fact that Principal Perez is a devout Catholic only perpetuates this 'school culture' of taking care of your own kind," retorted Ms. Yatar.

"We need to stand up for what is right," replied Mrs. Takagumi. "We are foolish to let it escalate further. We are no longer new teachers trying to pass our probationary period. We do not need to keep a low tone about this any longer. Either we are allowed the same no-leave policy to attend our religious services or else everyone has to sign for annual leave for any kind of absence related to attending a religious event."

"I see your point, Sashi," said Ms. Yatar. "But the real focus should be on what is the appropriate action to take as professionals. I mean, shouldn't church and state issues stay out of our public schools? I don't think that central office, in particular Superintendent Salas, will be happy to know that classes are being combined even if it is only for one hour. And what about the parents of these children in combined classes; what will they think? You know that regardless of what religion these children practice, their parents will be upset over lumping two classes into one huge classroom. It really has become more of a break period than a focus on teaching the curriculum for that hour. It is too difficult to oversee so many students and keep their concentration. By the time the classes combine, which usually means going to the library or study hall room, 30 minutes have gone by," explains Ms. Yatar.

"Yes, I agree with you Brindha," Mrs. Takagumi firmly stated. "We need to petition Superintendent Salas to investigate this 'time off without leave' practice. The children are the ones at a disadvantage with this practice, not us. We really should focus on doing our best job to educate our students."

Mrs. Takagumi and Ms. Yatar decided to write a formal letter to Superintendent Salas concerning this dilemma. In addition, they planned to attach a petition containing signatures of other teachers from Central Elementary School who were opposed to Principal Perez's "time off without leave" practice.

Four teachers in favor of the "time off without leave" practice heard about the petition and stormed into Principal Perez's office. One of these teachers, Mrs. Baza, began: "Principal Perez, you have to talk with Mrs. Takagumi and Ms. Yatar. If their petition ends up in Superintendent Salas' office, we all lose out on the practice of taking time off to show respect for the loss of loved ones."

"Yes," agreed Joe Cruz, another teacher and cousin of the deceased teacher, Maria. "You need to communicate our culture of caring and concern for others."

"Joe is right. However, Mrs. Takagumi and Ms. Yatar are still relatively new to our island and our school. We need to embrace their concerns too and let them know that the school respects their religious beliefs and practices," replied teacher Cecilia Mafnas.

"They have nothing to complain about," a fourth teacher observed. "You let them take time off when they need to pick up their children. It is not your fault, Principal Perez, if they submit a leave form to the payroll officer for taking time to attend a funeral service. They never asked not to sign one for their services. They do not understand the culture and tradition of the school. We care about our co-teachers. That is the kind of teacher we are. Regardless of the type of religious funeral services, we care enough to pay our last respects to the families of our deceased teacher."

On hearing the comments of these four teachers, Principal Perez called Mrs. Takagumi and Ms. Yatar into his office for a chat. "Sashi and Brindha, thank you for coming to my office. I know you are upset about the 'time off without leave' practice to attend religious services. You have been part of our school for five years. You should understand and be aware of the cultural tradition of paying last respects to a deceased teacher of our school. I understand your strong resolve to obey the rules and regulations of the profession and that any absence away from work should require signing a leave form. On the other hand, I am committed to the concerned and caring nature of this community and the traditions of our school. I ask that you give me two days to think over how to best handle this situation before you submit your petition to Superintendent Salas."

Mrs. Takagumi and Ms. Yatar were quite cordial with Principal Perez and respected him as the school leader. They agreed to wait for two days before submitting the letter and petition to Superintendent Salas. Now, Principal Perez needs to decide how to address this dilemma, as he sees the merits of both those in favor of and those against the "time off without leave" practice.

Questions for Discussion

1. Is there a legal issue here? If not, why not? If so, what is it and how would you resolve it? What is the fairest way to handle this situation? The most caring?

2. Why do you think the "time off without leave" practice has been allowed to go unnoticed for five years? Do you think the "culture" of the community and/or school should determine policy and/or practice? Explain your answer.

3. Does the ethic of the profession support Principal Perez in carrying out his "time off without leave" practice? Why or why not? How should Superintendent Salas respond to this dilemma, keeping in mind the best interests of the students?

4. What action would you take as a teacher who does not agree with the practice? Do you think Mrs. Takagumi and Ms. Yatar chose an appropriate strategy to address this dilemma? Why or why not? What else could they have done?

5. How do you think Principal Perez should respond to possible negative reactions from the parents of the children being placed in a so-called break hour period? Do you see an ethical issue here? If so, what is it and how would you resolve it? If not, why not?

CASE STUDY 7.4 RELIGION AND SOCIAL/PERSONAL CONTRADICTIONS

The day before the beginning of fall semester at State University, Dr. Diane Morgan, a professor in the Department of Women's Studies, was busily preparing for her courses. She sat in a small office which was strewn with hundreds of student papers she had collected over her past 10 years of employment at State. A number of papers were piled on the office floor, and the shelves were filled with many books about feminism, feminist pedagogy, gay and lesbian rights, women studies, religious studies, and psychological development. A big mirror hung on the wall with a huge colorful beaded necklace on the left side. Two nicely framed photos were on the desk (one of Diane and her son and the other of Diane and some of her friends). A number of certificates were hung on the wall with some thank-you notes from previous students. One read: "Thank you Diane for making me deeply reflect on my values and recognize who I am. Now I view things differently. My identity has shifted dramatically after taking your course. You helped me to critically examine who I am and to see other realities."

It was approaching 4 p.m. and Diane had been stuck in her office working since she had returned from her quick lunch at noon. She was preparing for her introductory class to women's studies. The department's administrative assistant, Sarah, knocked on her door. As Diane was deeply absorbed in reviewing her class textbook and did not hear her, Sarah pushed the door open while continuing to knock and began the following conversation:

Sarah: Hi, these are the copies you asked me to make.

Diane: Oh, thanks for bringing them in.

Sarah: I read over the syllabus while waiting for the copies. Do you mind if I ask how you handle such sensitive topics with all of the diversity concerns we are having on campus?

Diane: [Laughing.] Well, let me tell you it's not easy to do.

Sarah: One of the recent discussions in the alumni/ae association meeting with the university administration a few weeks ago was their concern that our university is becoming so far-out in some controversial issues.

Diane: [Sighing.] Unfortunately, many people like to ignore these issues and protect the oppressing social structure. Those who do not fit the dominant socially structured caricature are marginalized and oppressed. I want students to understand and challenge those power relations in our society that are based on gender, class, race, culture and sexual orientation. I personally think that they are breaking us apart instead of bringing us together.

Sarah: But how do you balance the conflict on these issues among students who come from diverse cultures and are of different gender, race, and sexual orientations?

Diane: That's what I was thinking of all day. On the first day of my courses, I open the class with an introductory background about myself. I am an Episcopalian woman who has a gay teenager. I come from a middle-class American family. I think declaring my assumptions and asking students to examine theirs is a first step.

Sarah nodded but was still puzzled as to how Dr. Morgan would handle the ethical and at times political concerns of students and administrators who do not agree with her.

Eight weeks have now passed since Diane's Introduction to Women's Studies class started. This class has been challenging at times owing to the great diversity of students. Even though Diane tries to provide a safe environment for all her students despite their gender, culture, discipline area, or sexual orientation, while facilitating their discussion of these issues, sometimes she feels student resistance to discuss certain controversial social justice issues. She included these issues in her course to help students ask hard questions and arrive at their own conclusions.

That morning, the class had been discussing homosexual marriage. Students were sitting in groups of four to a table. They were about to start discussing an article they had to read on the topic. Each group was required to present their reaction to the class after discussion. Diane interrupted the group work, remarking, "I know each of you has an opinion about this. However, please keep an open mind and respect for others' points of views. Just to get thinking about this issue, think of it in relation to our course. You might want to consider issues such as sex discrimination, identity development, gender social construction, legal regulations, and current social, political, and cultural changes."

Diane walked around the class to listen and to facilitate group discussions. One group attracted her attention owing to its diversity. It consisted of four students: Fatmah, an Arab Muslim woman interested in the oppression of women; Mike, a gay campus activist involved in a diversity initiative on campus that supports lesbian, gay, bisexual, and transgender students, faculty, and staff; Susan, a White American majoring in women's studies and interested in women's right to choose; and David, a fundamentalist Christian pastor and graduate student in religious studies, interested in developing community capacity to create venues for healthy adolescence gender identity development.

Their group discussion started slowly but quickly heated up as a result of clashing backgrounds and opinions. Diane noticed that Fatmah, who is usually active in group discussions, was strangely quiet. She was doodling in her notebook instead of giving her opinion to the group, looked uncomfortable and disturbed, and barely talked. When Diane asked her after class about the reasons for her lack of participation, she requested an appointment to talk to Diane privately about this later. Curious to know Fatmah's reasons, Diane agreed to see her at 3:00 p.m. that same day.

Later that afternoon, around 3:00, Diane was working in her office on the computer. She felt very tired because it had been a long day for her with three meetings, one class, and now her appointment with Fatmah. She heard someone asking Sarah about her office location, so she got ready to meet the student. She opened the door of her office and welcomed Fatmah.

Diane: So you wanted to talk to me about today's class.

Fatmah: Yes, Dr. Morgan.

Diane: Call me Diane.

Fatmah: Well, it's a little hard for me to do that. You see, in my society it would be very disrespectful of me to call you like that.

Diane: OK, I was surprised at your unusual silence today in class.

Fatmah: [Hesitating.] I don't know how to tell you this, but today's class discussion made me feel very uncomfortable.

Diane: That's great! I don't want you to feel "comfortable" in this class. I
think if you feel "uncomfortable," then you're actually learning. We talk
about controversial issues in this course and if they are not troubling to
you, then you probably shouldn't take the class. Having said that, tell me
what is uncomfortable for you?

Fatmah: I am really interested in the class because I think there are a lot of
social injustices for women, especially in my part of the world, and I am
troubled by that. However, Dr. Morgan, the issue of gays and lesbians
in my society is something that is not a subject for discussion. It's
outrageous to talk about.

Diane: Well, in this country this topic is still controversial for many people.

Fatmah: Yes. I could tell from one of my group members' opinion. But I
feel that this issue is putting me personally in both cultural and religious
conflict. Culturally, it's outrageous to talk about sex in general in my
society, let alone a topic like this. Sex education is not part of our
curriculum at any educational stage. It is really embarrassing for me to
be in a discussion like this. Please note that today's topic is even more
difficult for me because the issue is more than cultural; it's religious. In
Islam, we believe that homosexuality is against human nature, and it's
a great sin. We believe that people choose to become homosexual and
are not born that way. The environment plays a great role in shaping
such identities.

Diane: Let me ask you this: Do you think this is not an issue in your society
as well?

Fatmah: I don't know. But it is not something that my religion would allow
me to talk about, let alone fight for social justice on its behalf. Islam is
very strict about this issue. I totally understand the purpose of this
discussion for the class, but for me this is against everything that I was
raised to believe in and just by participating in this discussion I might
be committing a "sin." I'm facing a very difficult conflict. I was surprised
to know that one of my group members is "gay." I really adore this
person. He is one of the most considerate people I've met in this
university, but now I find myself in an awkward position. I don't want to
hurt anyone, especially this person, but at the same time, I can't depart
from who I am and what I believe in.

Diane was feeling a little hurt that somebody could view a gay person in this
way. It made her think of the many times her son had faced similar
opposition. She reminded herself that she is in the position of an instructor
who is willing to offer help to her students with a possibility of hope in
transforming their perspectives. Diane sighed inwardly and responded,
"Fatmah, the course is not about changing your social or religious beliefs.
The course is about examining them and broadening your understanding

of social justice. In this country, this is a big issue right now, and there are many people in the class who are interested in it."

Fatmah gazed at Diane in silence as she thought to herself, "You don't understand my situation. I think you're oppressing me by making it a course issue! The course is supposed to focus on women's issues, not gays and lesbians."

At the same time, Diane was thinking about other students she had in her courses over the past years with similar dispositions to Fatmah. She had used the same syllabus for the past two semesters. At the end of the course, she mostly received positive feedback from students about how the course helped them to confront their biases and form an opinion about important issues in their social lives. However, she had never had a Muslim student before in any of her courses. She was not aware of the concept of "sin" in Islam and its possible consequences for Fatmah's performance in her class. Diane strongly believed in the importance of this topic for her course content. She was very cautious about choosing academic literature for the course reading assignments. After a long silence, Diane asked Fatmah to sit out the next class and to come to see her at the end of the week.

Diane was looking for a way to help Fatmah deal with her struggle in class. When Fatmah came to see her at the end of the week, Diane said, "I remember your interest in women's oppression. I think one way for you to think about this is to focus on how this movement has socially and historically developed in the United States. You can look, for example, at how people organize themselves in social movements, divide roles, and the phases a social movement goes through. You can apply what you learn from it to issues of women's social movement in your country as the topic for your course paper."

As Diane spoke, Fatmah was thinking that this could be a reasonable assignment. However, she still felt strongly about issues of homosexuality being discussed in the class. She believed that other students on the course would raise this subject. Fatmah thanked Diane for her time and said she would have to think about this option for a few days since the deadline for dropping a course was in one week.

Diane struggled with Fatmah's comments about possibly dropping the course. Diane wanted to bring into the class discussions voices of those silenced by the social system due to sex discrimination, so she felt that the issue of homosexuality was an important topic for her class. She was aware that her decision "carries with it a restructuring of human life" (Foster, 1986, p. 33), although she hoped that Fatmah could reach a point of religious tolerance. She tried to find a solution to fit Fatmah's special concern, but she could not discard the topic.

Questions for Discussion

1. Discuss the multidimensions of Diane's ethical dilemma:
   - Discuss your reaction to Diane's decision to include gay marriage and homosexuality as issues for discussion in her women's studies class.
   - Explain what influence Diane's personal life and values had on her decision to include the topic of homosexuality in her course.
   - Discuss how this dilemma relates to academic freedom in higher education institutions.
   - Do you think Diane is breaking social system norms? Explain.
2. From an ethical perspective, why do you think Diane decided to continue to use a controversial issue in the course despite the fact that she had observed the discomfort of some students with this topic? Was she considering the greater good for the majority of her students? The best interests of each student? Explain your answer.
3. Discuss why Fatmah was the only student who felt she was not able to contribute equally to her group discussion even though the topic was of a sensitive nature to other group members as well.
4. How might one view this dilemma from a critical perspective? Are there concerns relative to power, privilege, and equity? If so, what are they and what could be done to address them?
5. What would be the most caring way to resolve this dilemma? Why? Do you think Diane's suggestion solves Fatmah's religious concern? Explain.
6. In light of the various ethical paradigms, what would you do if you were Diane? What alternative solutions might you offer the student?

Chapter 8

Equality Versus Equity

James K. Krause, David J. Traini, Beatrice H. Mickey,
Daniel L. Dukes, and Carly Ackley

In this chapter, the case studies presented deal with issues of inclusion, seniority, and access to educational opportunity. In all these dilemmas, the administrators and teachers in charge want to do the right thing. However, what is right for one person or group may not be right for others.

In the diverse and complex society of today, a paradox exists between the concepts of equality and equity. We define equality under the rubric of equal or even-handed treatment as discussed by Strike et al. (1988). They provided this definition: "In any given circumstances, people who are the same in those respects relevant to how they are treated in those circumstances should receive the same treatment" (p. 45). Equality, defined in this way, looks at the individual and the circumstances surrounding him or her. It does not focus on group differences based on categories such as race, sex, social class, and ethnicity. This view is one of assimilation because it assumes that individuals, once socialized into society, have the right "to do anything they want, to choose their own lives and not be hampered by traditional expectations and stereotypes" (Young, 1990, p. 157). It is a positive and inspiring concept—an ideal that is well worth attaining.

Equity, on the other hand, as we define it here, deals with difference and takes into consideration the fact that this society contains many groups that have not always been given equal treatment and/or have not had a level field on which to play. These groups have frequently been made to feel inferior to those in the mainstream, and some have even been oppressed. To achieve equity, according to Young (1990), "Social policy should sometimes accord special treatment to groups" (p. 158). Thus, the concept of equity provides a case for unequal treatment for those who have been disadvantaged over time. It can provide compensatory kinds of treatment, offering it in the form of special programs and benefits for those who have been discriminated against and are in need of opportunity.

Movements have had a profound effect in fighting for equity or social justice. In the case of the Native American movement, a battle took place against the concept of assimilation. This fight was for "a right to self-government on Indian lands" (Young, 1990, p. 160). It was also a desire to retain the language, customs, and crafts that gave this group its special identity.

Pressure from group movements has often led to legislation that has provided opportunity. To give an example of this, the women's movement fought for and eventually obtained the passage of Title IX of the Education Amendments of 1972. Title IX made it known that discrimination on the basis of sex was illegal in any educational program receiving federal funding (American Association of University Women, 1992, p. 8). The passage of Title IX opened the door for many gender equity programs and projects (American Association of University Women, 1995) enabling women and girls to be empowered and learn how to overcome the barriers that still exist today. But it is not only in the area of racial, ethnic, and gender movements that the paradox of equality versus equity may be found. If one turns to the umbrella term of *diversity* and defines it broadly, then a range of differences can be explored that includes categories not only of race, ethnicity, and gender but also of social class, disability, sexual orientation, and exceptionalities (Banks, 2001; Banks & Banks, 2006; Cushner et al., 1992; Gay, 2000, 2003; Shapiro et al., 2001).

The paradox of equality versus equity is treated differently under each of the four paradigms we use to analyze ethical dilemmas in this book. Turning to the first of the four paradigms, the ethic of justice is broad enough to include both equality and equity. This all-encompassing definition goes back as far as Aristotle. He "held that justice consists in treating equals equally and unequals unequally" (Strike & Soltis, 1992, p. 46). By this, Strike and Soltis felt he meant that "if high-school grades are the basis of admission into a university, then two people with the same grades should receive the same treatment. Either both should be admitted or both should be rejected" (p. 46). This illustration demonstrates the use of the justice paradigm for the principle of equality. But Aristotle also recognized that "when people differ on some relevant characteristic they should be treated differently." Strike and Soltis (1992), in this case, provided the example of a visually handicapped student who is not being treated fairly by being given the same book to read as a sighted student. "Here" they said, "fairness requires different treatment" (p. 46). This illustration utilizes the concept of equity in relation to the paradigm of justice. Thus, under the ethic of justice, both equality and equity are acknowledged.

The ethic of care, another of the four paradigms used in this book, challenges the impartiality and detachment of moral reasoning (e.g., Gilligan, 1982; Noddings, 1992, 2002, 2003). The concept of impartiality has tended to work by distancing oneself from others to enable an equal weighing of all interests. The caring frame would not be remote, but instead would be compassionate and place equity rather than equality at its center. No doubt, those who care would really listen to the voices of diverse groups— particularly those who have been discriminated against in the past. They would turn away from the ideal of impartiality that is inherent in our society and our beliefs (Young, 1990). Instead, they would recognize differences and the history of unfair treatment to different groups over time by trying to rectify past wrongs.

Under the ethic of critique, hard questions can be raised concerning the treatment of diverse groups in society. These questions can take into account the issues of oppression, domination, and discrimination. The myth of merit (Fishkin, 1983) and the problems of distribution of goods and services to all groups within our society may also be explored. In addition, within this paradigm, current demographic trends can be considered in critical as well as positive lights. The unprecedented expansion of our nation's racial, ethnic, socio-economic, and cultural groups can be discussed and questioned using this ethic, as can some of the accompanying problems of children of poverty, single-parent homes, and students of exceptionality (Hodgkinson, 1992; Utley & Obiakor, 1995).

Turning to the ethic of the profession, we know that how schools, colleges, and universities address the evolving needs of our students and society will determine, to a great extent, the success of our nation in this new millennium. A great challenge to be faced involves how educators balance the acceptance and support of difference without hurting the collective whole of our society. This is not an easy balance for educational leaders to attain, and the major question in this paradigm remains: Is equality or equity, or a combination of both, in the best interests of the students?

In this chapter, dilemmas are presented in an attempt to evoke analyses of ethics related to equality and equity issues. A range of approaches are addressed in the cases themselves and in the questions that follow each dilemma.

Case study 8.1, When All Means All, deals with a problem in a school that is beginning to serve as a model of inclusion for the state. In this dilemma, the problem centers on an emotionally disturbed child in a regular elementary school classroom who has caused chaos. Having worked with the child in the classroom for a time, a teacher has found him to be a constant source of problems. She feels that the youngster is infringing on the rights of others and is also not receiving the kind of attention he needs in an inclusive classroom.

In Case study 8.2, Black and White and Shades of Gray, new minority teachers are to be retrenched owing to economic reasons. The old rule, "last hired, first fired," is presented with all of its problems. The principal is placed in a very difficult position in a district in which minority students are increasing in number.

Access to Knowledge (Case study 8.3) is a case in which a principal is approached by Latino parents who want their child to take courses in the college preparatory track. The student has been discouraged by the guidance counselor and by his teachers from taking college preparatory work. The principal finds out that the student has not been doing well in his classes. Conflicting feelings on the part of the principal in handling the situation are discussed.

In Case study 8.4, Academic Integrity in a Deaf Education Setting, the assistant principal of a school for the hearing impaired must deal with standardized testing and how it is administered by two very different teachers. He has to decide whether both teachers should have followed test directions, as written, or modify them according to the needs of their students. This case asks: How should directions be administered to provide an equal playing field on standardized testing for students who are deaf?

Case study 8.5, When Fundraising and School Policy Collide, focuses on a small preschool center that depends heavily on donations. A grandfather, who gives money generously, wants his grandson to attend the school, but a child with spina bifida is next on the waiting list. The decision that must be made by the director is to determine who should be invited to enroll in the school, keeping in mind the consequences of that decision.

CASE STUDY 8.1 WHEN ALL MEANS ALL

As Jim Martin headed toward home, thoughts filtered back to better times. He found this occurring more frequently during the past few weeks. Three years had passed since Freedom Elementary School had implemented a full inclusionary model of educating students with disabilities. As director of special education for the school district, and with his office in the Freedom building, Jim had invested a great deal of time in developing the program and, thus, had a special interest in seeing it succeed. He also believed that the process of inclusion was a natural extension of the child-centered, collaborative approach the district and community supported. Here, the regular classroom would be the educational setting of choice for all students. However, after its early success, more recent struggles were now wearing on everyone. "How could something that unified everyone such a short time ago be so divisive now?" he wondered.

Jim had served as director of special education for 11 years. He was well liked and well respected by his staff and co-workers and had an excellent relationship with Rose O'Brien, the building principal. Jim had always prided himself on fostering the development of a highly skilled, caring faculty. He was able to do this by sharing leadership.

The idea of establishing an inclusive school stemmed from his work and that of a committed core of teachers. This team truly served as the driving force behind the exploration, development, and implementation of an inclusion model.

It was not easy to build this concept into a functional process, but everyone's hard work and steadfast belief provided the foundation for what would benefit all. Support soon grew from a small pocket of Freedom's staff to widespread support throughout the faculty and community. The vast majority of teachers genuinely believed that all children would be best served in a regular education setting with their same-age peers. Eventually, Freedom's effort to include students with disabilities began to draw attention from across the state. Educators from other school districts began to explore the "Freedom Model." Administrators and teachers flocked to the school in droves. Faculty members were asked to present at statewide conferences on inclusive practices. Jim had just recently received notice of the upcoming publication of an article he had written for a professional journal. It was entitled "Freedom: An Inclusionary Model for All." Advocates of full inclusion held up the Freedom Model as an example of successful practice that developed from the grass-roots effort of caring educators.

Momentum from the early successes, or the "Golden Age" as it later became known, carried staff through the first two years. Inclusion was not an easy process, but challenges were met with effective collaborative efforts. Staff and services were in place to prevent any child from needing to be pulled out of the regular classroom. Students were doing well, and the parents of students with disabilities were happier than ever. Although there were some parents who voiced concern about unfair levels of attention directed toward students with disabilities (and away from their own children), these parents remained the minority in the parent–teachers' organization. The school had established its identity as an inclusive school. This was a source of pride to the school and community.

At the start of the third year, Cody Smith, a fourth-grade student with serious emotional difficulties, enrolled at Freedom. Staff had included students with behavior problems in the past, but the level of Cody's conduct disorder was new to most. He had a long history of aggressive acting-out, disruptive behavior, and poor peer–teacher interactions. He had been previously served in a self-contained classroom for students with emotional disabilities. He had met with moderate success in this program, but the program's staff felt the need for continued extensive support.

The team met with Mr. and Mrs. Smith to review the wealth of educational and psychiatric information provided in Cody's file. Although there was some hesitancy, the team agreed that inclusion for all means all. If they were to be true to their established philosophy, they could not segregate certain students. The Smiths were somewhat confused by all this. Early on in Cody's school career, they had tried to fight his removal from the regular classroom. Just as they were becoming comfortable with the separate services, a new set of professionals were saying the regular classroom would be best for their son. They liked the idea of him being with "normal" kids, but would he fit in? They were finally convinced to try an inclusive class after speaking with other parents who advocated strongly for inclusive education.

The team assembled the following week to develop a plan outlining the supports and services necessary to educate Cody in the regular fourth-grade classroom. A range of supports involving additional staffing, curricular and instructional adaptations, and behavior support planning were developed. Jim swelled with pride as the staff met this challenge and developed a quality, individualized program. Cody's parents were fully involved and very pleased with their new-found empowerment. During the first month in his new school, Cody experienced only minor difficulties. Adjustments in supports were made to address his needs, and he responded well. Everyone was excited to be part of another success story. Cody was happy, learning, and making new friends.

As October arrived however, so did the firestorm of Cody's behavior. Almost overnight, he went from cooperative and pleasant to aggressive and disruptive. He threw books and food, cursed openly at adults, refused to comply with basic requests, and threatened to hurt other students. Mrs. Appleby, his teacher, often found herself at his side or in the hallway trying to calm Cody and prevent further disruption. Everyone now knew what a conduct disorder involved. The team immediately pulled together for the first of seemingly endless team meetings.

The team adjusted Cody's behavior support plan to allow for "calming" time when he became agitated. This proved unsuccessful. Individual aide support was assigned. Cody continued to disrupt class with his verbal outbursts. Teachers began to rotate one-on-one coverage. Unstructured time was studied and structured. The team studied factors in Cody's life that may have precipitated these difficulties. Profanity-laced tirades and noncompliance continued. Positive contingencies proved ineffective, family case management was fruitless, and medical intervention was unsuccessful. Consultation with social workers and psychologists led to little, if any, positive change.

After three months, the roof was about to blow off. Parents throughout the school demanded that Cody be removed. Others requested that their children transfer to other classes away from Cody. An undercurrent opposing inclusion started to surface for the first time. Jim Martin danced from fire to fire, trying to quell the rising displeasure of staff, students, and parents. Throughout all this, Cody and his parents remained pleased with the regular class placement.

Then it happened. The team wearily pulled together for another planning meeting. Jim was presenting his thoughts on the latest plan for intervention when Mrs. Appleby, Cody's teacher, stopped him midsentence and said, "I want him out of my class now! This is no longer fair to Cody or the other children." Two other team members concurred: "We cannot meet his needs in the regular classroom. He is too disruptive to the education of other students. This kind of class is too much for him to handle. He is too much for us to handle." Jim was completely caught off-guard by their comments.

"What about our philosophy that all our students will be included in the regular classroom?" Jim asked.

"Now!" they said with angry glares.

Several other team members, including Cody's mother, wanted to hear more from Jim about possible interventions. Heated arguments began to rise from the team. Accusations, name calling, and blame placing surfaced. Jim thought everyone could use a chance to cool off, so the meeting was rescheduled for the following morning. Members of the team stormed out, spewing threats involving the local teachers' association and disability advocates.

Word spread quickly within the school and community. Jim's office was transformed into a mission control center. Staff marched in to vent their frustrations. Even Principal O'Brien, who had been a steadfast supporter, expressed serious concerns. Parents called to address a number of rumors that they had heard. Advocates called for reassurance that inclusion would not be sacrificed. Cody's father even called to let Jim know his attorney would be attending the morning conference. What else could go wrong? The phone rang again and Jim recognized the superintendent's voice, and tone, on the other end. He didn't focus on every word, but the message came through clearly: fix this one immediately.

As Jim continued his drive toward home, he began to question his own beliefs regarding inclusion. "If we say inclusion is for all children," he thought, "is it right for us to separate some who are not experiencing success in this setting? Has all this work gone for naught? Is the process worthwhile if anger and resentment become pervasive throughout the school? How can this situation be 'fixed' as the superintendent instructed?" He wondered what would happen at the next morning's meeting and every day thereafter.

Questions for Discussion

1. Considering the support Jim has lost, should he continue the program? Discuss the pros and cons of program continuation that Jim should consider before he makes his decision.

2. Is it fair to sacrifice the needs of the individual even when he or she represents a voice not experienced by the majority? Is it ever fair to sacrifice the greater good for the individual? If so, under what circumstances? Is this the situation that exists with Cody? Does caring extend to the needs of the group, or is it restricted to the needs of the individual? Where and how does one draw the line between individual rights and the common good? In this case, is there an ethical choice that would support both sides? If so, what is it?

3 There are important laws to protect individuals with disabilities, but there are also laws that require teachers to educate all children. Do you see these laws as conflicting? Why or why not? Who made these laws? Who were they designed to protect?

4. Do you see any conflicts between Dr. Martin's personal beliefs about inclusion and his professional beliefs? What in this scenario leads you to draw your conclusion?

CASE STUDY 8.2 BLACK AND WHITE AND SHADES OF GRAY

Northern Regional School District had changed dramatically over the past 10 years. During that decade, the two townships it served had been transformed by a booming economy from a sleepy, rural, nearly all-White farming region into a bustling, quasi-suburban, multicultural area. One result of this economic expansion was a rapid growth in population and a concomitant change in demographics that had a profound effect on the composition of Northern High's student body. In the space of just 10 years, the racial make-up went from 98% White and 2% African American to 70% White, 22% African American, and 8% Asian. There had been little change, however, in the composition of Northern staff. Prior to the boom, all 30 teachers had been White. By 1991, there were 85 on the staff, and only two were minority: one was African American and the other was Asian.

Things began to change two years previously when Dr. John DiCaprio became principal. A graduate of Northern nearly 20 years before, he had returned with impressive credentials. A Harvard doctorate and five years of administrative experience in the prestigious suburban district of nearby Monroe City had assured the board of his competence, but it was his record at Northern as a student that had landed him the job. He had been student council president, a member of the National Honor Society, captain of the football team, and the only wrestler ever to win a state championship. His elevation to principal was hailed as the return of a favorite son.

Despite the support he enjoyed, John's tenure had not been without a few bumps. One of the most sensitive issues, and, in DiCaprio's opinion, one of the most critical, was the racial imbalance between the student body and the teaching staff. When he arrived, Northern High School had a staff that was 2.5% minority to educate a student body that was 30% minority. DiCaprio had pushed hard for increased minority hiring, but there was a great deal of resistance. A walkout by minority students in spring 1992, triggered in part by this imbalance, had been a wake-up call. The previous summer three new teachers had been hired, and two of them were African American. Minority representation on the staff now stood at 5.7%. Dr. DiCaprio was happy that the district was moving in the right direction.

According to projections by the state economic development authority, this part of the state of New Sussex had been labeled as the state's leading area of growth. Using data provided by the state, the district had estimated that the student population would continue to grow and eventually double within the next 15 years. Of greater significance was the forecast that a sizable number of new students would be African American and Asian. Dr. DiCaprio had seen in these statistics both a challenge and an opportunity. Increased enrollments translated into increased hiring, and it was through new hiring that Dr. DiCaprio planned to increase the number of minorities on his staff.

DiCaprio's best-laid plans now seemed like pie in the sky. The economic worm had turned. Much of the development in Jefferson County, where Northern's two feeder districts were located, had been fueled by growth in two areas. The first was the expansion of high-tech businesses in Monroe City, less than 20 miles away. The second was the increasing number of casinos in Pacific City, less than 30 miles away. The casinos had made shore property along the southern New Sussex coast too expensive for middle-income professionals, and so they had come to Jefferson County seeking affordable housing. With a recession in full swing, casinos went belly up, and the economic boom in Monroe City went bust.

The impact on Northern was immediate. The student population growth curve was, at best, expected to be flat for the next couple of years. Some even foresaw a decrease. To DiCaprio, the handwriting was on the wall; there would have to be a reduction in force (RIF). RIFing was anathema to the teachers' association because it made vulnerable teachers who had gained tenure and, presumably, job security. In deciding whom to let go, the union was adamant that the "last hired, first fired" rule be followed.

For DiCaprio, RIFing was the death-knell of his minority hiring program. He had searched far and wide to find the best qualified candidates, and his efforts had not been in vain. The two new African-American teachers had done a great job in their first year at Northern. He could easily think of a dozen tenured teachers he would rather let go. Although he would have dearly loved to violate the "last hired, first fired" rule, DiCaprio knew that to do so would create such a furor that the staff, usually complacent, would most likely rise up and take drastic action, possibly even strike.

It was the first week of April, and the district was required to inform all staff by the end of the month of their employment status for the upcoming year. DiCaprio had just met with the superintendent and received a directive: he would have to eliminate one position. As if that were not bad enough, the decision had been made to effect this reduction by increasing class size in either the Math or English Departments. What a setback! Of the two new African-American teachers hired, one was an English teacher, the other a math teacher. One would have to go. DiCaprio was incensed. He had argued for several other options, without success. He knew there had to be another way.

Peter Weiss was finishing up his second year in the Social Studies Department. DiCaprio had frequent conversations with Barbara Meyer, the department head, about him. Peter had been struggling somewhat with his teaching technique and his rapport with the students. One sore point was the fact that, although White, he was teaching the African-American history course that had been implemented the year after the student walkout. There was no hard evidence that he was insensitive to the minority students in the class. Complaints came mainly from parents and were philosophical in nature. "How could a White man understand the struggle of African Americans?" was a query that had been put to him many times.

Beyond this course, DiCaprio and Meyer had some misgivings about Weiss' capability, as evidenced by his mediocre course observations. Despite his concerns, DiCaprio believed that every new teacher should be given a fair chance to learn the craft of teaching. He remembered his own first few years in the classroom. His performance had been less than stellar, and he knew that he had needed those three years to develop into a good, solid teacher. He had intended to give Weiss the same opportunity. Now, however, as a principal, he had a different set of priorities. He certainly had doubts about Weiss' potential but had been willing to give him one more year. Given the need to reduce his staff by one, his thinking now took a different course.

George Taylor was the African-American English teacher who had been hired the year before. Fresh out of college and single, George had done an outstanding job both in and out of the classroom. He was co-advisor for the African-American Culture Club and had volunteered to run the "We the

Students" Committee. DiCaprio had founded this group after the walkout to promote understanding among the races at Northern. He had run it the first year but found that his busy schedule did not permit him to continue in this capacity. When George was hired, he was asked to take over and had done a first-rate job. George also had dual certification in social studies.

If Peter Weiss were not rehired, then George could switch from the English Department to the Social Studies Department. DiCaprio would be able to follow his superintendent's directive to reduce staff in the English or Math Department. He would be able to keep a gifted minority teacher, have an African American teaching the course in African-American history, and maintain what meager gains he had made in trying to establish a minority presence on the faculty. Of course, this could be accomplished only if he let Peter Weiss go after his second year; however, this would violate his long-standing belief that teachers should be given at least three years to prove themselves.

As he left the office that day, he was, for the first time in a long time, not quite sure what to do. As he rounded the corner, he bumped into Peter Weiss.

"Hey, Dr. DiCaprio, want to see something?" Peter said, waving a picture in his hand.

"What have you got there, Peter?" Dr. DiCaprio replied.

"It's a sonogram. My wife and I are going to have twins."

Questions for Discussion

1. What is the fairest decision Dr. DiCaprio could make? The most caring? Are they different? Is what is fair or caring for Peter Weiss the same as what is fair or caring for George Taylor? Are there others who should be considered in trying to determine fairness or caring? If so, who are they? Why those particular persons?

2. What do you assume would be the consequences for Dr. DiCaprio if he broke the "last hired, first fired" rule? Are there times when rules or laws must be broken to achieve a higher moral level? Do you think this situation is an example of one of those times? Why or why not? Explain.

3. Where do you suppose the "last hired, first fired" rule came from? Could you speculate as to what its original purpose may have been? Do you believe it is a just rule? If you believe the rule is just, do you believe it is absolute? Or are there circumstances under which the rule might be applied differently or not at all? Whose rule is this? Who benefits from the rule in this scenario? Who, in general, would benefit from such a rule?

4. What do you believe is the most moral decision that Dr. DiCaprio could make in this situation? What would you do if you were in his place? Why would you take such action? In this circumstance, are your personal beliefs the same or different from your professional beliefs? Explain.

CASE STUDY 8.3 ACCESS TO KNOWLEDGE

Mackenzie High School, the only high school in Harford County, is a growing comprehensive public high school comprising Grades 7 through 12 with an enrollment that fluctuates between 2,500 and 3,000 students, of which 55% are minority. The student population varies greatly, based on the demographics of the five elementary schools from which students come to enroll in Mackenzie.

The school district in which Mackenzie High School is located comprises a tri-county system of one high school with a lower division for grades 7 through 9 and an upper division that serves students in grades 10 through 12, and the five elementary schools. All the schools except the high school are located in a geographically contiguous radius of approximately 25 miles.

The elementary feeder schools are quite diverse with regard to socio-economic status. The two elementary schools that serve the highest socio-economic community have a combined minority population of less than 20%. On the opposite end of the socio-economic ladder is Adams Run Elementary School with a minority population of approximately 90%. In the middle are Brown and Jackson Elementary Schools, which serve a low to moderate socio-economic neighborhood with minority populations of about 30% and 40%, respectively.

Although the students are diverse in terms of ethnicity, socio-economic status, and educational need, the faculty of Mackenzie High School is quite homogeneous. Of the 120 professional staff, consisting of administrators, counselors, a librarian, and teachers, less than 15% are minority, of which 75% are female.

Mackenzie High School is situated in the center of Harford County, a blue-collar community that is highly active politically. Harford County is populated by citizens with varying ethnicities including African Americans, Asian Americans, Hispanics, and European Americans. The community is nicely balanced in terms of young couples who are just starting out, well-established families, and senior citizens. Harford County is primarily working class with a number of prosperous businesses nearby. The Aerospace Jet Plant, the Harford County Medical Center, and an auto plant that is a subsidiary of General Motors provide the economic base for Harford County. These businesses have provided employment for a large number of residents of Harford County generation after generation.

Harford County, originally a predominantly White, working-class community comprising citizens from Irish, Polish, and German descent, has changed appreciably over the past decade. Although there has been a significant influx of people from diverse backgrounds, Whites have remained in the majority. Nevertheless, the minority population has had a powerful impact on the town and on Mackenzie High School. This presence has affected the cultural life of Harford County as well as the educational mission of Mackenzie High School.

Ruben and Gabriella Soler moved to Harford County from Puerto Rico approximately a decade ago. The Soler family is typical of the people from diverse populations who gradually migrated to Harford County. Alberto is the youngest of three children. His older brother and sister graduated from Mackenzie High School and obtained employment in the nearby medical center and General Motors plant. However, Alberto's parents wanted a lot more for their youngest son. They were relying on the school to provide the kind of education Alberto would need to get beyond the factories of Harford County.

When Alberto was small, and from the time he could remember, his parents instilled in him the desire to set his goals high. Moreover, they implored the school to provide programs designed to improve English fluency. They knew that being able to speak and write English was Alberto's ticket out of Harford County, and lack of fluency in English was the main stumbling block that had held back his brother and sister. Even though Alberto was a very conscientious student, learning did not come easily because his language and his culture were different from the majority of students. As a result, Alberto had been placed in low-ability groups since first grade. By the time he entered Mackenzie High School, he had spent approximately eight years in the lowest functioning group.

Mackenzie High School played an important role in the Harford County community. When the racial make-up of the community began to change, Mackenzie High School attempted to ease the process of assimilation by emphasizing language instruction, offering remedial classes, instituting a more comprehensive vocational educational program, and establishing multicultural courses. Yet, despite all the recent innovations, there has been a growing concern about the future. The White majority, who have worked in the factories and surrounding businesses for decades, have become concerned about the future opportunities for their children, especially in view of the recent migration of new residents. They see the changing economy and increasing population as signs of a future struggle for their children.

Parents of students represented in the minority population feel the same pinch. Both groups want more for their children, and they look to Mackenzie High School to provide the educational preparation children will need for a better tomorrow. They want their children to make better lives for themselves by attending college; consequently, the demand for access to college-bound programs has intensified. In recent years, parents' desires to have their children attend college have been reflected in an increased commitment to academic counseling and college preparatory courses. Moreover, the demand for college-bound classes has focused tremendous attention on the selection process for the placement of students in various programs as well as assignment to tracks.

Issues of access to knowledge and equality of educational opportunity for the minority student population have come to the forefront, and competition has escalated. Minority students make up the majority enrollment in vocational educational classes. Many teachers believe that, on the whole, minority students perform poorly academically because they are below average in intellectual ability. They subscribe to the findings of the research of Jensen, who argued that because average IQ test scores of certain groups (African Americans and Latinos) are consistently below those of other groups (Whites and Asian Americans), it is likely that there is a real genetically determined difference in intellectual ability among members of these groups (Jensen, 1969).

The Mackenzie High School community is satisfied with the state of affairs. The staff feels that the school provides an adequate, and in some cases an excellent, education for its students and that it serves Harford County in a fitting manner. The curriculum is balanced so that students can pursue individual interests, and teachers can provide for individual educational needs. The guidance department takes an active role in the process of program selection and placement.

Dr. Patricia Meyerowitz, principal of Mackenzie High School for eight years, is characterized as a fair-minded, no-nonsense, yet quite compassionate administrator. She exhibits a strong sense of authority, passion, and commitment to the educational mission of Mackenzie High School. During the past five years, she has observed a gradual shift in teacher attitude and performance, noticing that many teachers have accepted the idea that minority students cannot be expected to learn at high levels. This notion is reflected in the manner in which students are placed in programs as well as in the quality of instruction offered to them.

Given these circumstances, it is not surprising that Pat Meyerowitz welcomed the concern of Mrs. Gabriella Soler, mother of Alberto Benito Soler, a ninth-grade Latino student who had previously attended Jackson Elementary School where, as indicated earlier, he had been placed in low-functioning groups for most of his educational life. Alberto entered

Mackenzie High School in seventh grade where he continued in the lowest functioning group.

Mrs. Soler was mindful of the attitudes of staff at Mackenzie High School. She had had numerous meetings with the guidance counselor during the previous two years and, based on her past experiences, she had little doubt that minority students were not treated fairly at Mackenzie High School; moreover, Mrs. Soler had grown to distrust the judgment of Alberto's teachers. Despite unwavering effort and pleading to have her son placed in a higher group, Alberto spent two years in classes that did little to meet his interests or his educational needs.

Now, Alberto is preparing to enter the upper division of Mackenzie High School. His ambition is to go to college; therefore, he wants to be placed in the college-bound program. Mrs. Soler has determined that Alberto has not been treated fairly by the chairperson of the guidance division, Maryanne Polkalsky, because she has denied him access to the college-bound program.

Maryanne Polkalsky, a pillar of the community, is widely known in Harford County. It seems as though she has been at Mackenzie High School forever. She has advised most of the students' parents and, throughout the years, has assigned many working-class and poorer students to non-academic tracks. She is powerful and uses this power masterfully to maintain control. Ms. Polkalsky is accustomed to being bombarded by parents and students, and uses the authority of her position to skillfully maneuver students into programs to which she feels they are suited. Her decisions have made it generally impossible for minority students to escape a lifetime of work in the factories that surround Harford County.

In recent years, resentment has mounted because many of the minority students and their parents have been denied access to an equal educational opportunity, and they have openly discussed Maryanne Polkalsky's misuse and abuse of power and authority. As judge and jury, Maryanne has decided that Alberto would not do well in the college-bound track and should register for the vocational program.

Mrs. Soler feels that Ms. Polkalsky has no right to thwart Alberto's dream of going to college when most of the non-minority students are given a fair chance to prepare for college by their placement in the college-bound program. Furthermore, Mrs. Soler has observed that a disproportionate number of Latino and African-American students are enrolled in vocational education courses. In fact, Mrs. Soler is convinced that Ms. Polkalsky's treatment of Alberto is based on prejudice, and that this is but one example of the treatment of minority students at Mackenzie High School. She is cognizant that most of the minority students are advised to join the work-force, to apply for apprenticeship programs, or join the armed services. Few, if any, are recommended for college.

Mrs. Soler is convinced that minority students do not achieve at high levels at Mackenzie High School because the school culture favors the White majority, which places minority students from other backgrounds and cultures at a serious disadvantage. Teachers do not create a democratic environment in their classrooms, nor do they exhibit attitudes of caring and concern. Alberto has a fundamental right to the same opportunities afforded to White students, and Mrs. Soler is demanding that her son be given equal access to knowledge and the same educational opportunity that non-minority students receive so that Alberto can acquire the background, skills, and knowledge necessary to fulfill his dream of going to college after high school.

Principal Meyerowitz conveyed Mrs. Soler's sentiments to Maryanne Polkalsky. Ms. Polkalsky assured Dr. Meyerowitz that her decision was made in Alberto's best interests. Alberto was recommended for the vocational education program based on his record of prior academic achievement, including standardized test results and recommendations from his teachers. An objective evaluation revealed that Alberto was in the lower quartile of his class, and Maryanne was confident that he did not possess the aptitude and the language development required to do well in college.

Moreover, she emphasized that in light of the financial burden of college, it would be an injustice to mislead Alberto and his family. She felt it was her professional duty to guide Alberto toward an attainable goal, namely joining the workforce after graduating from high school. Pat Meyerowitz did not doubt Maryanne's sincerity or her goodwill. Nor did she think for one moment that Maryanne's decision was in Alberto's best interests.

As an educator, Maryanne Polkalsky is in the position of deciding what path Alberto's life will take. She is considered an expert in her field. This is a job that she has done for years, and as far as many people are concerned she has done it well. On the other hand, Pat Meyerowitz, as principal, is the instructional leader of the school. She recognizes that Maryanne is strongly influenced by past practices that have had an unsympathetic outcome for minority students.

Is Alberto entitled equal access to good instruction and equality of opportunity so that he can gain the skills and knowledge necessary to attain his goal? What should Dr. Meyerowitz do?

Questions for Discussion

1. One could argue that because Alberto had been tracked into low-ability groups since first grade, he had received an inequitable education from the beginning and, thus, was not given the preparation he needed to compete for a college preparatory program. Do

you agree with this statement? Assuming it is true, does the school have a moral obligation to rectify this situation? If so, how?

2. Is tracking just? Is tracking in the best interests of students in general? Any students? Are there types or methods of tracking that are fairer than others? If so, what are they? If not, why not?

3. What are the benefits of tracking? What are the detriments? Is tracking mostly an economic issue? If so, in what ways? If not, why not? What else needs to be considered in educating students? Who makes the rules about tracking and to what purpose?

4. What would a caring administrator do in this situation? A caring guidance director?

5. What is your view of the ethics of tracking from a professional point of view? From a personal point of view?

6. In this particular scenario, do you agree with Pat or Maryanne? Explain your reasoning. If you were Pat, what would you do to make an ethical decision? If you were Maryanne, how would you handle this situation in the most ethical manner?

7. What would you tell the Solers? If you really believed that Alberto could not make it through a college preparatory program, would you tell him? Do you believe that Alberto has a right to fail? Do Maryanne or Pat have a responsibility to protect Alberto from failure? If so, what course of action might they take? If not, why not? Should all students, regardless of academic success, be permitted to take whatever courses they wish? Why or why not? If not, how does one decide where to draw the line?

CASE STUDY 8.4 ACADEMIC INTEGRITY IN A DEAF EDUCATION SETTING

Ms. Johnston pulled into the school parking lot earlier than normal on a brisk March morning. This was the first day that the students at Fairway High School, a large public school in a growing suburban area, would be taking the high stakes state assessment. Just like other teachers in her school, Ms. Johnston had been working tirelessly all year to teach and reteach the essential skills covered in the high school graduation test. However, one important difference between other teachers and Ms. Johnston was that she had been using two languages to instruct her students: English (for reading and writing purposes) and American Sign Language (ASL). As a deaf teacher who is a native signer and a well-known teacher-leader in the field of American Sign Language, Ms. Johnston realizes the importance of her deaf students learning both languages, and had established a classroom in which both languages are valued and studied intently.

As she walked into the building to prepare for the arrival of her students on this particularly important morning, Ms. Johnston began to remember a poignant conversation she had with Mr. Humphries, the assistant principal responsible for overseeing the special education programs at the school. During their intense discussion on testing accommodations for deaf students, Ms. Johnston pointed out her concern that the deaf students who use ASL were at a disadvantage over the deaf students in the school in which she had previously taught. In Ms. Johnston's eyes, the biggest struggle had to do with the translation process of English print into sign language, which is viewed as the equivalent of reading aloud the test to hearing students (both accommodations are for those students reading significantly below grade level, as documented in the students' IEPs).

According to the state's testing manual, teachers must sign the questions and answer choices verbatim as they are written in English. Ms. Johnston elaborated that because ASL is not signed English, then signing the print words "verbatim" in English order would be like taking each printed English word and translating it word-for-word into spoken Spanish, instead of using correct Spanish grammar. Ms. Johnston compared this policy with the policy in her previous state, which allowed signing that is consistent with the sign language used during classroom instruction (ASL in Ms. Johnston's class). The premise was to make sure that deaf students had the same accessibility to the printed information that hearing students would have to an exam which was read aloud to them. By the end of this conversation, Mr. Humphries expressed his understanding of Ms. Johnston's perspective on signing accommodations, but emphasized that because the state's policy says "verbatim," they are required to follow this requirement.

As the students began to walk to their rooms on this first morning of testing, Mr. Humphries stood in the hallway near the deaf/hard-of-hearing classrooms and began to think about how truly diverse the deaf students are in this school. Some students would receive their accommodations through spoken English (often called the "oral" approach to deaf education), some would rely on a cued language transliterator (called "cued speech"), and yet another group would receive their accommodations through American Sign Language. It was this last group that raised Mr. Humphries' curiosity.

. For this day's testing, the students who use ASL were divided into two classrooms; half were with Ms. Johnston in her classroom and the other half were with Ms. Smith, the other deaf education teacher in the department who uses ASL. Mr. Humphries first stepped into Ms. Smith's classroom to check on their testing progress, and could tell that everything was going smoothly. Although he was a beginning signer himself, he was confident that Ms. Smith was signing the test "verbatim." However, when he walked into Ms. Johnston's classroom, he noticed that her signing was very different from Ms. Smith's. Ms. Johnston seemed to spend more time signing each test item, and Mr. Humphries wasn't sure if she was really signing "verbatim," as her signing seemed to create more of a visual picture for the students. Out of fear of offending Ms. Johnston because she is deaf and is a leading expert in the field, he did not say or report anything related to this situation.

Three months later, Mr. Humphries sat in his office closely reviewing the test results for the deaf students in the school. He was stunned to see how significantly better the students in Ms. Johnston's testing room scored, as compared with those in Ms. Smith's. This was especially surprising, considering that all the students were at relatively similar ability levels. Immediately, Mr. Humphries remembered back to the testing day when he noticed what looked like Ms. Johnson giving more of a visual explanation to the students while signing the questions and answer choices.

Mr. Humphries scheduled a meeting with Ms. Johnston to ask her about this. During the meeting, Ms. Johnston admitted that she did sign "conceptually accurate" American Sign Language instead of "verbatim" English word order, because she feels that signing correct ASL gives her students a clearer picture of the questions, and helps level the playing field for deaf students who use ASL. She also noted that this is an issue of equity for her students and that their state is behind the times by requiring "verbatim" signing. Her final comment left Mr. Humphries wide-eyed: "I have a moral obligation to fight for the rights of deaf students, and to ensure that they are given the same opportunities and advantages that are given to hearing students. If you want to report me to the state, then you have my permission. But I know in my heart that I did the right thing."

When Ms. Johnston left the room, Mr. Humphries realized he had a difficult decision to make. He knew that Ms. Johnston had violated policy, and that it appeared to have increased scores. He also knew that Ms. Johnston was not ill-intentioned in her actions, and only wanted the best for her students. Finally, he admitted to himself that because so few public school educators have any knowledge of deaf education, it is highly likely that no one would ever learn of this situation.

Questions for Discussion

1. Which of the four ethical paradigms is most applicable to this situation?

2. Which solution to this ethical dilemma would be in the best interest of the students in Ms. Johnston's testing room? Ms. Smith's testing room?

3. During his decision-making process, Mr. Humphries brought the situation to the attention of a fellow assistant principal, who then stated, "When in doubt, report! High stakes testing is about following the rules. Period." If you were Mr. Humphries, how would you respond to this statement?

4. Suppose you are the principal of Fairway High School, and Mr. Humphries sat down with you to discuss the situation. You realize that you have very little knowledge about the needs of deaf students. How would you give advice or make decisions in this situation?

5. Do you believe there are times when teachers and administrators have an ethical obligation to make decisions that go against local, state, or federal policy? If yes, do these times include situations involving high stakes testing?

CASE STUDY 8.5 WHEN FUNDRAISING AND SCHOOL POLICY COLLIDE

Ms. Ross had been Director at The Small School for four years and loved the work that took place there. The Small School, a private early childhood center that promised kindergarten readiness for its population, prided itself on creating classrooms of diverse learners. To that end, The Small School offered youngsters from ethnically diverse backgrounds, special needs children, and those who do not come from English-speaking homes priority when determining the potential admission of a given child. The waiting list to get into the center is long, but every once in a while a spot other than those for the infant room would open up so that someone on the waiting list could enroll their child.

While the school is well known in the local area for providing high-quality early childhood programs, the center is also staffed with special educators, a school counselor, and a social worker who work individually with children in order to identify any special learning needs early on in a child's academic life. Parents from the most affluent backgrounds like their children to attend the center, as recent studies by a local university have shown that children who attend the program are more developed cognitively and socially and are generally ahead of their peers upon entrance into kindergarten.

Ms. Ross knew that her school was not like every other preschool in town and that the work she and her teachers were doing with children in their youngest years was something that she found both exhilarating and fulfilling. This was Ms. Ross' first administrative position since leaving the classroom as a teacher at The Small School, and she had made the transition easily, so far.

As Director, Ms. Ross holds many roles, one of which was to be the "face" of the center within the local community. Within the center, Ms. Ross was in charge of not only operational leadership but also supervising teachers, providing professional development to her staff, and maintaining close relationships with the families of children that attended her center. In addition, it was her responsibility to work closely with the development office and to meet with potential donors, since much of the funding for the center came from external gifts.

Because the economy was not what it had been at the beginning of her tenure as an administrator, Ms. Ross was finding that many donors could not give as much as they had in the past. Still, she remained optimistic that the unique mission and population of the center would help the development department reach their goal as usual.

Unfortunately, Ms. Ross received word from the development office that she would need to look over her budget for the coming fiscal year. They did not reach their fundraising goal, and it was going to impact the children if she did not make some changes. Ms. Ross had just brought up her budget on the school computer when she heard three heavy knocks on the door. "Come on in," Ms. Ross called.

In walked Mr. Simmons, grandfather of a past student at The Small School, and reoccurring donor. Ms. Ross was surprised to see Mr. Simmons, though he did come by from time to time with good news about a significant gift he had just given to the school. By the look on the man's face she could see that this was not one of those conversations.

"Hi, Ms. Ross, I am going to get right down to business," Mr. Simmons explained as he sat down in the chair across from her desk without being asked.

"No problem, what can I help you with today? Would you like some coffee or something to drink?" Ms. Ross faked cheer as she tried to lift the negative feeling in the room. Mr. Simmons replied, "No, I am fine, I am going to make this quick. I saw one of your teachers at the grocery store last week and she informed me that there is a spot opening in your 2-year-old classroom. First of all, I do not know why this information was not provided to the donors. Why wasn't it in the newsletter? Second, I want my grandson, Harrison, to be put in that position. His mother is ready for him to enter an early childhood program, and obviously we want him here."

Ms. Ross was furious: which of her teachers would that have done that? One of the issues she talked to the teachers about in their staff meetings was the need for confidentiality, especially when it comes to enrollment. The waiting list for the Small School was very long, and the next child on the list, Caleb, had visited the school twice, and as a child with spina bifida would benefit from the social interaction, resources, and opportunities at the school.

"I completely understand, what you are saying Mr. Simmons, but we do have a waiting list and I would need to look that over again to see where Harrison is on the list, I'm sure you understand that."

"No, actually I do not understand that, Ms. Ross. I have given over three million dollars to this school in the past two years, and I need to make sure that this happens."

Ms. Ross had never seen Mr. Simmons quite this hostile before. "It's just that we have another child on the list who, because of certain circumstances, cannot get into another program like this one. He has visited the school twice with his family and plans to enroll in two weeks when the other child leaves."

Mr. Simmons paused to think for a minute then rose to his feet and walked to the door. He turned back toward Ms. Ross while grabbing the door handle. "Well, I understand your situation, Ms. Ross, and here is mine. I usually give a lot of money to this school, you know this, and if Harrison gets in, I will give you double what I gave last year. If he does not, please take me off of your donor list because I will not be giving to this organization any longer."

As Ms. Ross watched Mr. Simmons leave the office, she put her head in her hands and considered her options. She could call Caleb's family and say that she was wrong and that the position was filled and allow Harrison to enroll or she could call Harrison's mother and tell her that the position was filled, and work closely with the development department to try and make up for the lost resources.

If Ms. Ross chose to put Caleb in the class, she knew that he would immediately receive the attention and services he needed. She had previously seen children with special needs grow and develop because of their experience in this center and that was what she wanted to do. On the other hand, if she did not put Harrison into the class, she could risk losing a substantial amount of money for the school. This kind of money ultimately allows the school to provide these exceptional services to children. Without Mr. Simmons' money, many of those services may have to be cut, which would influence all of the children. No matter what happened next, Ms. Ross knew that she was in a dilemma for which she had no immediate answers.

Questions for Discussion

1. Does Mr. Simmons have a right to expect that his grandson will be enrolled in the school? If there are no clear expectations for a donor's role in the school, how should Ms. Ross address these concerns? Through a justice paradigm? Through the ethic of care?

2. Should Ms. Ross follow the waiting list policy and enroll the next child on the list, namely Caleb? Why or why not?

3. If Ms. Ross chooses to place Caleb in the classroom and the school is negatively impacted because of this, do you think this will affect whether or not Ms. Ross should keep her job? Why or why not?

4. How could Ms. Ross' decision impact and/or change the culture of the school? How would this dilemma be viewed through the ethic of critique?

5. When a decision is made, what is at stake for the Small School? Ms. Ross? Mr. Simmons? Caleb? Harrison?

Chapter 9

Accountability Versus Responsibility

Susan A. Rosano, David M. Gates, Lindy Zaretsky, Elizabeth A. Santoro, and Mary Beth Kurilko

This chapter presents dilemmas that deal with different aspects of accountability in relation to responsibility. In each of the five cases, high stakes testing is central to the problem and gives rise to a variety of ethical issues focusing on equity, equality, individual rights, professional ethics, and the best interests of the student.

There is a strong focus on accountability in U.S. education. However, this concept is not new. It has been with us since the 1970s and has increased over time. Some say it was taxpayers in California who led the way to this emphasis when they complained that they were not getting their money's worth in public education and opted out of paying taxes through Proposition 13, passed in 1978 (Shapiro, 1979). Others believe that *A Nation at Risk: The Imperative for Educational Reform* (National Commission on Excellence in Education, 1983) was the cornerstone for the accountability movement. Additional national reports, such as *America 2000: An Education Strategy* (1991), *Goals 2000: Educate America Act* (1993), and *No Child Left Behind* (NCLB) (2002) continue to include accountability. In fact, NCLB asks for stronger accountability than previously required for better test results.

Although all the reports include accountability, it is important to understand that this concept comes from an accountant's ledger that all too often places the budget at the center of the decision-making process. Despite its derivation, with a stress on the budget, the term itself is complex and has numerous meanings. In fact, there are as many as 10 kinds of accountability. They include political, legal, bureaucratic, professional, and market accountabilities (Darling-Hammond & Snyder, 1992). Added to these are parent, student, fiscal, and personal forms of accountability (Gross,

Shaw, & Shapiro, 2003). Finally, there is public accountability (Gold & Simon, 2004).

Despite the diversity inherent in the term, accountability, in all its forms, is seen by many to be a significant factor in school improvement. Not only the general public, but also numerous educators, have found it to be a much-needed factor leading to positive changes in the schools. In particular, strict accountability makes certain that budgets are kept in check, meeting the approval of many taxpayers.

Currently, high stakes, standardized test results are most often used for accountability purposes to determine how successful an educational institution or district has been in educating its young people. However, it is not only the institution or district that is affected, but the individual student as well. For students, the number they receive on a high stakes test frequently determines their educational opportunities in the future. Over time, tests do more than provide a number for how successful a school or student has been. Frequently, these tests drive the curriculum. More and more, teachers and administrators turn to the test to guide what they should teach in schools. Some people perceive the continual testing, the reporting of scores in newspapers and magazines, and the tests driving the curriculum to be positive accomplishments, whereas others consider them to be negative activities, publicly punishing students and educators alike and, in some instances, encouraging students and school personnel to cheat (Nichols & Berliner, 2007).

Thus, while accountability is often associated with educational achievement, it is also frequently thought to be a concept that creates a great deal of blame. By turning to numbers alone as guides, through standardized test results, taxpayers, legislators, and the nation believe that they are able to determine how students are doing, and many are ready to place the blame on schools. All too often, other factors, such as poverty, drugs, environmental pollutants, and crime, with their negative effects on learning, may be ignored.

There is another term, however, that is not used enough with regard to school success or lack of it. This concept is responsibility (Gross & Shapiro, 2002). Responsibility, while similar to accountability, may be perceived as more inclusive and places the answerability for the success or failure of young people's learning on all of society—the public, legislators, parents, teachers, administrators as well as the schools. This term does not always connote blame, nor does it put a budget at the center of the decision-making process. Instead, it offers another concept with regard to education that asks everyone to share responsibility for young people's learning and to place students at the center of the educational process. It is a much broader term that not only encompasses the results of high stakes tests but also can include evidence from authentic and alternative types of assessment in determining what students have learned.

In the case studies presented in this chapter, the paradox of account-ability versus responsibility is highlighted. In each of the five cases, testing is a central issue. However, the cases are different in that four of them are located in K–12 settings (one of which takes place in Canada) and the final dilemma occurs on a college campus.

In the first dilemma, The Secret Society of Test Givers (Case study 9.1), a teacher feels under pressure to make certain that students in her class do well on high stakes standardized tests. She has been told by her school administrator that unless her students obtain passing results, there is a good chance of a state takeover, a resulting budget cut, and inevitable loss of jobs. Because of all the accountability pressures on the school principal, he has urged his teachers *to do what they need to do* to make certain that students do well. Now the teacher faces the decision as to what she should do as a responsible, professional educator.

In Case study 9.2, Whose Best Interests? A Testing Dilemma, a school administrator has been told that while his district is currently doing well on the standardized tests, it has been projected, within the next two years, that many of his students will not pass the exam. In response to this informa-tion, the superintendent, with the encouragement of the board of school directors, has been proactive and has devised a new curriculum with test-specific courses. When the principal explains the proposed changes to the department chairs, the idea is met with resistance. The chairs are angry because they have developed courses by turning to research and using best practices, and they believe that these carefully crafted courses are good for the students now and ultimately will be beneficial for their futures. Thus, they are reluctant to make the substantial revisions requested. The principal is facing an ethical decision that pits policy against best practice and pits teachers against administrators and the school board.

Case study 9.3, Testing High Stakes, focuses on the administering of a mandatory high stakes literacy test and the problems that those students who are slow learners face. In this instance, a principal must deal with parents who demand that their children be given special accommodations for taking the high stakes test. However, she is aware that the test guidelines do not allow for these privileges. The principal is very concerned about the parents' expectations and the reality of the test-taking situation. She is especially worried about the climate change in her school from one of care, cooperation, and respect for all learners to that of performance, efficiency, and economy.

In Case study 9.4, Ability, Maturity, and Parental Perspectives, which is an early childhood dilemma, there is a disagreement between parents and teachers. The parents have been in conflict with the administration since their child was in first grade and, now that he is in the third grade, they want him once again to be retained because of immaturity. The teachers, on the other hand, feel he is ready to move on to the next grade. Should the principal succumb to the demands of the parents and choose education retention or accept the decision of the teachers, which is based on best professional judgment as well as testing results, but still may be viewed as social promotion? In this era focusing on accountability and meeting proficiency requirements, a decision of this nature is not treated lightly.

Case study 9.5, A Merit-based Scholarship, deals with the fractious issue of affirmative action with regard to college opportunities. It takes place in a small Midwestern college. It involves a merit-based scholarship with two finalists who are both outstanding. However, there are differences between the candidates: their results on a standardized test for admissions into the college, their race/ethnicity, and their gender. This case pits the college president, pressured by an outside group, against the admissions director, who has always made the scholarship decision. Breaking with tradition, the president is attempting to override the professional judgment of the admissions director in the scholarship selection process.

CASE STUDY 9.1 THE SECRET SOCIETY OF TEST GIVERS

June Lopez was a teacher at an urban elementary school, PS 235. Although she was considered to be a new faculty member at this school, she was really a seven-year veteran from a private school system. This was her first assignment in a large, urban, public school system, but she felt ready to work in this high poverty area. At the outset, she was greatly impressed with the school's atmosphere and, in a short time, she developed a fine working relationship with her colleagues, the students, their parents, and the administration. However, she was never in this school at testing time. Thus, she was surprised at the amount of anxiety and tension that seemed to be surrounding this event. In the faculty lunchroom, not much was said. In fact, she noticed how quiet it was around the table. However, in some of the classrooms, as she passed by the closed doors and peeped through the window panes, she was getting the distinct impression that all was not as it should be.

James Rose was the principal of PS 235. He had been in charge of this school for the past 10 years and was a seasoned administrator, having served as an assistant principal and a supervisor of English teachers. He was not new to poverty in education, since he had worked in a couple of schools where there were a substantial number of low-income families, and this school was no exception. In PS 235, all the children qualified for free breakfast and lunch. Many of the youngsters were being raised by single mothers or grandmothers, or were in foster care.

Approximately a quarter of the parents did not appear for report conferences, despite the many outreach activities the school provided to involve them. For example, and most recently, the school received new books, and once the teachers were prepared to handle the material, the principal offered training sessions for the parents. Although few parents or guardians turned up, he knew how important it was to keep teachers and families working together, and he fully recognized the need for parents to be part of their children's education. However, despite his continuing attempts to take the role of instructional leader seriously, his school was considered to be *failing* based on only one criterion: low test scores.

Although the school was labeled as *failing*, what Ms. Lopez saw, taking into account her own background in private education, was that her colleagues in PS 235 provided a supportive and caring environment for students. One indication of this was that attendance was good, usually between 92% and 94%, for both teachers and students. Another reason for her faith in the school was that she had overheard visitors saying that the children seemed happy and also appeared to be at ease and secure. Although she felt confident in the abilities and sensibilities of her colleagues and her principal, the problem with the test scores continued to cause concern within the faculty.

Despite their worries, the majority of the teachers appeared to believe that they were doing the very best they could with the resources and circumstances they had been given. They also felt that they had a responsibility toward the students and community that went well beyond reading, writing, math, and science. The majority of them believed in developing the whole child, and that included instructing students in music, art, athletics, and citizenship, to name but a few areas. However, no matter what their beliefs might be, the fact remained that children in the school were doing poorly on standardized tests, and they all knew that something had to be done.

It was at Friday's faculty meeting when the concerns about testing rose to the surface. This occurred when Mr. Rose reminded his staff that the test scores must go up or there would be serious consequences. He stated in a hushed voice, behind the closed meeting room door, "Do what you have to do." The teachers groaned and many started talking among themselves. At June Lopez's table, this is what they said:

Ms. Greene: Last year, Mr. Rose sent tests back that students had not completed, and he told me, "Do what you have to do to get these completed."

Ms. Golden: Oh please, I'm going to leave the calculators out during the test.

Ms. Davis: I'm going to not only read the directions to my students but the questions and the answers as well. I know a teacher at PS 92 who frowns to let the students know which are the wrong answers and smiles for the correct ones.

Ms. Greene: They [the administration] seem to care more about raising the test scores than whether or not the students are actually learning the material. I can't stand it anymore. I'm putting in for a transfer.

Ms. Davis: [Looking at Ms. Lopez]. You heard Mr. Rose say, "Do what you have to do." And that's exactly what you have got to do to survive in this crummy school.

Ms. Lopez: But aren't you concerned that you could lose your job if this got out?

All teachers: [In unison.]   No! They don't care. Just raise those scores.

Ms. Golden: Oh June, you may want to leave the dictionaries out on the desks. And, if they [the students] ask questions, don't hesitate to answer them. Remember June, it's all about the test.

Ms. Greene: Besides, do you really believe that some of these other schools are not doing the exact same thing?

Ms. Davis: You know they are.

Ms. Golden: Our school has been playing by the rules for a long time and look where it's gotten us.

Ms. Sanford: [Who has been silently listening to all of this.] You all can do what you want. But this is my teacher's license, and I'm not losing it for anyone. I have heard that one teacher, not here, but in another school, erases answers. This is treading on very dangerous ground. I understand why someone might go to these lengths, but it ain't gonna be me!

June Lopez left the meeting feeling very upset. It appeared that the majority of teachers, at least at her table, were planning to cheat, and she did not know what to do. She was not sure how her students would do; in particular, if the other teachers were cutting corners, how would those students' test results affect the scores in general? She could not help but ask: If she followed the letter of the law in giving the test, would her students' results be lower than the others'? How would those results make her look as a teacher?

Questions for Discussion

1. In light of the circumstances described in this dilemma, what would be the fairest course of action for June to take for: The teachers? The principal? The students and their parents? The community? Would it make a difference if she knew that everyone else in other nearby

schools were doing the same thing? Does it matter that a state takeover would spell disaster for the district, end in loss of jobs for the teachers and would likely make matters worse for the students? If this were the case, would the teachers' actions be justified?

2. Would it be more caring for June to report Mr. Rose's and the teachers' actions to someone higher up the chain of command or to remain silent? Why? If you believe she should report the problem, whom should she tell? Explain your rationale.

3. What actions might June take if she were coming from a critical theory perspective? What issues of power and domination might she identify?

4. What would the profession expect of June in this case?

5. What actions on June's part would be in the best interests of the students? Why?

CASE STUDY 9.2 WHOSE BEST INTERESTS? A TESTING DILEMMA

The meeting could have been worse. That thought provided Central High School Principal Charlie Franken little solace as he sat in his office reflecting on the discord created in the just concluded meeting with his department chairs. Their responses to the proposed curriculum change approached open revolt, and Charlie felt trapped with few good options.

Central High students always performed well on the state's standardized tests by maintaining scores that were equal to or above state averages. The school continued to meet state-defined, adequate yearly progress targets. Unfortunately, it was the school's future performance that most concerned the board of school directors. With each passing year, the state's goals for acceptable scores became more aggressive. Due to such high expectations, it appeared that a large number of districts would not meet state goals in the coming years. The school directors wanted to ensure that their district would not be among them.

If the number of Central High students achieving acceptable scores increased, at the current rate, the school would be placed on the state's "at-risk" list in two years' time. Such an action would eliminate state funding incentives for good performance and open the door for a state takeover of the school district. With such dire consequences looming in the future, the directors thought it prudent to increase student performance on the state test. The board charged the district superintendent, Dr. Carl Horne, to design and implement a curriculum that specifically addressed state standards. Appreciating the gravity of the situation and the serious concern of the board, Dr. Horne developed a plan that he presented to Charlie Franken.

In a meeting with Charlie, Dr. Horne presented an outline of the curriculum changes that the board of directors agreed would address their concerns. Courses designed specifically to address the state standards would be created in each of the four core disciplines for grades 9 through 12. These eight new courses would provide intensive training in test-taking skills. The curriculum would be centered on the material covered by the state standards and would be mandatory for students who failed to meet acceptable levels of achievement on the state exams. Because there was no federal or state funding provided to support such an initiative, these changes were to be implemented utilizing current staff.

Charlie's reaction to the proposal was less than enthusiastic. Sensing his opposition, Dr. Horne explained how such a curriculum was in the best interest of the school district. The community respected the accomplishments of the district and was proud of its standing in the state. The threat of falling below state expectations and being placed on an "endangered list" would undermine the trust and support of the community. The turmoil that would result from such a situation would be unthinkable; consequently, it was necessary to take action before problems developed. Dr. Horne's parting words were clearly etched in Charlie's memory. He stated, "You're either part of the problem or part of the solution. Keep me informed of your progress."

Now that he had his "marching orders," Charlie's first action would be to meet with his department chairs. Because of their previous work on developing the curriculum, he knew the meeting would not be pleasant.

Under Charlie's collegial style of leadership and with the notable support of the department chairs, especially the respected English chair, Alicia Weston, the faculty developed a curriculum to best serve the needs of all Central High School students. They researched and worked with a strong sense of purpose nurtured by an altruistic desire to give their students "the best." Developed and implemented over a five-year period, the curriculum identified three directions of academic preparation based on students' post-graduation plans. Each discipline offered courses designed to prepare students for college, vocational/technical school, or direct entry into the workforce. At each grade level, an interdisciplinary relation among the core disciplines was established. Students were free to choose from among the offerings in order to create an individualized plan that best suited their needs. Although subject to ongoing evaluation and revision, the current curriculum appeared to be successful in achieving the desired objectives and was highly regarded by the staff. It was with this in mind that Charlie presented the new curriculum revision plan to the department chairs.

As anticipated, the chairs were not receptive to the proposed change. The impact on the current curriculum would be significant. At first, discussion centered on a practical consideration. With no new staff, the courses offered for vocational/technical school students and those desiring to enter the workforce on graduation would be virtually eliminated, as many of those students would most likely be candidates for the new courses. This trend would be exacerbated in future years with the relentless raising of state targets for successful achievement.

The discussion then took a more philosophical turn. The validity of teaching test-taking skills was questioned. How were such skills useful in the real world? In addition, the practice of "teaching to the test" was anathema to educators interested in providing their students with the knowledge and skills necessary for success in their chosen areas. Further more, by identifying which students were assigned to the courses, the school would be eliminating student and parental choice by subjecting them to mandatory tracking. It was no surprise that Alicia Weston was particularly vehement in her objections by suggesting that teachers were not needed to fulfill the processing demanded of the new curriculum; trainers would be sufficient.

What did surprise Charlie was Alicia's threat to resign her position as chair and revert to being a regular classroom teacher if such curriculum changes were mandated. She did not want to be in a leadership position for the implementation of a program that she considered to be unethical. While proffered in the heat of the moment, Charlie knew her well enough to realize that this was not a mere bluff. Trying to gauge the reactions of the other chairs to her pronouncement, Charlie could not discern if any were inclined to follow her lead.

Sitting in his office, Charlie considered his dilemma. He knew he was bound to carry out the mandates of the school board and the super-intendent, but what if he believed that a particular directive was not in the best interests of the students? Then he paused to reflect: Who is the ultimate judge of what is in their best interests? The authority certainly resides with the board, but are the directors the best qualified to make curricular and pedagogical decisions? What would be the effect on the school's students, morale, and culture if the curriculum changes were unilaterally mandated? Would siding with his chairs in a unified front delineating the shortcomings of the proposed changes influence Dr. Horne and the board to reconsider their position? These questions preoccupied his mind as Charlie tried to formulate the first report of this progress for Dr. Horne.

Questions for Discussion

1. What actions might Charlie take that would be fair to both the students and the faculty? Would you recommend that he take these actions? Why or why not?
2. Is caring for the school district synonymous with caring for the students? What is the principal's best course of action according to the ethic of care? Should the ethic of care be the primary lens through which to view this dilemma? Why or why not?
3. Why is accountability so important in education today? Who benefits from an educational curriculum and system based on uniform standards?
4. What is Principal Franken's ultimate responsibility? What should be in his first progress report to Dr. Horne? Should he take the chair's side on this issue? Why or why not?
5. What would the profession expect Charlie to do in this case? What action would be in the best interests of the students?

CASE STUDY 9.3 TESTING HIGH STAKES

Gillian Goodwin's head ached. She tossed the four letters from parents into her "priority response" bin. Ms. Goodwin, the principal of Roselawn Secondary School located in a western province of Canada, had just hung up the phone with her superintendent of schools. They had discussed at length the issues the parents had raised in the letters and how the school would strategically be responding to the parents' requests. Although somewhat reluctant, Ms. Goodwin had agreed with her superintendent that they needed to "nip this one in the bud" as quickly as possible. She leaned back in her chair and closed her eyes.

The letters were from four parents of children in the tenth grade who had recently received a memorandum from the school notifying them of the scheduled dates and times of the mandatory Secondary School Literacy Test (SSLT). Each letter asked for special and different privileges for their child with regard to the exam.

Passing this test was essential for graduation. It was based on reading and writing skills, and if students did not pass, they could take the examination as many as three times before the end of grade 12. The four parents, including the chair of the parent council, Carol Johnson, had written the letters after a meeting in Ms. Johnson's home where they discussed the problems their children faced in taking the exam. Ms. Johnson's son was diagnosed with attention deficit hyperactivity disorder (ADHD), and he had an individual education plan (IEP).

At the meeting, Gillian told the parents that she planned to ask the school to administer the examination to her son in two afternoon sessions and not during the one day that the other children had to take the exam. She believed that her son did much better in the early afternoon after he took his medicine. The other children did not have a diagnosis, but they simply did not do well in exams.

After their conversation with Ms. Johnson, each of these parents felt that their child should have some special accommodations, such as additional time, breaks, assistive devices, or technology. Ms. Johnson had told the parents that all their children needed was an IEP to receive these accommodations. To obtain an IEP, each parent was considering hiring a private psychologist to test their child and hopefully make a diagnosis that would require special arrangements for the examination.

After reading letter number four, there were many questions racing through Gillian Goodwin's mind. She pondered: How did the principalship become so removed from the instructional and relational leadership role she had so enjoyed in the past that she had already agreed with the superintendent to nip this problem in the bud? When did her role become such a prescriptive and technical data-driven, number-crunching game? Was the role so narrowly defined by and confined to reacting to problematic issues that appeared messier and more taxing with each passing day? Did she, in fact, really have any freedom or professional autonomy left to creatively explore with parents alternative solutions that served the best interests of the students? This latest dilemma had her doubting her capacity, willingness, or ability to muster the energy to engage in this latest round of negotiation and compromise tactics.

Enough reflection, Ms. Goodwin thought. She quickly sat upright in her chair and retrieved the four letters from her response box. It was time to move into action. She contacted each parent and gave them the times she could meet with them the following day. She then asked her special education department head, Mr. Jenkins, to come to her office as soon as he could manage it. Once he arrived, she briefed him on the contents of the letters, explained about the meeting for tomorrow, and gave him time to read the four letters. What follows is part of the conversation Ms. Goodwin had with Mr. Jenkins.

Ms. Goodwin: I can see that you are upset by the letters and rightfully so. However, the superintendent and I have agreed that we will stress that the testing agency's guidelines clearly state that in order to protect the security of test materials and to ensure the validity and reliability of the results, all students across the province must write the SSLT at the same time, and that includes Mrs. Johnson's child. As for the other parents, I have already pulled their children's school records that clearly demonstrate our teachers have been addressing both strengths and needs of these students in their instruction and in the work assigned. There is absolutely no evidence to support the parents' claims that their children are in need of IEPs. To calm the parents' fears, we will remind them that if their children do not do well, they are entitled to retake the test.

Mr. Jenkins: While I am relieved to hear what you have to say, what if the parents will not back down? Who is going to write these IEPs if that happens? It is not the responsibility of my special education teachers since these children are not formally identified through the IPRC process. We can barely manage to complete the paperwork required of us right now. These accountability measures are just going too far!

Ms. Goodwin: The superintendent and I have played out all the scenarios that you have described. In regard to Mrs. Johnson, we do not believe she will be granted her request through the testing agency. As for the other parents, we will emphasize that all evidence to date does not indicate a need for the development of IEPs or for further accommodations for their children. This will be the primary message we send to them tomorrow. It is of paramount importance that we take a "divide-and-conquer" approach here.

After Mr. Jenkins left, Ms. Goodwin had to admit that she was not looking forward to the confrontational and adversarial approaches she knew would be adopted the following day when she informed each parent that their request was denied. She did not blame the parents for trying. Why shouldn't they try to position themselves at an advantage in this competitive school climate that valued performance, efficiency, and economy over the ones she had worked so hard to cultivate in her school—those of care, cooperation, and respect for all learners?

What had really unsettled her was hearing herself say to both her superintendent and Mr. Jenkins, "We take a 'divide-and-conquer' approach," and they had both been very supportive of this stance. How had she arrived at such thinking? It went against all her beliefs and values associated with inclusive leadership that she had tried so hard to live out in her practice.

In thinking through her beliefs once more, one unexplored option came to mind that had not been discussed with the superintendent or with Mr. Jenkins. Ms. Goodwin remembered that she had a small amount of discretionary monies. She could, she realized, consider using these monies to accommodate the concerns of the three vocal parents who did not have IEPs for their children. Those monies could be utilized for some special sessions of test preparation for the students and could even help Ms. Johnson's child as well. But what would other parents say if word got out? What of the needs of their children? In particular, what about the multicultural parents, who were not vocal and yet had children in her school, whose first language was not English? Did they not deserve some special consideration too?

Intuitively, she knew that if she did not provide some kind of accommodations, this particular story was not going to have a very happy ending tomorrow for either the parents or the school system. She knew that more meetings would be requested and coalitions of allies on both sides would argue their respective cases in such meetings. Requests were no longer really requests because "no" was no longer an acceptable response. Demands were only masked as requests with much posturing on both sides regarding honoring differences of perspectives.

Taken aback by her own escalating cynicism, Ms. Goodwin had to ask herself: When exactly had she begun to doubt what had been her unshakable belief in the ability to achieve equity and excellence in education for all through collaborative problem solving among parents, educators, and other stakeholders in education? Called on to handle another school problem, she continued to wonder how she should handle tomorrow's meeting and if she should alert Mr. Jenkins and the superintendent to any change of strategy.

Questions for Discussion

1. How might Gillian Goodwin handle this situation if she were trying to abide by the letter of the law? The spirit of the law? Would these approaches be the same or different? Why?

2. What is the most caring action that Gillian can take? Who should this ethic of care be directed toward? Why that person(s)?

3. Who has determined these guidelines? Why must standardized tests be administered? Why must they count as a requirement for graduation? In this situation, who is in a position to benefit the most? The least? Explain your answer. What, if anything, can be done to equalize this situation?

4. Is it in the best interests of each student to treat everyone the same or to make accommodations for those who need more assistance? Why?

5. What might the profession expect of Gillian? What obligations, if any, does she have to the multicultural community as well as to the community in general?

CASE STUDY 9.4 ABILITY, MATURITY, AND PARENTAL PERSPECTIVES

John Dolan is currently a third-grade student at Happy Times Elementary School, a large suburban district outside of a Mid-Atlantic city. John enrolled in this elementary school in first grade; he attended a Montessori program in his pre-first-grade years. While in first grade, the teacher noticed early on in the school year that John was struggling with his readiness skills in reading. John was recommended for services with the reading specialist where he met the eligibility requirements to receive such service. Beginning in mid-October of first grade, John began to receive 30 minutes of remedial help with the reading teacher daily. John began to make small strides with his reading skills. He was proficient or above average in all other subjects.

During a mid-year conference with the teacher and the counselor, Mr. and Mrs. Dolan requested that their son be retained in first grade. Their basis for retention stemmed from their concerns about his immaturity. Mr. and Mrs. Dolan are in their early fifties. John's other siblings are 12 to 14 years apart in age. John has no children in his neighborhood near his age to socialize with after school and on the weekends. The teacher and counselor explained to Mr. and Mrs. Dolan that John was making progress in his reading; they believed the reading support intervention was working. They also shared with the parents how well their son was doing in his other subject areas such as math, science, and social studies. However, the staff did express their concern about his tantrums when he was corrected or did not get his way. To address these concerns, the staff devised a behavior plan. Mr. and Mrs. Dolan supported the behavior plan and indicated that they would partner with the school on the plan. Mrs. Dolan indicated that she had arranged for a teacher in another building (the one where she is employed as a cafeteria worker) to tutor John once a week in reading skills. The team agreed to revisit his progress again in late April with a comprehensive review of his data.

At the end of April, the teacher, principal, counselor, reading support teacher, and parents met to review John's progress. The school team provided the parents with reading data reflecting the progress being made; however, the strides were minimal and slow. His teacher could also observe daily John's frustration with his reading and his poor self-esteem concerning his reading ability. The team was beginning to conclude that perhaps John had a specific learning disability in reading since he did very well in other areas but continued to perform below grade level benchmarks in reading. Mrs. Dolan requested retention for her son while Mr. Dolan was not in agreement with her. The school team was concerned because repeating the grade would serve no benefit to John in the other subject areas, since he was doing well, as indicated by his scores. The principal and the team recommended a psycho-educational evaluation by the school psychologist to rule out any learning disabilities. The parents agreed with the recommendation and signed the permission to evaluate.

John was found to have a specific learning disability in reading comprehension, decoding, and written expression. John's overall IQ was 121. The IEP was developed with the parents, and John began receiving services in the beginning of second grade. During second grade, John started to make steady gains in his reading ability. The outbursts were still occurring, but nothing was at a level to warrant serious concern. The parents continued to "baby" him. Once again, at the end of second grade, the parents wanted to retain John due to his immaturity. The parents did not seem to be aware that they were contributing to his behavior problems.

Now, this school year, the school team is once again faced with the request from both parents to retain their son based on his immaturity. The dilemma for the principal is complicated in a variety of ways. Mr. and Mrs. Dolan requested a meeting with the special education teacher and the regular education teacher to discuss progress and asked the special education teacher not to include the principal in the meeting. Dismayed by the parents' request, the principal advised the special education teacher to include the special education supervisor in the meeting in case the issue of retention was discussed.

The meeting had occurred several weeks before. The parents brought along the teacher, from another building, who is tutoring John. During this meeting, the team reviewed John's progress and shared the gains he has made in reading this year. He is only six months behind in reading. The teachers also shared that John has demonstrated progress in all academic disciplines; they were even pleased with his improved behavior. The teachers believed the special education intervention, coupled with their effort and care, provided for such strong gains. The parents were adamant about the retention to the point of their becoming belligerent. The tutor was also adamant and expressed to the team the idea of retention as the only solution. The supervisor informed the parents of their rights to place their request in writing. She shared with them that after the request is presented to the Child Study Team with data, the principal would make the final decision. However, it was clear at the meeting that the parents believed they had made the final decision based on the information given to them by John's tutor.

The parents are angry, demanding, and now refusing to meet with the principal, special education supervisor, and director of elementary education to discuss their concerns. Numerous attempts have been made to schedule an appointment. The parents continue to ignore the outreach efforts being made by the school.

The dilemma now exists because the parents believe strongly that retaining their son will "make him more mature." The school team has the data to support his gains. The interventions provided academically and behaviorally have worked. Retaining this student would be of no benefit to him. Needless to say, under these circumstances, questions remain.

Questions for Discussion

1. Do the parents have a right to demand retention based on immaturity?
2. Do you think an exception should be made in this case to grant the parents' request for retention? How does this relate to the ethic of justice for the child, parents, teachers, and administrators?
3. Are all the professionals described in this dilemma operating under the ethic of the profession? If not, explain with examples.
4. Is it fair to retain a student based solely on immaturity? How does this notion relate to the ethic of critique?
5. Are the parents operating under the ethic of care for their child to request the retention? Explain. Have they considered the feelings of their child to be retained and its impact on him?
6. Is the school team (principal and teachers) demonstrating the ethic of care with regard to their opinions on retention for this youngster? Explain.
7. What decision should the principal make? State specific reasons for your response.

CASE STUDY 9.5 A MERIT-BASED SCHOLARSHIP

Jessica Walters stared at the two files on her desk. As director of admissions at a small, liberal arts college in the Midwest, she and her staff were faced with tough admissions decisions each day, but this case was the most difficult she had dealt with in her 20-year admissions career, and it was certainly the thorniest she had ever experienced here at Midvale College.

The applications in question were from two top-achieving students competing for a unique scholarship offered to a single high school senior from the town. Each one had attended strong schools, taken challenging courses, led clubs, started organizations, and were in the top 10% of their graduating classes. Despite their similarities, their family situations, their gender, and their racial and ethnic backgrounds were different. The

Hispanic male candidate, Juan Hernandez, came from a single-parent home; however, that single parent, a father, was a lawyer. The White female student, Courtney Rolands, came from an intact home, but both parents were in blue-collar hourly wage jobs and neither had attended college.

Academically, while these students were both strong candidates, there was one key difference: their ACT scores. The Hispanic male student's score was four points—a substantial difference on the composite ACT scale —below that of the White student. Jessica knew that if she followed the college's written guidelines for this scholarship, Courtney Rolands, the student with the higher ACT score, would get the award. Jessica reviewed the files again. This time she looked for any other serious differences in the students' applications. She could not discover any particular challenges that might be considered as a plus factor in the scholarship consideration. The only significant difference was their ACT scores.

This case was exacerbated by the fact that Jessica's college had been enjoying record enrollment numbers during her tenure. She was a shrewd marketer, and she and her team had been able to attract more and better qualified students. Unfortunately, with increasingly higher ACT scores from their incoming freshmen, more students of color were denied admission. Jennifer's graduate work had been in the area of standardized test differentials, so she was acutely aware of students of color having admission difficulties. Admittedly, the decline in Hispanic numbers was slight, but some people were starting to notice. Student groups and faculty were beginning to agitate about the declining number of Hispanics admitted to Midvale College, and the president of the college was feeling the heat. The issue was compounded by the fact that the town, like many other towns in the Midwest, had been experiencing a Hispanic population boom.

On the one hand, Jessica could understand their concerns. Enrolling a diverse student body was a compelling issue and important enough to allow colleges to consider race as a plus factor in admissions. However, University of Michigan U.S. Supreme Court cases (Gratz v. Bollinger, 2003; Grutter v. Bollinger, 2003) gave Jessica pause; colleges and universities across the country were re-evaluating their admissions policies to ensure they were legal. These court decisions addressed the use of race in admissions, but much of the discussion surrounding them indicated that minority scholarships and financial aid would be the next targets. In sum, what the decisions said was that race could be a factor in assuring diversity in admissions but that there could not be a quota system to ensure minority representation. The policy needs to be flexible and highly individualized in that a number of factors are considered. The admissions policy in Gratz v. Bollinger (2003) was illegal because, among other things, it automatically gave applicants an additional 20 points if they came from underrepresented minority groups.

Midvale College had never used an affirmative action policy in admissions, and the information distributed to the public indicated that the college did not consider race in admissions decisions. In the case of the Midvale scholarship application it did ask for race, but the form clearly indicated it was optional and would have no impact on the scholarship decision. If Jessica started to use that piece of information as part of the scholarship decision process it would feel to her to be unethical, and possibly it might even be illegal. However, Jessica wondered if she could consider race in this situation because it had to do with a scholarship award as opposed to admissions. After all, both students would be admitted to the college.

As she was still considering which student should win the scholarship, the college president contacted her to say that he had just received an angry call from a member of the college's board. The Hispanic member was outraged at the possibility that a minority student might be passed over for the scholarship due to a lower test score. He pointed out that a minority student had never received this scholarship (in fact, few had ever applied), and this year it was important that someone who was not in the majority should receive it.

The president was tired of all the pressure and effectively told Jessica that she "should" award the minority student the scholarship. As she put down the phone, Jessica knew she had to make the most ethically challenging decision of her career. Traditionally, it had always been the admissions director who made the decision about the scholarship. Should she allow the president and the pressure group to determine the recipient of the award, or should she make the decision herself?

Questions for Discussion

1. Which ethical paradigm(s) does the president of Midvale College seem to be most influenced by? Is his directive legal? Is it just?

2. If we only had the ethic of justice as a paradigm, what decision would Jessica have to make?

3. How might Jessica use the ethic of care in this case? Is it possible to care for all parties in this case? If so, how? If not, why not?

4. From a critical perspective, what are the ethical issues in this scenario that relate to social class, racial/ethnic equality, power, and oppression?

5. Imagine that you are the admissions director. Choose the student you think should win the scholarship competition. Carefully consider which ethical paradigm(s) you are using as you make your decision. Explain.

Chapter 10

Privacy Versus Safety

*Hollie J. Mackey, Addie Daniels-Lane, Jason Rosenbaum,
Christopher S. Weiler, and Dipali Puri*

**In this chapter, we explore the extent to which privacy rights need to be sacrificed
in order to keep schools safe. Five cases represent a gamut of school safety dilemmas
ranging from gang membership and suspected drug use to cyber-bullying, sexting,
and cell phone use. Each dilemma juxtaposes the privacy rights of the individual—
parent, student, teacher—and the threat of danger to the student body.**

While educational leaders have as their primary charge to ensure that the
students in their schools are provided with high-quality instruction, this goal
cannot be achieved if schools are unsafe. Keeping schools safe and providing
the school community with a sense of security is an important responsibility
which, if not carried out, can cause serious repercussions. At the same time,
most of us would agree that personal privacy is one of the most important
rights we possess. Justice Brandeis observed that:

> they [the framers of the U.S. Constitution] recognized the significance
> of man's spiritual nature, of his feelings and of his intellect. They knew that
> only a part of the pain, pleasure and satisfactions of life are to be found in
> material things. They sought to protect Americans in their beliefs, their
> thoughts, their emotions and their sensations. They conferred, as against the
> government, *the right to be let alone—the most comprehensive of rights and the
> right most valued by civilized men.* To protect that right, every unjustifiable
> intrusion by the government upon the privacy of the individual, whatever the
> means employed, must be deemed a violation of the Fourth Amendment.
> (Olmstead v. United States, 1928, p. 478, Brandeis, J. dissenting [emphasis
> added])

Indeed, our Bill of Rights guarantees individuals the freedom from
warrantless searches and self-incrimination; however, the framers of the

Constitution could not anticipate how large our public school system would become or the threats to safety that would challenge those fundamental rights (Stefkovich & Miller, 1999). Thus, in the school context, there is a fine line between privacy and safety. Creating this context is the widely accepted fact that school is one of the few places where parents are, for the most part, compelled to send their children for most of their childhood (Levin, 1986). Further blurring this line is the precedent set by Justice Abe Fortas in Tinker v. Des Moines Independent Community School District (1969) that "special characteristics of the school environment" (p. 506) provide schools with the ability to limit students' and teachers' rights. This notion of special characteristics "has been central to judicial reasoning about individual rights in schools" (Warnick, 2009, p. 200).

From a practitioner's perspective, educators have always been concerned about maintaining order and discipline in the schools. The issue of school safety, however, reached a peak in the 1990s. The Gun-free Zones Act of 1990, ruled unconstitutional in U.S. v. Lopez (1995), was followed by the Gun-free Schools Act of 1994 (GFSA), which mandated that states pass legislation requiring schools to expel for at least a year students possessing weapons on school property. While exceptions could be permitted on a case-by-case basis, this law resulted in states enacting zero-tolerance laws, which began with guns but often expanded to other student behavior (Smith, 2009). Repealed in 2002, the GFSA was re-enacted under No Child Left Behind (NCLB, 2002). Around the same time, the 1999 shootings at Columbine High School in suburban Colorado reminded Americans of the potential horrors of school violence. Here, two high school students killed 12 students and one teacher and injured another 23 people (Associated Press, 2009). While not the first incident of its kind, Columbine was one of the most publicized, attracting widespread media attention which brought up crucial issues of bullying, discipline, and weapons in schools.

Efforts were also ongoing to eradicate drug use in the schools. In 1994, the Elementary and Secondary Education Act (ESEA) authorized The Safe and Drug-free Schools and Communities Act (SDFSCA) State and Local Grants Program. Providing financial support for programs that would prevent drug and alcohol use among youth, this initiative was "a central part of the Federal Government's effort to encourage the creation of safe, disciplined, and drug-free learning environments that will help all children meet challenging academic standards" (Bilchik, 1999). Within the next eight years, the U.S. States Supreme Court issued two decisions which permitted, under certain circumstances, random drug testing of students in public schools. The first decision, Vernonia v. Acton (1995), allowed schools to randomly drug test student athletes. The second, Board of Education v. Earls (2002), ruled as constitutional random drug testing of students involved in extracurricular activities. Language in both opinions viewed drug use as a threat to keeping schools safe.

In 2009, the Supreme Court heard Safford v. Redding, a case involving the strip search of a middle-school student for possession of prescription-strength ibuprofen. While the court ruled for the student, the justices were hesitant to say what they would have decided had the search been for more serious drugs. They did, however, grant the school district immunity from money damages, noting that school authorities would not have necessarily known that the strip search was illegal because the law was unclear. Indeed, there are lower court opinions that have condoned such practices as legal and necessary for the safety of the school (Cornfield, 1993; Williams, 1991). All these decisions are based on a standard of reasonableness set forth in the Supreme Court's ruling in New Jersey v. T.L.O. (1985) where the Court balanced the privacy rights of students against school officials' duty to maintain order and discipline in the schools, a responsibility which has come to be equated with school safety.

School safety has become a primary issue to which both educators and policy makers have responded with increased attention to safety technology, law enforcement officers in schools, and revised school discipline procedures including zero-tolerance policies. In some instances, the "special characteristics" of schools have been used to place safety ahead of individual rights. In this respect, some scholars have questioned the necessity for this erosion of rights in the name of security (Casella, 2003; Chen, 2008; Martinez, 2009). In addition, rather than resting blame solely on the perpetrators of a crime, the notion of collective responsibility for ensuring the safety of America's children has emerged (Lickel, Schmader, & Hamilton, 2003).

Rapidly advancing technology has only added to school safety problems with issues of cyber-bullying, social networking websites, and cell phones with instant messaging, texting, and digital photo-sharing capabilities. Shaheen Shariff, a Canadian scholar who has written extensively on topics related to technology, is one of a growing number of scholars (Gorman & Pauken, 2003; Noddings, 2002; Starratt, 2003; Stefkovich, 2006; Stefkovich, Crawford & Murphy, 2009) who see a moral dilemma beyond the legal dimensions of school safety. In her book on cyber-bullying, Shariff describes this challenge for educators and policy makers:

> Maintaining civilization and civil behavior is difficult enough in organized society, even when the rule of traditional law is supposed to prevail and order and authority exists to protect innocent citizens. What happens when traditional rules and the authority are removed . . . ? This is the dilemma that schools confront as they attempt to navigate the legal and moral challenges around responding to cyber-bullying and, ultimately, developing in students appropriate moral compasses for an electronic age. (Shariff, 2009, pp. 2–3)

This chapter contains five case studies dealing with issues of personal privacy versus safety in the schools. Case study 10.1, Keeping Children Safe: When is Enough, Enough?, addresses the sensitive issue of drug use and the extent to which school leaders are willing to go to keep schools safe and drug free. Here, based on her demeanor and changes in her physical appearance, it is clear that a student is experiencing some type of crisis in her life. The school counselor and administrators assume that the student is using and possibly distributing illegal drugs. In reaction to the pervasive use of drugs in school and to keep both the student and the school community safe, the counselor conducts a highly intrusive search—one that reveals something very different. This case illustrates how a seemingly pervasive fear of drugs may overshadow other equally if not more important student concerns.

Gangs pose an enormous threat to school safety, an issue that is explored in Case study 10.2, Punishment, Rehabilitation, or Mitigating Circumstances? Here, both the greater community and the school community are committed to eradicating a serious gang problem and have developed policies to address this threat. The school's policy requires, among other things, the suspension of any student promoting gang activity. In this scenario, a middle-school student is trying to recruit some of his classmates for gang membership and is suspended. Before the student can return to school, a parent must be present. School leaders find an even more compelling dilemma when they realize that the student's mother, who they were counting on for support, has not only been extraordinarily difficult to contact but may also be part of the problem. In addition to disciplinary issues, this situation explores the larger problem of where to draw the line between the privacy of families and the safety of the individual student and of all students.

Technology plays a critical role in the remaining three dilemmas described in this chapter. The use of technology has grown exponentially in the past 30 years, bringing with it many advances to our society and enhancing the ways in which we learn. It has also spawned new concerns related to privacy and safety as well as exacerbating old problems. These scenarios address some of the fairly prevalent issues that few school leaders could have anticipated in earlier times. For example, Case study 10.3, School Discipline, Criminal Complaint, or Compassionate Intervention?, involves sexting, i.e., the transmission of sexually explicit photos by telephone. This situation involves a middle-school student who sends this information in response to what he construes as a dare on the part of a female classmate.

Case study 10.4, New Bullying for the 21st Century: Cyber-bullying in the Middle, adds a twist to traditional bullying problems as the bullying is done on the internet. This dilemma involves Sam Walsh, a middle-school student who is being harassed by Babe-ah-licious555, an anonymous person who says she is in one of his classes. This student taunts Sam and then takes the humiliation to a public level by photographing and recording him in embarrassing situations and then broadcasting this information and her unkind e-mails to other students in school. Here, the school authorities must contend with issues of the student's safety and possible classroom disruption juxtaposed against where to draw the line with respect to students' free speech rights and privacy in their own homes.

Finally, Case study 10.5, All's Fair in Love and School, concerns a teacher's private life that inadvertently, and suddenly, becomes public. In this dilemma, a young, very popular teacher who has done much for the school in his five years of employment now finds his job in jeopardy after private information is discovered on his cell phone. In this instance, the cell phone dropped out of his pocket as he left the classroom to gather up some papers he had left in the teachers' room. Class had not yet begun but the students had started to arrive. One student found the cell phone, looked inside, and discovered private pictures which he shared with other students revealing the teacher's sexual orientation, an event that caused the teacher to lose control of his class and ultimately affect his teaching. Thus, an issue of privacy becomes a safety issue as parents complain not about the teacher's sexual orientation but about the disruption in the classroom.

CASE STUDY 10.1 KEEPING CHILDREN SAFE: WHEN IS ENOUGH, ENOUGH?

Dr. Matayo walked slowly through the reception area and down the hall to his office before entering and gently closing the door. Hand still resting on the handle, he let his head drop slightly to rest against the back of the door. Nine years of teaching and four years as a principal had not prepared him for the events that had just transpired under his watch. While still a little unclear about what he needed to do, the one thing he knew was that within minutes he would have two angry parents, a contrite school counselor, and one scared high school senior waiting for him outside his office. He took a few deep breaths and recalled what had led to this disastrous day.

Ironside High School was located in a relatively well-populated mountain state area. Although the community was technically considered rural, Ironside accommodated over 1,200 students who came primarily from families associated with the mining industry on which the town had been built. This industry provided a tax base that afforded the school district resources well beyond those of most schools in the state. These included an indoor track and swimming pool, enough money in the budget to maintain smaller class sizes, a "serenity garden" for students and staff, and the space and funding for three full-time school counselors specializing in academic advising, emotional support, and drug and alcohol education. Most recently, the school had used surplus budget money to expand and refinish the student parking lot to accommodate the increasing number of students who were driving to school.

With the good always came the bad, it seemed. Many of the students at Ironside had access to a lot of money, not a responsibility that they seemed to take seriously. Dr. Matayo was always mildly surprised when the students arrived in their shiny new cars that made the faculty and staff vehicles look like they belonged in a junk yard. He was also saddened by the number of students who had been caught with illegal drugs in the community. Unfortunately, the town was situated along an interstate corridor known to be used for moving drugs between Mexico and Canada. It seemed that their location was a nice resting spot for some of these dealers and the city was suffering. Dr. Matayo was thankful that they had not yet discovered any drugs in the school but he knew it was only a matter of time. His students had both the money and the resources to get just about any drug they wanted. He thought about how times had changed. When he was in school it was obvious which students were involved with drugs and alcohol and those who were not. Now it seemed that it was mostly athletes and honor students. It was a painful memory that just two years ago they lost a student to drug use. He was a good student, an all-conference athlete whose mother had found him dead on the garage floor. He had seemed fine at football practice that day, only to suffer a heart attack 30 minutes after practice, Methamphetamines.

Dr. Matayo turned back to the matter at hand. Mrs. Teahorn, the extremely competent and caring drug and alcohol counselor, had stepped up her efforts to educate students in the hopes of preventing drug and alcohol use. She had also tried to keep a vigilant eye on the student body to try to recognize signs of drug use and get students help if they needed it. Over the course of the previous month one student, Natasa Kadiev, had shown some classic signs. Typically an outgoing and friendly girl, she had become withdrawn and rarely spoke to anyone. Her cutting-edge fashion sense had been traded for a uniform of sweatpants and a hooded sweatshirt. Her haphazard ponytail appeared to have been pulled up as an afterthought and she no longer wore any make-up. Mrs. Teahorn had overheard students talking about Natasa, some even implying that not only was Natasa using drugs but she was probably getting them for her friends as well.

Mrs. Teahorn tried talking with Natasa many times and had even pulled her from class on several occasions to try to develop a closer relationship with her in the hopes that she would disclose the cause of her rapid transformation. It appeared that the opposite had occurred. Natasa had complained to Dr. Matayo that she felt "picked on" and that she wished Mrs. Teahorn would leave her alone. She resented being pulled from her favorite class. After talking with Mrs. Teahorn he had decided that while she needed to ease off of Natasa, it was certainly a good idea to keep an eye on her for her own safety. If she was using drugs she was putting both herself and others at risk.

Dr. Matayo moved the chairs in his office around to accommodate the unplanned meeting between himself and the four people he could hear gathering outside his office. Mrs. Teahorn entered first, making brief eye contact and then quickly averting her gaze to a painting on the back wall as she took her seat. Mr. and Mrs. Kadiev came through the door next, his arm protectively around her shoulder and a look of anger and determination in his dark brown eyes. Mrs. Kadiev cried gently into a handkerchief. Trailing in last was Natasa, whose hand was carefully encircled by the hand her mother had dropped behind her to cement the solidarity of their little family through touch.

Dr. Matayo: Let's start at the beginning. Mrs. Teahorn, would you please explain what happened? Natasa, if you want to add anything you are entitled. Your side of the story is important too. If you feel Mrs. Teahorn is not accurate please speak up.

Mrs. Teahorn: This morning I passed Natasa in the hallway and her eyes were all sunken in and red like she had been crying or something. I know you told me to give her some space but my heart just broke for her; so I decided to pull her from third period, her study hall, to talk with her.

Dr. Matayo: Please continue.

Mrs. Teahorn: Once we got to my office she started yelling at me to mind my own business. I told her what I knew about the signs of drug use and asked her if she had been using drugs. She told me "no" but I didn't think she was telling the truth. I could see I wasn't getting anywhere and decided to send her back to class. She had tossed her backpack against a chair in my office and some of its contents had fallen to the floor. I leaned down to help her when she jerked the bag away and told me to leave her stuff alone. I raised my hand to touch her shoulder to reassure her that I was only trying to help when she quickly moved her bag behind her. That made me think she had drugs, so I asked her to empty the contents of her bag. She refused and said I had no right. I explained to her that I did as per district policy. She then started tugging at her sweatshirt that had gotten twisted with all her jerking around. She kept trying to put it over her hips so I thought she might have drugs in her pockets. I asked her to take off her sweatshirt knowing she had a T-shirt on underneath and to then empty her sweatpants pockets. . . .

Dr. Matayo: So you were concerned that she was both using drugs and that she had them in her backpack or pockets?

Mrs. Teahorn: Yes, absolutely! We have seen so much devastation due to drugs the past few years, I thought I was doing the right thing.

Dr. Matayo: Please continue.

Mrs. Teahorn: Well, I guess she knew I was not going to let her leave so she pulled off her sweatshirt and dumped her backpack out all over my floor. And then . . .

Natasa: And then I said, "Are you happy now?"

Dr. Matayo: Is that when you called Mr. and Mrs. Kadiev?

Mrs. Teahorn: Yes.

Natasa: Must have been SOME surprise to see that the perfect counselor was WRONG! Tell them what you found Mrs. Teahorn . . . wait, let me . . . she found this stupid big round belly and a pregnancy book in my backpack! Some drugs, right?

Dr. Matayo let this all sink in and wondered what he was going to do. He knew that Mrs. Teahorn was only doing what she had felt she needed to do to protect Natasa and perhaps other students from drugs. He also knew that the Kadievs were a very prominent family and Mr. Kadiev would want heads to roll for this. He glanced up once more and saw before him a counselor who knew she had erred, two parents who just found out that their daughter was pregnant, and one young woman whose troubles had just been compounded by humiliation and broken trust.

Questions for Discussion

1. What is the ethical dilemma presented above? Analyze this scenario through the lenses of justice, care, critique, and profession.

2. Discuss how the scenario illustrates the tension between students' safety and their right to privacy within schools. Which is more important?

3. Was Mrs. Teahorn justified in her assumption that she might find drugs either in Natasa's backpack or her pants pockets? If you were Dr. Matayo, how would you explain this justification to Natasa's parents? The school board?

4. What are the implications for Dr. Matayo should he decide not to strongly reprimand Mrs. Teahorn? Should she be reprimanded?

5. How does this scenario challenge the conflict between personal and professional ethics?

CASE STUDY 10.2 PUNISHMENT, REHABILITATION, OR MITIGATING CIRCUMSTANCES?

Wilbur Meadows Elementary School is located in a mid-size urban area. The city population is about 55% African American, 30% Caucasian, and 15% Hispanic and other. Recently the city has seen the proliferation of gang activity and a number of gangs have been identified as being active in the city. An upsurge in violence and drug activity has been recorded. Initially the city leaders denied there was a problem. More recently, they have acknowledged it and begun taking aggressive action against gangs. The Board of Education has also reacted by establishing an anti-gang policy. This policy requires a five- to nine-day suspension, notification to the local gang task force, a possible legal hearing, and referral to an anti-gang program. The district is also establishing its own anti-gang program under the guise of the Phoenix Curriculum. This program focuses on goal setting, personal choice, and developing responsibility (Youngs, 1989). The curriculum is being used to target students in grades 4 to 8.

Recognizing that Wilbur Meadows serves a troubled community known for drugs and violence, Ms. Smith, the school's principal, and the School Leadership Team believed it was time for the staff to know as much about gangs as the children. They invited the State Police Gang Unit to conduct an in-service for the staff. They also invited incarcerated gang members who have turned their lives around to engage and dissuade students.

Jamal Sanders, a seventh-grade special needs student at Wilbur Meadows Elementary School, was suspected of flashing (gang-related) signs. Ms. Smith and the school counselor, Mr. Alex, had several conversations with Jamal about gangs. When Jamal's mother was asked to come in for a conference, she sent representatives in her stead. Jamal was eventually caught in the act of trying to encourage other students to become part of a local gang, the Junior Hoods 301 Sect. Consequently, Jamal was suspended and his name was sent to the local gang task force. Ms. Smith and Mr. Alex met again with Jamal to impress upon him the seriousness of the situation. Jamal's mother was notified that a mandatory parent conference would be required before Jamal could return to school. Several messages left for her went unreturned. The school's social worker hand-delivered the letter. It was apparent that something had to be done with Jamal, some type of intervention with parent input and support. Ms. Smith wondered if Jamal's family had any idea where he seemed to be heading and how much support she could expect from them.

When Jamal's mother reported to the school office for the conference, Principal Smith and Mr. Alex looked at each other with stunned expressions. Ms. Delores Sanders entered the room wearing a sleeveless, low-cut blouse.

The upper part of her arm was encircled by a tattoo of cat paws (the symbol of the Hoods); at the center of her cleavage was an additional cat paw. Principal Smith's head began to spin. Nothing in her training had prepared her for handling this. Where and how to begin? These were just two of the questions looming in front of her. A strategic diplomatic approach would have to be the order of the day. She hoped Mr. Alex had some insightful strategy to contribute or at least was ready to follow her lead.

Questions for Discussion

1. How can Principal Smith protect Jamal given the circumstances? Should she confront Ms. Sanders for her possible involvement in gang activity?

2. What type of disciplinary action should be taken against Jamal? Should Ms. Smith refer Jamal to the district for a hearing to expel him or should she report him, or his mother, to the police?

3. Given the circumstances, is rehabilitation possible for Jamal? What is the most caring way to handle this situation? Should Principal Smith report Ms. Sanders to Child Welfare for possible child endangerment?

4. Is the district's policy fair to students like Jamal? Should there be exceptions to the rule? If so, how would you craft these rules/policies?

5. How might this situation be handled from a critical theory and/or social justice perspective?

CASE STUDY 10.3 SCHOOL DISCIPLINE, CRIMINAL COMPLAINT, OR COMPASSIONATE INTERVENTION?

In her office at Community Hall Middle School, a morning cup of coffee still hot in her hand, Principal Rondell hung up the phone and stared blankly at Assistant Principal Park as she issued her instructions: "Please get Grace from class." Seeing her principal's expression, Park asked no questions and returned a few minutes later with a confident eighth grader who could not quite hide the embarrassment and awkwardness she knew she was about to encounter.

Despite her 20 years in public education, and eight as principal of the school she and Ms. Park had turned into the most desirable middle school in this urban district, Principal Rondell was facing a new kind of problem. With the increase in student use of social networking websites and camera phones over the past few years, there had been some instances of students using these technologies in inappropriate ways. However, these had been relatively mild infractions and fit well within the kind of social posturing, bullying, and moments of poor judgment that any experienced middle-school educator is accustomed to addressing. Aware of how such technology opens up delicate challenges to the school disciplinary code, Principal Rondell has managed to address those past instances through private conversations with students and sometimes parents about respect, privacy, and the culture of personal responsibility at Community Hall Middle School.

The poised eighth grader stood in front of Principal Rondell and Assistant Principal Park. "Hi, Grace," the principal began. "I just got off the phone with your mother. You knew she was going to call?" Grace sat down and nodded almost invisibly. "Do you have your phone with the picture?"

Grace nodded again as she handed over her phone. "Will Ms. Park be able to find the picture herself or do you have to open it for her?"

"I deleted all the others. You'll see it. It has the date and time it was received. But I don't think you really want to see it. I mean, it must be weird for you to see an eighth-grade boy naked."

Ms. Park held her breath for a moment as she finally realized what the situation entailed. She had heard about the increasing frequency among teens of sexting one another, of sending sexually suggestive, and sometimes explicit, pictures by cell phone, but was nonetheless surprised to encounter it among her own students.

"Don't worry, Grace," said Ms. Park, "I've dealt with enough bad behavior by school boys that you might be surprised what I've seen."

Grace looked up, stared Ms. Park straight in the eye for a moment without speaking. She broke the silence in a low, exactingly clear voice "I hope you haven't seen a student this way."

Ms. Park saw no way around having to see the picture that Bob, Grace's classmate, had sent to her. Once the evidence had been confirmed and Grace told her side of the story, she was sent back to class, leaving the leadership team alone to form a plan of action. After she interviewed Bob, and another eighth grader, Rachel, the story seemed to come together clearly. No one was debating the actual events and how they unfolded.

The story matched what Grace's mother had explained on the phone. Two days earlier, Bob had made a sexually inappropriate comment to Grace while they were in art class which insinuated that she show him her breasts. Grace tried to deflect the comment with humor by responding flippantly, "Yeah, you first." That evening, Grace received on her phone a photo message from Bob showing his erect penis.

Grace would later report being quite disturbed by this, but out of fear and anxiety had not at first told anyone about it. She discussed it the following day in school with her friend Rachel, who convinced Grace to send her the photo that evening. Unknown to Grace, Rachel had sent the photo to most of the eighth-grade class by the end of the following day. Upon discovering this, Grace was horrified and told her mother about the whole episode. The next morning, Grace's mother called Principal Rondell to see that Bob and Rachel's appalling behavior was appropriately addressed.

Ms. Rondell and Ms. Park had difficult decisions to make. These decisions were compounded by the fact that Grace's mother said that she was deciding whether or not to press criminal charges against Bob and Rachel. Ms. Rondell called a Department of Education attorney to discuss the possibility of criminal charges, and he confirmed that there is precedent for children being charged under child pornography laws for photographing and/or distributing nude photographs of themselves or friends. Grace's mother could file a complaint that would not necessarily involve the school. As far as school discipline was concerned, Rondell and Park tried to ascertain whose actions would fit various infractions, including sexual harassment. The situation was complicated by the fact that the picture was taken and sent outside of school and school hours. They wondered if they were mistaken in even considering this a matter of school discipline.

Principal Rondell and Assistant Principal Park were convinced that they could, legally speaking, wipe their hands clean of the issue and tell Grace's mother that they have no authority over Bob's actions that were taken outside of school. However, they realized that saying that would likely push Grace's mother toward a criminal complaint and create an extremely serious situation for the two families. In addition, it would do nothing to address the fact that the entire eighth grade was now tangentially involved and the situation might poison the positive school atmosphere that the two school leaders had worked so hard to build over the past eight years. Then again, wouldn't addressing the actions of these students confirm in some parents' minds that it was in fact a school-based disciplinary situation and thus force Rondell's hand in administering the consequences?

In addition, Principal Rondell and Assistant Principal Park were concerned about Bob's antisocial behavior and how rattled Grace had been, and wanted to be sure these children would get the support they needed in order to learn from, heal, and move on from this whole episode. The school leaders were also considering how to better educate students about making smarter choices around cyber safety.

Principal Rondell and Assistant Principal Park shut their office door and sat at their conference table to make difficult decisions before students, parents, teachers, and possibly the police became further involved. Time was short, as the phone would surely start ringing any minute with any or all of those stakeholders expecting answers.

Questions for Discussion

1. Should Principal Rondell have left viewing the picture to Assistant Principal Park? Why do you think she avoided viewing it herself? Was it right to pass on this responsibility? Was Park obligated to see the picture as evidence?

2. Should Principal Rondell have avoided the school's involvement by encouraging Grace's mother to work things out with Bob's parents since the situation did not occur in school or during school hours? Is it ethical for the principal to dissuade a parent from contacting the police? Would your answer be different if the picture did not involve nudity or another potentially criminal act?

3. What is Rondell's responsibility to report the incident to higher authorities in the school district? What reactions or actions would be appropriate for the district superintendent if parents call the district office complaining about a sexting incident between students?

4. If disciplinary action is taken against any student, would Grace, Bob, and Rachel all have to receive punishments, or can you punish one without the others? Should they receive the same punishment?

5. If Grace's mother was president of the PTA, would it change Rondell's response? Should it? What if the PTA president was one of Bob or Rachel's parents? What if Grace or Rachel had a history of suspensions due to bad behavior, and Bob was a popular, straight "A" student? And vice versa?

6. What advice would you give the school leaders? What would be in the best interests of the students while also balancing the school leaders' professional and legal ethics?

CASE STUDY 10.4 NEW BULLYING FOR THE 21ST CENTURY: CYBER-BULLYING IN THE MIDDLE

Dr. Jack Web, principal of Henry Mercer Middle School (HMMS), became involved in this situation three weeks earlier, following a call from a concerned father. Edward Walsh explained that both he and his wife noticed that Sam, their only child, who was normally a reserved, shy, 12 year old, had been acting strangely for about a week. The Walshes had often worried about their overly sensitive son. Sam frequently reported that he was "unpopular" in school. He was insecure about his weight, his lack of athletic prowess, his intelligence, and his love of, and talent for, singing. Glee Club, he often remarked, was not for the popular boys in school.

When Sam presented Mr. and Mrs. Walsh with his first pre-algebra grade of the second marking period, 53%, it increased their concern. It was quite odd, since he had achieved an "A" on his recent report card. They wondered how his grade could drop so precipitously. Although this could explain his unusual behavior they continued to watch Sam, whose state of mind continued to deteriorate. On Sunday evening, right after Sam got off his computer, Mr. Walsh found him sobbing in his bedroom.

"Sam," he said, "please tell us what's wrong. We just want to help you."

"I can't," managed Sam through his tears. "It'll make it so much worse! Can I please stay home from school tomorrow? I can't go in there."

"Sam, it can't be that bad," his father replied. "You can't start to miss school, especially with your pre-algebra grade right now. You have to tell me what is wrong."

To this, Sam erupted into tears again. Alerted to the situation by Sam's sobs, Rebecca appeared in the doorway of his bedroom. She motioned to her husband and whispered, "Edward, go check the computer's history. I'll stay with him."

Mr. Walsh had set his computer to be able to check Sam's chatting on Yahoo!® Messenger. He read the chats and immediately understood. Sam was being bullied online. Edward related to Dr. Web that he printed the offending conversations and went back upstairs to Sam's bedroom. Sam was curled up in a ball, still whimpering.

After being presented with the evidence, Sam finally confided in his parents. He had been in a chat room and received an instant message (IM) from a girl who identified herself as a student in his pre-algebra class. She did not use her real name, but her screen name, Babe-ah-licious555, was provocative enough to pique Sam's curiosity as to her real identity. The girl had flirted with Sam, who was not yet ready for the interest of girls. The mystery girl's flirtations grew more and more provocative, sexually explicit, and personal. Babe-ah-licious was quite advanced for her age. Sam explained that he simply did not know how to handle the content of the girl's messages. In addition, he was also hesitant to get his parents involved because he feared he would be banned from using the computer, and that he would be bullied worse if his parents contacted the school.

Sam had been unable to find out the true identity of the girl, whom he had asked repeatedly to stop her online advances. The scorned Babe-ah-licious assured Sam that she would ruin his reputation at school by telling everyone that he didn't "even like girls." Sam was, after all, in the Glee Club. She punctuated her point by ending with a gay epitaph. Sam was devastated at the thought of being labeled by everyone at his school. "And," Sam cried, "she's in my pre-algebra class and I don't even know who she is!"

After relating the story, Edward Walsh tried to enlist Dr. Web's help. Mr. Walsh opined that, in addition to having his home computer privileges revoked, the issue also needed to be dealt with from within HMMS. Sam was being victimized, which was affecting his pre-algebra grade, as he was understandably distracted during class. At this point, Edward Walsh demanded that Dr. Web find out the identity of Babe-ah-licious555 and ensure that she would be properly punished through expulsion from school.

"Mr. Walsh," Dr. Web interjected, "I'm very sorry that Sam has gone through this. However, other than referring Sam to his counselor, I don't believe I can help you. True—the incident involves at least one of my students, but it clearly occurred outside of school. I can't see how I have any jurisdiction there. In fact, with the anonymity of the chat world, we can't even be sure that this girl is a student at HMMS. I'm afraid I can't go on a hunt for her identity, and even if I found it, I certainly can't suspend a student for things she did outside of school." Although cordial, Edward had ended the conversation and hung up the phone in frustration.

On reflection three weeks later, Jack Web wished he had been at least a little more involved in helping Sam and his family. He had been thinking about the issue in terms of all of his students. The faculty had recently brought the issue of cyber-bullying to his attention, and asked if they could research programs to help the students deal with the problem. Still, he had remained ambivalent about the school's need to be involved in a problem that occurred largely outside the walls of HMMS. Today, however, he wondered if he should have been more proactive. That morning, he had received a surprise visit from the entire Walsh family. Mr. Walsh was obviously irate. Mrs. Walsh, whom he had not previously met, was definitely calmer, but also agitated. Sam looked miserable.

In the three weeks since Dr. Web had spoken with Edward, things had gotten worse. At first, all seemed better. Sam was more confident because he was no longer alone in the knowledge of what was happening online. He had thrown himself into practice for a musical at the local community theater, in which he was the male lead. He was even making some friends in the cast. In addition, encouraged to do so by his parents, he spoke to his pre-algebra teacher, who allowed him to retake his last exam. Sam passed with flying colors thanks to increased homework time, which had resulted from less computer time.

Everything changed, however, on the opening night of his play, which had been the previous Friday. Sam was excited and ready. The performance began well. The audience seemed to love his acting ability. However, during his "big number" his voice, which had recently begun changing, cracked. It happened only once, but it threw Sam off for the remainder of the song. He left the stage in a state of utter embarrassment, which was magnified when Sam noticed some of his classmates in the audience.

The rest of Sam's performances went off without a hitch. He was great— and it thrilled him so much that he seemed to have forgotten about the voice crack. Then things got worse again. The previous night, he had asked for and been granted permission to use the computer for a report he was working on in social studies. When his mother left the kitchen, he quickly logged on to Yahoo!® Messenger. He later explained to his parents, all the while blushing, that he and his female co-star had exchanged information and were hoping to chat online. She, however, was not the first person to IM him—it was Babe-ah-licious. She wasted no time in continuing her reign of terror over Sam. "Thought you'd want to see this dork-brain, I'm sending it to everybody you know!" said the message. Accompanying the message was a link to "YouTube." Sam quickly clicked on the link and his worst fears were realized. There he was, on stage, on the opening night—and there it was—the voice crack! "No!" Sam yelled. His mother ran back into the room to find her son crumpled on the kitchen desk wailing.

When Mrs. Walsh finally convinced Sam to let them watch the video, they were shocked, appalled, and furious. As they were watching, another message popped up on the screen. "That wasn't so 'gleeful' was it?" it said. "Here's another link I thought you'd be interested in, you little. . . ." At this point, Mrs. Walsh remarked that the final word of the message was a word that she would not repeat. She continued, and related that Sam was promptly sent to his bedroom before his parents clicked on the link. They did not want him to be further humiliated. Babe-ah-licious had opened an eponymous and unprotected Facebook account, in which her first and only post was the offending YouTube video. She had obviously sent out friend requests to everyone she knew. There were about 10 comments under the video. Many of these used foul language, and all of them scoffed at Sam. Some made fun of how poorly he dressed. Others blasted him for being overweight. Still others attacked him for a lack of masculinity. The worst were the ones that used the same homosexual slur used in the IM. All of these kids, led by Babe-ah-licious, were really set on making Sam's life miserable.

Sam had refused to come to school that morning—and truthfully, they couldn't blame him. As such, his parents had accompanied him to Dr. Web's office. Mrs. Walsh confided in Dr. Web that they had entertained the possibility of withdrawing Sam from the school, but had decided against it on principle.

Dr. Web replied, "I'm glad. That seems a bit hasty, don't you think?"

Jarringly, Sam's father banged his fist on the desk and yelled, "Web, I asked you to help three weeks ago and you refused. Now my son thinks he's the laughing stock of the school. He's being terrorized beyond belief. To me, there's only one reason to keep him here. It's his home school, and he has a right to a free and appropriate education, doesn't he? But you're not meeting his needs or keeping him safe. I've contacted a lawyer to discuss our rights in this situation. You just may have a lawsuit on your hands. What do you intend to do? At the very least, this girl has to be found and punished."

The worst part for Dr. Web was the end of the conversation. Sam had looked him right in the eye and quietly begged, "You have to stop her, sir. You just have to. Please help me." Jack Web had no idea what to do next.

Questions for Discussion

1. In this situation, none of the bullying has actually occurred in the school. As such, do school officials have an ethical responsibility to get involved? Why or why not?

2. Through which ethical paradigms does Dr. Web seem to make his decisions? Has he demonstrated the ethics of care and the profession to Sam and his parents? If so, in what ways?

3. Does the responsibility of the school rest on whether or not the offender attends the school? What if the identity cannot be ascertained?

4. How can the school, through the ethics of care and profession, help its students develop a healthy identity of "netizenship"?

5. Although he is repeatedly labeled as gay, Sam's sexual identity is unknown. If Sam identified himself as a gay student, would that make a difference in how to deal with the situation? Why or why not?

CASE STUDY 10.5 ALL'S FAIR IN LOVE AND SCHOOL

Dr. Meena Patel anxiously turned the key in the ignition of her car as she mentally arranged what she was going to say to her school board that evening. She had been principal at Crest Ridge High School for the past 10 years and, before that, had taught tenth-grade social studies for 12 years, specifically United States history, a subject near and dear to her heart. Dr. Patel enjoyed her administrative position immensely because she was able to make a real difference in the lives of students, parents, and faculty. Now, she was starting to have second thoughts.

Over the years, her high school, Crest Ridge, had struggled to meet academic standards and maintain a satisfactory level of educational excellence. The mission of Crest Ridge High School was to "provide students with an excellent education while helping each and every child realize his or her full potential to become a productive and responsible citizen and lifelong learner." The school, even though located in a small, rural community, had a diverse faculty and staff which paralleled the diversity that existed among the students. Dr. Patel had worked hard to increase the level of teacher quality in the school by reducing the high teacher turnover rate and attracting new high-quality faculty members who were passionate about teaching. As a result, student achievement had improved dramatically.

With both pride and a profound sense of sadness, Dr. Patel reflected back on one of her most impressive hires, now the center of the turmoil she must address that evening. Over the past five years since his hire, David Wilson had gained a reputation among the faculty as a dedicated and well-respected ninth-grade social studies teacher. Beloved by all his students, he was one of the most popular teachers at Crest Ridge. He was known as the teacher who challenged and pushed his students academically but also treated them with respect and kindness. Mr. Wilson had been instrumental in making changes in the curriculum, spearheading the department committee, and taking on various leadership positions within the school. He designed, developed, and piloted an after-school "Literacy for All" program, for which he had recently gained substantial state funding, thus providing desperately needed resources for students in need of extra help with their academic studies. He had also started an intramural basketball program in an effort to provide students with a safe, non-academic activity they could enjoy after school.

As a teacher, Mr. Wilson was approachable—always willing to talk to and listen to his students. Despite his open door policy with students, he liked to keep his own life private including his personal relationships. All the other teachers knew he was single and were constantly trying to "set him up" with one of their friends or relatives. He always declined, stating he believed that it was important to keep his professional life separate from his personal life. This only strengthened people's admiration of his dedication to his profession.

The problems began with a single incident several weeks earlier. As usual, Mr. Wilson was at work early and, that day, was getting ready for first period. As he was making a final check of any text messages or voicemails before complying with the mandatory "phones off while teaching" policy, he remembered that he had left copies of the social studies quiz he needed for his third period on the copying machine in the teachers' lounge. With a few minutes remaining before classes started, he rushed to get the copies as his first few students began trickling into class. In the teachers' lounge he realized that, in his haste, he had forgotten to turn off his phone. When he reached into his jacket pocket, he discovered that the phone was missing and realized that it must have dropped out of his pocket.

While Mr. Wilson was gone, one of his more outgoing students, Tyler, noticed a cell phone lying on the floor. He picked it up and flipped through it, both out of curiosity but also to determine the owner. Tyler got much more than he expected. Shocked, he discovered several highly compromising pictures of Mr. Wilson and another man kissing. In the most explicit picture they were on the beach, one sitting between the other's legs, leaning back and tilting his head up to kiss the other one. Both men had their shirts off so it appeared that they may have been completely nude. Tyler was stunned, not believing what he saw. Shock turned to anger and images of betrayal as Tyler thought back to the times Mr. Wilson had volunteered to privately tutor him and his friends and all the time spent in the locker room under Mr. Wilson's supervision for the after-school basketball program. As more students entered the room, Tyler decided to share his discovery with his classmates. They began passing the cell phone around so that everyone could see the pictures.

As Mr. Wilson walked back to the classroom he noticed quite a bit of commotion the closer he got. The students started whispering when he walked in and, while it seemed odd, he dismissed it as normal teenage drama. He then noticed the furtive glances they were shooting at Tyler and two students who were gathered around his desk. Tyler quickly flipped the cell phone shut as Mr. Wilson approached: "What is going on here? You need to be in your seats so we can start class. Tyler, what is that in your hand?"

Tyler said that he had found this cell phone on the floor. "OK, well, you know cell phones are not allowed in class," David Wilson calmly replied, hiding his impatience well. "Please put it on my desk."

Then Tyler said: "I wanted to see who it belonged to, so I opened it up to see. Turns out it's *yours*, Mr. Wilson." At that moment, Mr. Wilson realized that not only was the phone his, but it was obvious by his students' faces that they had all seen the pictures in his phone. He felt violated, but knew that he had to address the issue immediately.

Deciding that it would be best to be direct and honest with his students, Mr. Wilson took the phone from Tyler and said calmly, "I understand that all of you must be curious about the pictures in my phone but certain items are private and I would like to keep it that way and not discuss my personal life." He put the phone in his desk drawer and then asked his students to return to their seats, take out their social studies books, and get ready for class to start. He really did not feel comfortable discussing his personal life with his students and hoped that his students would respect his right to privacy.

Despite his efforts to move on and put the incident behind him, the students in his class continued to carry on about the pictures on the cell phone and Mr. Wilson's sexual orientation. He had a difficult time keeping the students focused on social studies. Throughout the day, Mr. Wilson's students had become increasingly disruptive and frequently acted out. He finally gave up and called Dr. Patel to his classroom because he could no longer facilitate his lessons. The students had become either uneasy and distracted or angry and belligerent about the cell phone incident. He no longer had control and, as the weeks passed, the situation worsened.

Word of the incident spread quickly around the school and throughout the community. Dr. Patel started receiving phone calls from irate parents. Some reacted to the incident itself and a few went so far as to ask that their child be moved out of Mr. Wilson's class. The vast majority of complaints, however, came from parents who were truly concerned about their children's safety. Since the incident, Mr. Wilson had been unable to control discipline in his classes. Moreover, there were frequent disputes among the students in the class, with some who felt betrayed intimidating those who supported Mr. Wilson's need for privacy and his sexual orientation.

When she was called down to Mr. Wilson's room, Dr. Patel found a situation more serious than she could ever have imagined. She located a substitute teacher and asked Mr. Wilson to join her in her office. Mr. Wilson explained that he had wanted to keep his personal life private but since the students had seen the picture he had needed to address the issue. He then detailed what was said and the behavior he had had to deal with after he thought that he had taken care of the incident.

Dr. Patel believed that teachers have a right to privacy and should not be punished based on what they do in their personal lives, especially considering nothing illegal had occurred. She also knew that Mr. Wilson had a right not to be discriminated against based on his sexual orientation. Yet this incident had affected Mr. Wilson's teaching, and the lack of discipline in his classroom was starting to result in safety concerns. She was forced to admit to Mr. Wilson that she had no choice at that point but to put him on leave until the issue could be resolved. Now, with a sad heart, she dreaded the evening's board meeting.

Questions for Discussion

1. Did Dr. Patel make the right decision to put Mr. Wilson on leave? Based on the facts, do you think he had completely lost control or that the students were in danger?
2. As an educational leader, ensuring the safety of the students is important. At what point does a teacher lose his or her right to privacy when it comes to matters of safety?
3. Analyze this dilemma through the ethical lenses of justice, care, and critique. What decision would be in the best interests of the students?

4. What should be expected of Dr. Patel through the lens of the ethic of profession?
5. Discuss the conflicts between personal beliefs and professional ethics in this situation.

TEACHING AS SCHOLARLY WORK

Part III is meant to assist anyone who might be teaching or who wants to teach ethics to educators. We begin by focusing on instructors, and in this particular case on ourselves as professors of ethics in educational leadership. We take the reader on a reflective journey. During this journey, we describe how we thought through our own personal and professional codes of ethics, and we reflect on the critical incidents in our lives that shaped our teaching. This self-reflective process helped us determine what we privileged in our classrooms. This section also deals with our approaches to teaching ethics, the issues we faced, the theoretical underpinnings behind our pedagogy, and the value of ethics in educational leadership programs and in education in general.

In addition, in this part of the book, we attempt to provide one model to illustrate the concept of scholarly teaching that was introduced by Boyer (1990), in the Carnegie Foundation's report, *Scholarship Reconsidered: Priorities of the Professoriate*. Through a form of self-reflection and peer review that we developed during a 13-year period, we began to define our teaching of ethics as scholarly work. In fact, some of our published writings on ethics contain sections where we speak of our pedagogy and what we have learned through self-reflection and peer review. This concept of teaching as scholarly work continues to be recommended by Shulman (1997, 1999) and by Hutchings (1998, 2000, 2002) of The Carnegie Foundation for the Advancement of Teaching. It is a concept that we take seriously.

Part III also covers our experiences in teaching ethics to diverse educational practitioners. We explain how we have come to believe that this preparation is needed for educational leaders, especially in our changing and chaotic society, in this new millennium.

Chapter 11

Ethics, Ourselves, and Our Pedagogy

We know precious little about how professors balance the academic ideal of rigorous scholarship with what might be called a core pastoral concern to nurture and challenge the ethical values and world view of their students. Furthermore, we know precious little about the attitudes, beliefs, and personal journeys of educators practicing in educational administration programs. (Starratt, 1994a, p. 100)

Even though scholars may recognize the importance of ethics for educational leaders, they have not yet been able to resolve how this subject can or should be taught. In addition, little research has been conducted on this question (Beck & Murphy, 1994b). This chapter is meant to encourage self-reflection on the part of instructors. It is also intended to serve as a rubric to discuss our methods of teaching ethics and how this approach is carried out with diverse students.

THE TEACHING OF ETHICS: OUR PERSPECTIVE

In this age of uncertainty, with all of the problems that confront us, we think it is extremely important for those of us carrying out instruction in ethics to have a sense of who we are and what we believe in both personally and professionally. In our case, we realized inasmuch as we ask our students to embark on difficult soul-searching assignments, such as developing their own personal and professional codes, it is important that we do the same. Furthermore, as two professors who taught basically the same content in an ethics course in different academic years to similar educational administration doctoral cohort groups, we feel that such explorations may have profound effects, enabling us to compare and contrast how we teach such a course and why we choose to teach it in the ways we do.

We tend to believe what Witherell and Noddings (1991) have written: "To educate is to take seriously both the quest for life's meaning and the meaning of individual lives" (p. 3). We have been affected by the works of Beck (1994), Belenky et al. (1986), Gilligan (1982), Gilligan et al. (1988), Ginsberg et al. (2004), Maher and Tetreault (1994), Noddings (1992, 2002, 2003), Shapiro and Smith-Rosenberg (1989), and others who have stressed the importance of developing a voice and have come to realize that life stories and personal experiences can be powerful. Such stories can help determine who we are today both personally and professionally.

We have also been affected by the work of Bakhtin (1981), Buber (1965), Freire (1970, 1993, 1998), Kohlberg (1981), Purpel (1989, 2004), and others in their quest for dialogue and knowledge of "self" in relation to others. Difficult dialogue leading to self-disclosure can be a most trying process, but it can also assist us in making our once hidden ethical codes explicit. Furthermore, it can take what might be deemed a selfish process of focusing on the "self" and use it as a way to serve and care for others by helping them find their voices and their values.

Before we discuss our course and its pedagogical implications in more detail, we would like to spend a little time providing an overview of our backgrounds and a few critical incidents that have shaped our lives. After considerable reflection, we believe that these stories have led to the development of both our personal and professional ethical codes. We also believe that such self-disclosures are needed to assist us in a better understanding of our pedagogical approaches and how we influence our students (Stefkovich & Shapiro, 1994).

THE PROFESSORS' STORIES

On the surface, the two of us seem to be quite similar. We are both White females; we are both from the northeastern seaboard; we both have doctoral degrees in educational administration from Ivy League institutions; and we are both middle class and about the same age. However, that is as far as our similarities go.

In fact, we are very different individuals. Part of the difference is explained in our education and professional preparation, but this formal education and its socialization does not tell enough. Our stories and the critical incidents within them have tended to shape who we are. We have chosen parts of our lives that we feel have had an impact on how we came to approach the same ethics course in different ways. Rather than pretend that we came to the course with open minds, we think it is important to indicate some of the experiences and perspectives we brought with us.

Joan's Story

When I reflect on my own personal ethical code, I know that I have been shaped by my religious roots as a Jew, and by the area where I grew up, in the northeastern part of the United States, which stressed the Puritan work ethic and a form of Social Darwinism in which individual hard work and competition were thought to be healthy values. The notion seemed clear at that time, growing up as a middle-class child in Connecticut, that we all had opportunity, if only we worked hard.

However, I know that my code of values and ethics has been deeply shaped by the years I spent in college—a time when the Civil Rights Movement was growing. While in college, I gave considerable thought to the concept of discrimination, and I remember many a holiday having verbal battles with my parents about the Civil Rights Movement and civil disobedience. In fact, soon after graduation, during my honeymoon, my 18-year-old British brother-in-law accompanied my husband and myself in singing peace and Civil Rights songs. The three of us were so keen that we were the only Whites attending a rally in Washington, D.C., at which Martin Luther King Jr. spoke. My family and friends thought that I had had a very strange honeymoon indeed.

My ethical code was also shaped by teaching British history in London, England, for a few years to working-class children who had little chance to advance because they had not passed the 11+ exam, a high stakes test that determined if they were university material or not at the tender age of 11 or so. I taught in a secondary modern girls' school composed of students who were either from working-class White Anglo-Saxon families or from working-class families of color from diverse Commonwealth countries. The options for students in this school were generally to become hairdressers, shop assistants, or at best secretaries in the high road nearby. Even when we "went comprehensive" under the Labor government, a tracking system prohibited my students from having opportunities to move toward higher education. In England's secondary schools, I saw injustices based primarily on the intersection of social class with race, ethnicity, or both.

Some years later, I returned to the United Kingdom to spend a postdoctoral year at the University of London's Institute of Education. There I was exposed to the rich tradition of the philosophy of education that seemed to permeate all of education. The philosophical works of Peters (1973) and Hirst (1974), for example, were held in high regard. Peters and Hirst were able to combine the liberal tradition of justice with more of an emotional and caring quality. Their respect for both the cognitive and affective domains had a positive effect on me.

Most importantly, beyond the formal classroom, during the four years I lived in the United Kingdom, I was impressed by British society's ability to combine socialism with the *noblesse oblige* spirit that still existed from the Middle Ages. The government provided national health care, generous university grants for poor students, and welfare benefits that did not stigmatize people. Unlike many Americans schooled in Social Darwinism, I began to feel that society had an obligation to look after its people in appropriate ways, if at all possible, from the cradle to the grave.

Thus far in my life, my consciousness had been raised in the areas of religion, race, and social class, but it took a critical incident for me to focus on the category of gender discrimination. It was Uncle Max's funeral that was the turning point for me in the area of gender.

Uncle Max's funeral took place in the northern part of England, in which a very fundamentalist sect of Jews lived. When my husband and I arrived at Uncle Max's home, the women were moaning and wailing around a hearse that waited outside the door. This seemed strange to me because Uncle Max was well into his eighties and had not suffered unduly before his death. Accompanied by my husband, I went to the burial grounds for the ceremony. At the grounds, much to my surprise, I turned out to be the only woman present and was told not to leave the car. Apparently, women were not allowed on the burial grounds lest they "sully the soil."

This was a painful experience for me. I had only recently buried my father in the conservative Jewish tradition, and my mother, sister, and I had been free to mourn publicly and on the cemetery grounds. It seemed to me that the humiliation for women continued that day when the Rabbi told Auntie Minnie, Uncle Max's wife of 45 years, that she missed an excellent speech he had given on behalf of her husband on the burial grounds. All the women around me seemed to accept, without comment, what I perceived to be an insult, but I was never the same. Gender became an overriding category of difference and discrimination in my life, making me into a feminist.

Seven years of co-directing a women's studies program at the University of Pennsylvania continued to raise my consciousness toward injustices—not just in the area of sexism but in the realms of race, ethnicity, social class, sexual orientation, and disability. In reflecting on patriarchy, power, and hierarchy, I began to realize the great impact of society and how it can manage to keep diverse groups in their place. Dealing with issues of oppression, victimization, and difference, I began to understand how groups have been socially constructed by those in power and the effect of that construction on individuals within the group. Collectivity, social responsibility, and care of others were concepts that struck a chord with me, moving me away from "rugged individualism" and Social Darwinism. Thanks to studying feminist scholarship, I began to question abstract justice, rights, and law.

My background, the numerous critical incidents in my life, the years I spent in England and in the area of women's studies led me to focus heavily on the underdog in society. I seem to care deeply about injustices of all kinds. I ask constantly: Who has been omitted? Whose voice is missing? Whose ethical values am I privileging? Whose ethical values is society privileging? I often think about the good of the whole community as well as the good of different groups within the community.

However, my code of ethics, I now realize, is not simplistic. On issues related to one's body and one's life, I am very much committed to individual liberty and privacy. Thus, in all cases, I do not disdain the rights of the individual. I am, then, a situational ethicist, who leans toward a belief in our need to have a moral commitment beyond self toward those less fortunate and those who are different from us—toward the concepts of social justice and social responsibility.

Privilege

> Leaders need to be deeply reflective, actively thoughtful, and dramatically explicit about their core values and beliefs. (Bolman & Deal, 1991, p. 449)

Initially, I tried to make certain that the graduate students in my course had some introduction to traditional ethics. I provided an overview of the major Western thinkers in the field, focusing on utilitarianism, consequentialist and non-consequentialist theory, and basic liberal tenets of Western philosophy based on individual rights.

The language of rights was further discussed as we sorted out moral dilemmas raised by Strike et al. (1988), and I asked the students to use the step-by-step process advocated in their book. This process moved from the presentation of a case, to the establishment of the dispute, to the setting forth of different arguments, and finally to resolving the dilemma. Although this framework was used, I spent considerable time critiquing the arguments put forth in Strike et al. (1988). It seemed to me important for students to see that a basic text was not the gospel and that there were other approaches that could be used to answer the dilemmas discussed in the book. In many ways, I sought to raise questions that would challenge the liberal democratic philosophy espoused in this text.

Although I did not leave out the language of rights, justice, and law, I had my students listen to other voices and turn to the language of critique and possibilities as well as the language of care, concern, and connectedness over time. These forms of ethics are presented by alternative ethicists.

In particular, to introduce the students to alternative forms of ethics, I spent considerable time in class focusing on the work of Purpel. In his book *The Moral and Spiritual Crisis in Education*, Purpel (1989) described a complex form of ethics that made an excellent bridge from traditional to non-traditional ethics. Purpel himself indicated that he borrowed from "two ancient traditions, the Socratic and the Prophetic and two theological movements: Liberation Theology and Creation Theology" (p. xi). This mix enabled students to move from liberal democratic ethics focused on law and justice to areas of social justice and compassion.

Throughout his work, Purpel challenges us to deal with the complexities and the contradictions of the modern world and leave behind any simplistic notions of right and wrong or good and bad. He introduces important paradoxes, and, in so doing, highlights areas of miscommunication that frequently lead to misunderstandings. These paradoxes include concepts of control–democracy, individuality–community, worth–achievement, equality–competition, and compassion–sentimentality. These paradoxes are maintained by society and they trickle down to our schools. Although Purpel does not classify himself as a critical theorist, he does set the stage for those who challenge the current system, and he makes us reflect on the important concepts of democracy, social justice, privilege, and power as they relate to schooling. Through Purpel's work, I was able to turn to the writings of critical theorists as I felt that the class and I were ready to discuss the writings of Giroux (1991, 1994) who not only challenged the system, but also offered promise through the concept of "the language of possibilities."

Under the concept of the language of possibilities, a number of critical theorists recommend activism and social change. Collective effort, learning through service, and local involvement—what Welch (1991) might call working toward solidarity within one's own community—are parts of the message. In many ways, Purpel, as well as the critical theorists, moves away from the remote, neutral, seemingly objective discussions of rights, law, and justice that tend to be ethical arguments of the traditional liberal democracies and toward the inclusion of feeling, emotion, and compassion in ethics.

Other non-traditional education ethicists I privileged in my teaching were feminist ethicists. To illustrate feminist ethics, I turned primarily to the works of Gilligan (1982; Gilligan et al., 1988) and also to a study (Shapiro & Smith-Rosenberg, 1989) carried out when my colleague, Carroll Smith-Rosenberg, and I taught a women's studies ethics course. Prior to examining the works of feminist ethicists—in particular, Gilligan—I spent time discussing the writings of Kohlberg. I discussed Kohlberg's groundbreaking work based on an analysis of 84 children's (boys') responses to moral dilemmas over a 20-year period and his design of six stages of moral development.

Although I admire Kohlberg's work, I tended to use his scholarship as a way to introduce Gilligan and her inclusion of girls into the moral development stage theory. I then turned to Gilligan as a scholar who was able to critique Kohlberg's stage theory. In so doing, she revealed responses not taken into account by Kohlberg. She introduced us to the voice of concern, connectedness, relatedness over time, and caring. She felt this voice to be important and yet, in Kohlberg's stage theory, it was invisible—hence, many girls and boys who were caring young people often received low scores using his stages.

Gilligan's critique and the work of scholars such as Noddings (1984, 1992), Belenky et al. (1986), and others made me aware that all voices need not be categorized in traditional ethical ways focusing on justice, law, and rights. There are indeed other voices that are important in this society and should be valued. My own experiences in the three years I taught ethics to undergraduates with Carroll Smith-Rosenberg led me to believe that what Gilligan and Noddings had written had meaning.

Furthermore, in Shapiro and Smith-Rosenberg (1989), we discovered in our own classes many illustrations of alternative ethical thinking. We were able to give examples of students' approaches to solving moral dilemmas through their writings in journals that showed how powerful the voice of care, concern, and connectedness was within our women's studies classroom.

On reflection, then, it seems clear to me that I tended to privilege the voice of critique and possibilities and the voice of care, concern, and connectedness over the voice of abstract rights, law, and justice. Nevertheless, it also became clear that although the majority of graduate students whom I now teach could hear all of these voices, some could not. This proved to be somewhat disappointing. However, judging from the course evaluations, the journal entries, the personal and professional codes, the ethical dilemmas, and the comments in and out of class, overall, I noted that most of the graduate students were able to at least stand back and reflect on the concepts of the "rugged individual," individual rights, and abstract justice that previously many of them accepted, without question, as the best principles for our current society.

Of late, owing to terrorism, wars, and financial instability, Steven Jay Gross, from Temple University, and I began to explore links between his concept of Turbulence Theory (Gross, 1998, 2004, 2006) and the multiple paradigm framework in the teaching of ethics. According to my current students, who have begun adding turbulence gauges to the Multiple Ethical Paradigms, this combination has proved to be valuable (Gross & Shapiro, 2004; Shapiro & Gross, 2002, 2008). By becoming aware of the turbulence level, and by sometimes even managing it, educational leaders have another tool, beyond the four ethical lenses, to help them solve ethical dilemmas.

Beginning in 2004, Steve Gross and I also founded an educational movement which we call the New DEEL (Democratic Ethical Educational Leadership). With core values emanating from democracy and ethics, the New DEEL has attracted faculty from over 30 universities and colleges, and practitioners from Canada, England, Australia, Taiwan, Sweden, and Jamaica. Many of them attend the New DEEL Conference held annually at Temple University. Most recently, the New DEEL has become a part of a consortium of international universities under the UCEA Center of Values and Leadership.

A major thrust of the New DEEL is to reintroduce ideals that were meaningful to many of us when we first became educators. Hopefully, the effects of returning to our roots will enable us to critically evaluate external standards, high stakes testing and accountability, and to reinvigorate the values of civic responsibility and social justice. In addition, this movement offers guidance toward developing new courses and programs as well as research and scholarship.

Jackie's Story

My own values and ethical code have evolved through the years. I was raised in a Catholic working-class family in a rural community in western Pennsylvania. It was here that I learned the importance of honesty, respect for others, and hard work. Mine was the first generation in that town that went to college, and my family viewed an education as the most important goal that one could achieve—both as an end in itself and as a way up and out of a tough life.

In the 1920s, the community where I grew up had been a bustling coal town, but the Great Depression hit hard and the mines closed. Most of the men in the town—those of my parents' generation—turned to labor jobs in neighboring steel mills while their wives stayed at home raising the children. The men of my generation—if not college-bound—took on the hard and often dangerous life of an iron worker. The women married young and became hairdressers or, if they were lucky enough to be educated, teachers. There was a definite pecking order in this town. Those who had been fortunate enough to immigrate first, namely the English and the Welsh, owned farms with large houses and a great deal of land. The Irish came next and often had jobs working for the township. At the bottom of this ladder were those who carried with them the stigma of long, funny last names—the Italians and the Eastern Europeans. These were the majority, and I was one of them.

"You have really got to get that name changed," the town pharmacist said to an 11-year-old me as he stumbled over the name while filling my prescription. "Perhaps you will marry someone with a shorter last name." That was the first time I remember the sting of discrimination. It always struck me as odd that my grandmother—who came from Czechoslovakia in 1916, played the piano, spoke five languages, and raised seven children alone after her young husband was killed in a mine cave-in—was somehow inferior because she carried the badge of a long last name. I also shared that disdain from others—and that limitation—because of my name and my ethnicity. This was only one of a number of similar childhood incidents, but it remains most vivid in my mind because it was the first time I came head to head with the painful realization that I might be limited because of something I could not help—because of who I was. Even at age 11, I realized that to be considered as good as other people I would need to do more than change my name; I would need to deny my identity, my culture, my background, and my family.

This denial of self was something that I have never been prepared to do —either then or now, decades later. But I always carried that memory with me and vowed that I would never, at least intentionally, impose that pain or stigma on any other human being. It was not until I attended college in the late 1960s that I was exposed to people of other races and other cultures and, after hearing their stories, realized how insignificant my pain must have been compared to that of so many others.

Thus, a respect for human dignity and a focus on the worth of each person as a unique individual have always been important values for me. These values began early on, but took shape during my college years. I majored in psychology at a time and at a university where a strong liberal arts education was stressed. And quite by accident, I happened to be at one of the few universities in this country that approaches psychology from the European tradition of existentialism. So, instead of running rats in mazes, I studied Kant and Sartre and pondered the meaning of existence, something that, at the time, seemed quite exotic for a first-generation, college-educated female from a blue-collar background. Nonetheless, this experience greatly influenced my present view of life as well as my approach to teaching.

Formal education as a personally enriching experience, as a key to open doors of opportunity, and as compensation to counter perceived short-comings (with regard to ethnicity and gender) has always figured large in my life. I earned a Master's degree in counseling immediately after undergraduate school and, after some 13 years of working in public schools and in state bureaucracy, I quit what my family perceived as a "good" (meaning "stable") job to attend graduate school full time. During the next seven years, I completed a doctorate in educational administration as well as a law degree.

Each of these educational experiences taught me important lessons, and each shaped my values in different ways. It was through my counseling program that I learned the meaning of empathy, a key concept in the profession. "It's not the same as sympathy," I remember my professors saying. "It's being able to put yourself in someone else's shoes, to feel as they feel." It is no wonder that today one of my favorite contemporary philosophers is John Rawls, who believes that a just outcome is one that a person would arrive at having no idea which role he or she played in any given moral dilemma.

As part of my doctoral program in educational administration, I took an elective course with Kohlberg and learned about the longitudinal studies that gave rise to his theory of moral development. It was here also that I was first exposed to the works of Gilligan. It was during this program that I wrote a doctoral dissertation on students' privacy rights and, in my first class in school law, began to understand both the limitations and the power of the law in remedying social inequities. I learned about issues of equity and inequity and about the obligations that we as educated people have to right these wrongs.

At law school, I learned about justice or at least what I have come to realize as a manmade version of justice. I took courses with Lani Guinier and worked as her graduate student studying the Voting Rights Act and pondering the mechanisms of our democratic system. It was also in law school that I began to realize that my long-held beliefs in individual rights could come into conflict with my concerns about equity. This intersection of civil liberties and civil rights continues to influence my teaching, my research, and my personal and professional values. I see the conflict between the two as a source of concern, as a mystery yet to be solved.

Although I have alluded to gender, I mention it this late in my story because I never perceived it as an influential or limiting factor in my early years. I was the older of two children—four years older than my brother—and, in many ways, I was my father's first "son." Thus, expectations for me, as for all first children, were high. I often teased my parents, saying that they wanted a son so badly they named me "Jack," something that my mother —who chose my very feminine first name (Jacqueline) and who spent a great deal of her twenties searching out frilly dresses for me and curling my straight hair—denied vehemently.

The upshot of this juxtaposition between Jack and Jacqueline, between the identity of first-born "son" and Shirley Templesque daughter, was that I grew up seeing myself as androgynous. Obviously I was female, but I never viewed it as a limitation. I felt competent and respected, both at home and at school. When I read about male heroes, I always identified with the main character. When I watched my favorite swashbuckler movies—*Robin Hood* and *Captain Blood*—I was Robin Hood as much as Maid Marian. I was Errol Flynn as much as Olivia de Havilland. To me, neither role seemed inferior; they were instead complementary.

My parents' attitudes about hard work and education as a way to improve social class influenced me deeply. These aspirations affected me no less, and possibly more, than my brother because I was the first-born and also more interested in academics. It was only as I grew older and entered the workforce that I saw my gender as a limiting factor. It was with some dismay, and a great deal of incredulity, that I realized an individual's worth could be diminished and opportunities determined solely because of x and y chromosomes.

Thus, I entered the teaching of ethics coming from a background in psychology and law that stresses a traditional, liberal democratic philosophy combined with values that have shaped my thinking. The latter include, above all, a respect for each individual's worth and contribution, a desire for justice, fairness, and equity, and a high regard for the ability to empathize. How these values are translated into my teaching is probably best reflected in what I privilege, that is, what I emphasize in the classroom, just as Joan's values influence what she privileges.

Privilege

> Ethical education is not a simple training in the predisposition to be ethical, the lessons of which, once learned guarantee an ethical adulthood. Ethical education is lifelong education. It takes place simultaneously with our efforts to be human. (Starratt, 1994b, p. 135)

I began my class much the same as Joan had with an overview of traditional ethics and an exploration of the concepts of utilitarianism as well as consequentialist and non-consequentialist theories. In the beginning, my students were confused when we discussed traditional ethics; they asked for more—more readings, more clarification, more discussion. After all, we had condensed the whole of Western philosophy into one or two short lessons. To compensate for what I saw as an overly brief introduction and to make sure that the students would feel grounded in the traditional approach, I stressed these theories throughout my teaching and tried to reinforce their significance in relation to the more modern, less traditional works of Gilligan, Foster, and Purpel.

I also used several dilemmas set forth by Strike et al. (1988) as a starting point for discussion. Unlike Joan, I did not follow the step-by-step process set forth in the text, but instead made up my own questions. These inquiries generally focused on issues of "What does all this mean?" and "What does it mean to you, personally?" This approach to ethics is advocated by Starratt (1994b) and articulated in his book, *Building an Ethical School.*

Although Strike et al. (1988) come from the same type of liberal democratic tradition that I espouse, I did not always agree with their analysis or with the way the dilemma was constructed. This was particularly true with respect to one situation that involved a principal stopping by a bar on the way home from a meeting only to find his prim English teacher working there as a topless dancer to support her sick mother. The principal was not even sure that it was she until the teacher came up to him later to talk, still dressed in her "costume," a sequined G-string.

The overall situation seems conceivable, but this type of "Marian the Librarian" story in which a woman sheds her conservative clothing and turns into a vamp, although interesting, struck me as lacking verisimilitude. In addition, as a number of students in my class pointed out, Strike neglected to broach the ethical issue of what the principal was doing in a topless bar. If there was an ethical problem here, was not the principal as ethically bound as the dancer? Would the situation have been different if the principal had been a woman and the teacher a man? In a later edition of his book Strike addressed this issue, but at the time of his first edition these questions prevailed.

In spite of the fact that my approach, and my analysis, often differed from that of Strike and his associates, I was fascinated by many of the dilemmas they presented because they were very close to legal cases I had taught in my class on school law. For instance, one such scenario involved a teacher writing a letter, to the local press, that criticized the school. "That's the Pickering case," I thought—or at least a modified version of it. Indeed, Strike pointed out that ethical problems and legal problems are often the same. When I first read this statement it did not quite ring true to me, but I was not sure why. However, after thinking long and hard, I have come to at least a tentative resolution.

Court opinions often talk about justice, a concept that Kohlberg (1981) characterizes as a higher stage of moral development. Indeed, the symbol for the legal system is a blindfolded woman holding evenly balanced scales. Consequently, legal opinions handed down by the courts are considered to be just decisions. This interpretation makes sense to me in relation to Strike's statement. As a lawyer as well as an educator, I believe in the power of the law and witness its justice. I see the good that has come from important legal decisions, such as Brown v. Board of Education (1954), the U.S. Supreme Court's famous school desegregation decision, and Brown's progeny, as well as subsequent federal legislation, which secured the rights of women, linguistic minorities, and persons with disabilities.

However, as Starratt (1994c) pointed out, "What happens when the law is wrong?" Indeed, the law is sometimes wrong, as evidenced by the Jim Crow laws requiring racial segregation and the Plessy v. Ferguson (1896) decision which upheld the notion that separate is equal. Moreover, sometimes the law is left open to considerable interpretation and consequently leaves government officials (e.g., public school administrators) with a great deal of discretion in carrying out legal mandates. Therefore, I agree with Starratt and ask a related question that can be easily applied today to court decisions following Brown as well as to many students' rights cases: "What happens when the law does not go far enough?"

This last question is one I posed to the second ethics class I taught in one of their final lessons. Here, I diverted from Joan's original syllabus and added the facts only (not the legal analysis) of Cornfield by Lewis v. Consolidated School District (1993), a court opinion that I often include in my legal research. This case involved a total nude strip search of a male high school student for drugs. I gave my class the following instructions: "Here are the facts of a court decision. Assume the actions the school officials took were legal. (The federal appeals court for the seventh circuit said they were legal in that jurisdiction.) Are they ethical? And, given similar circumstances, how would you act if you were the school administrator?"

I used this exercise as a vehicle to encourage the students to explore traditional conceptions of justice as well as to apply non-traditional views such as feminist and critical theory. Unlike Joan, I spent little time lecturing on critical theory. Early on, I assigned the same chapters in Purpel's and Foster's books that Joan did, but only used them as starting points for discussion of students' personal and professional codes, and ultimately for analysis of the strip search case. As time went on, I replaced these chapters with articles on social justice, particularly those emphasizing servant leadership and authenticity.

Conversely, I spent a great deal of time on Gilligan's work, but I approached it only after an extensive overview of Kohlberg's theory and his stages of moral development. Probably because of my earlier training in psychology, I liked the idea of developmental stages. In addition, as I mentioned before, I had taken a course with Kohlberg and have always respected his work. Thus, I presented his theory in some detail, noting that his earlier research was seriously called into question as it relates to women because his sample consisted only of men. I also spent considerable time encouraging my class to discuss caring as part of ethics and how this concept fits with notions of justice.

My latest teaching and research efforts have emphasized issues related to the intersection of law and ethics, particularly as it applies to the best interests of the student, a concept that lies at the center of our paradigm of the profession. This is the focus of both my seminar on law and ethical decision making and two of my latest publications (Stefkovich, 2006; Stefkovich & O'Brien, 2004).

Starting in 2007, I have had the privilege of team teaching a course in law and ethics as part of the Summer Principals' Academy (SPA) at Teachers College, Columbia University. During this first summer, I had the delightful experience of co-teaching the SPA course with Tom Sobol, former Commissioner of Education for New York State, former Superintendent of the Scarsdale School District, and currently a faculty member at Teachers College. Tom generously shared his syllabus with me. Through working with him, I was able to gain insights into many of the classical ethics philosophers as well as contemporary scholars. His reflections on the nuances of Nel Noddings' work greatly enhanced my own understandings of the ethic of care and his discussion of authors such as Sergiovanni (1992) and Badaracco (1997) expanded my understandings of both the care and justice paradigms. His knowledge and wisdom gained from years of study and practical experience at the highest levels of education resulted in a truly precious and memorable experience both for myself and for our students.

As is generally true with all my classes, I learned as much (or more) from the students in the SPA program than they learned from me. These students were from all over the country, but most were working in the New York City Public Schools. Some had come from "Teach for America," a program that prepares non-education majors to teach in high-need areas. A large number worked in charter schools and/or had started their own schools. During the past few years, I have modified my courses to include new information and insights as well as to accommodate changes in the student body both at Teachers College and at Penn State and in our society. In essence, my classes have taken on a distinctly global quality reflecting ethical decision making across nations and cultures.

Much of this global approach was also an offshoot of my work with the University Council for Educational Administration's (UCEA) Center for the Study of Leadership and Ethics (CSLE). Joan and I started attending and presenting papers at the Center's annual conferences in 2000. In 2003 with our department's hiring of the Center's director, Paul Begley, CSLE moved from the University of Toronto to Penn State. Through Paul's leadership in the Center, we were able to work with educational ethicists from around the world and directly expose our students to cutting-edge work in applied ethics. In 2009, with Paul's return to Canada, the UCEA center expanded to include our center (which I co-direct), Penn State's Rock Ethics Institute, the New DEEL at Temple University, and associate groups from Australia, Canada, Hong Kong, and Sweden. Currently, I am working closely with this group, as well as with Nancy Tuana, Director of the Rock Ethics Institute, on issues related to moral literacy in the schools.

OUR PEDAGOGY AND THE ISSUES WE FACE

Initially, our teaching of ethics involved a seven-week course, required of all doctoral educational administration students at Temple University. Since many of the students felt that one half of the semester was not sufficient, this course is now 14 weeks in duration. Most recently, at Temple University's College of Education, Steve Gross has presented a New DEEL (Democratic Ethical Educational Leadership) graduate course focusing on exemplars and their values. More New DEEL graduate courses are being designed. In addition, Joan served as the Ethical Threader for the planning process of Temple University's Academic Strategic Compass. In this capacity, Joan and Laurinda Harman, a colleague in Health Information Management, are developing an Applied Ethics Certificate for Temple undergraduates. In preparation for the Certificate, new professional ethics courses and co-curricular activities will be introduced across the undergraduate curriculum.

At The Pennsylvania State University, a new course in ethics was instituted in fall 2004. This course is offered to educational leadership doctoral students for a full semester as part of their cohort experience but is also available to other graduate students. Begun in 2003, Penn State also offers an elective seminar on the law and ethical decision making. Open to all graduate students, this course addresses ethical issues related to court decisions and focuses on the "best interests of the student." Starting in spring 2010, Penn State initiated a course in ethics and education (taught by Angel Duncan), aimed at students in a new undergraduate major focusing on educational policy studies as well as students in teacher preparation majors. In summer 2010, Jackie will begin her fourth year teaching law and ethics for Columbia University's SPA program. The last three years involved team-teaching with Mario Torres, Associate Professor at Texas A & M University.

Although we believe that ethics may be taught effectively in many ways, we have found that dealing with the issues we have come to face—concerns about diversity, prior preparation, and an ever-evolving view of ethics as a process requiring self-reflection—are handled more easily when adequate time is allotted. Recognizing that the teaching of ethics can be difficult, it is our desire to share our experiences with others so that they might learn from both our successes and limitations. It is in this spirit that we describe our pedagogy and the particular issues we faced in teaching ethics.

Pedagogy

Although Joan privileges the ethic of care and critique and Jackie privileges the ethic of justice, our approaches to pedagogy are remarkably similar. We envision our instruction to be reflective, process oriented, and constructivist in that we encourage students not to memorize class notes and ethical codes, but to reflect on their own experiences and through them derive meaning from what they have learned. Our aim, then, is to empower our students and/or practitioners so that they in turn will empower others. We use many of the same readings and take into account diverse perspectives of ethics through the use of the paradigms of justice, caring, critique, and the profession. We employ a variety of teaching approaches including lectures, class discussions, internet discussion boards, and small group activities.

We expect students to keep personal journals as an aid in helping them to reflect on their experiences. In addition, they are required to write reflective professional ethical dilemmas, which use the four ethical lenses to analyze the cases and resolve them. Joan also includes a reflective personal dilemma in her assignments. All dilemmas are presented orally to the class. We encourage students to compare and contrast written ethical codes, both personal and professional, and share their similarities and differences. Of late, Joan and Jackie are including more of a hybrid model of teaching allowing for the use of new technologies and for some student-to-student interactions through discussion boards. As we have taught ethics, we have also encountered challenges, issues that needed to be addressed before we could proceed.

Diversity as a Strength and a Challenge

During the period from 1990 to 1999, when we worked together at Temple University, we taught more than 150 graduate students as part of their doctoral cohort requirement. Joan has continued to teach the ethics course from 2000 to the present, and Jackie has taught an ethics course for doctoral students in Penn State's educational leadership program since 2004, as well as a graduate seminar on law and ethics since 2003.

Probably what has been most striking about our students is their diversity. Temple is an urban university and has been fortunate in attracting students from a variety of racial and ethnic backgrounds. At Temple, some students came from Philadelphia, the location of the university and the sixth largest city in the United States; others came from smaller Pennsylvania cities such as Harrisburg and Scranton. Some students came from other states such as New Jersey, Delaware, and Maryland. Some students commuted from very rural areas, whereas others lived in wealthy suburbs. In one class at Temple, there was a woman from Trinidad, a man from Ethiopia, a relocated New Yorker, and a student born and raised in Pennsylvania Dutch country (home of the state's substantial Amish and Mennonite populations). Temple students frequently come from the Temple Japan campus and from an educational program that is currently being taught in Jamaica.

At Penn State, on this rural campus, Jackie teaches a variety of students as well. A number of students come from the central Pennsylvania region, others commute two to three hours to attend classes, and a substantial number of full-time students come from across the country and the world, representing a wide range of racial, ethnic, and religious backgrounds. Penn State has a well-established Comparative International Education (CIED) dual-degree program and for years has hosted mid-career professionals from emerging nations as part of the Hubert H. Humphrey Fellowship Program. Jackie's ethics classes have attracted international students from both of these programs as well as from more traditional majors. Her international students often come directly from their home countries with the intention of either returning to serve in their universities or ministries of education or to seek education as a means to stay in this country. Penn State also trains individuals in the longest continually running American Indian Leadership Program (AILP) in the country. Here, students may earn Master's and doctoral degrees in educational leadership. These students, most of whom will return to work in their tribal schools, have brought their perspectives to greatly enrich Jackie's classes.

Besides having racial and ethnic diversity, students in our ethics classes have also been different in many other ways. During her years at Penn State, Jackie has taught classes with (to name only a few) American Indian teachers and administrators from tribal schools; students representing ministries of education in countries as diverse as Saudi Arabia, Brazil, and Korea; educators from Guam, Cyprus, India, Kazakhstan, and various African countries; teachers from China, Japan, and Taiwan; as well as many teachers and administrators born and raised in central Pennsylvania, and educators relocated from cities such as New York and Philadelphia.

Turning to religious diversity, although primarily Christian or Jewish, Temple students represented a variety of factions within these religions. These factions, we believe, tend to influence students' personal and professional codes that, more often than not, sound like some version of the Ten Commandments. For instance, some students belonged to Philadelphia's Black Baptist churches. Others were White Christian fundamentalists from a Bible belt part of Pennsylvania. We taught Catholic nuns and a priest, Orthodox, Conservative, and Reform Jews, Black Muslims, Hindus, and Mennonites. We also taught students from a wide variety of Protestant religions, as well as individuals who never mentioned religion as part of their identity. At Penn State, most of the regional students were Christian, but the American Indian and international students represented a variety of religions with the latter including, among others, a number of Buddhists, Hindus, and Muslims.

Graduate students at both universities ranged in age from the mid-twenties to almost 60, and their professional experiences were often just as diverse. As might be expected, we had our share of public schoolteachers and administrators; however, others did not necessarily fit the mold of what might be expected in a doctoral program in educational leadership. Some came from business; others worked in higher education institutions. There were counselors, psychologists, biologists, and English and physics teachers. And, just as we, the professors, came to this experience with certain predilections, so did our students. It was through our pedagogy that both we and our students came to understand our values and the critical incidents in our lives that shaped them.

We believe this quality of diversity accounts for the classes' greatest strength in that it enables different perspectives on ethical issues to be discussed. It also presents the greatest challenges to us as teachers because this diversity proved to be a complex phenomenon that was neither easily defined nor easily handled. As we taught our classes, it became readily apparent that diversity was not so obvious.

We could never really resolve the differences among our students, nor should we. What we could do, though, was employ strategies that would draw students out and force them to reflect on their own ethical codes as well as the perspectives of others in the class.

In teaching ethics, we also had to be very careful to guard against stereotypes of any kind, not just the most obvious—for example, along race and gender lines—but also the more subtle stereotypes based on religion, culture, sexual orientation, geographical location, profession, and previous training. We not only had to check ourselves, but also our students, always challenging preconceived assumptions and ingrained notions. Dealing with diverse cultures, backgrounds, and opinions meant that we, as teachers, had to be constantly alert to what was happening in our classes.

As we taught ethics in educational leadership, we found ourselves grappling with clashes of culture regarding diverse student populations and ultimately acting as translators for our students, crossing borders of gender, race, social class, and other categories of difference to make meaning of others' values, morals, and ethical codes. Through this process, we, too, benefited, growing—as teachers and as human beings—from these experiences.

These strengths of diversity in our classrooms, the challenges diversity has brought, and how we met these complexities in our pedagogy reinforce our earlier discussions on privilege and pedagogy and our acceptance that there can be no "one best model" for the teaching of ethics.

Prior Preparation in Ethics

In addition to these aspects of diversity that provided us with many challenges, another important difficulty we faced in our teaching, and one related to difference, was that most of our students had little or no background in ethics. Consequently, these students were often not quite sure what was expected of them; ethics was very different from the "typical" educational administration courses to which they were accustomed.

In some of our classes, there were also a few students who represented the other end of this spectrum in that they had been exposed to numerous ethics courses, sometimes as a by-product of religious training. However, they, too, faced ambiguity when dealing with our class because, for the most part, their training had been in the liberal democratic tradition as well as the Judeo–Christian tradition.

The first group, the majority, reacted to this ambiguity by seeking more structure. For instance, when asked to write a personal code, there were always questions as to what this would entail and, in each of our classes, someone inevitably asked if we could provide a sample personal ethical code as a model. On the other hand, the few who had had ethics training generally seemed comfortable with this task. For them, the challenge was to broaden and possibly shakeup preconceived notions of "truth."

In the end, as the students grew accustomed to new ways of thinking and became more comfortable with the introspection so critical in this process, they began to see the merit in what had first appeared to be a most unusual classroom experience. It was at this point that many of our students expressed appreciation for this opportunity, some wishing that there had been more time. At Temple, this led ultimately to expanding the original ethics course from a half semester to a full semester.

In her journal, one student neatly summed up this sentiment by reflecting on her own experiences as well as the diversity she encountered:

> A course such as this, with the participants we have in class, would be beneficial to everyone. How many of us get the opportunity to really "hear" the beliefs and thoughts of people different from ourselves in an academic, nonthreatening atmosphere? In truth, this . . . cohort is the first time that I've encountered such diverse people in all my graduate courses. I am constantly amazed at the responses of some of the people in class because they are so different from my own experience and way of thinking. This is truly energizing and I am enjoying the exchange a lot.

Ethics as a Process

We have come to see the teaching of ethics as an ever-evolving process on the part of the professors as well as the students. We believe that conscious reflection about our pedagogy should enable us to be more honest with those we teach and also help us to decide if the pedagogical approaches we select are appropriate for the material to be taught. Self-reflection by professors also models ways to carry out students' own moral self-assessments.

For instance, our students gave us excellent feedback as we modified our courses. They also seemed enthusiastic about the various approaches we used. As one student pointed out, "Each assignment caused me to think about what I thought was important both as a human being and as a reflective practitioner." Another mentioned that "the journals were an

excellent way of keeping track of the cognition and the developing awareness of the participants." A third student added, "This journal . . . [has] . . .
allowed me to read articles and pieces much more critically. It was a
necessary part of my intellectual growth." Others reflected on the need for
codes of ethics. As one student, a White male administrator, confided,
"Often administrators go on 'gut feelings'. . . . This course has been
somewhat difficult for me since it has forced me to think systematically and
reflectively about my motives and actions with respect to values and ethics."

Although we do not advocate "one best model," in our case, we did find
that a substantial block of time devoted to ethics enabled our students to
move beyond their initial discomfort with the reflective nature of the class.
In fact, as these students grew accustomed to the ethical paradigms and
to the introspection so critical in this process, they began to see the merits
of such an approach, and many wished that there had been more time in
the curriculum devoted to ethics. As one student, a female administrator
in her forties, pointed out, "At first I thought perhaps the idea of changing
one's ethics was 'unethical' and perhaps meant that you weren't 'well-
grounded'. But now I think that for some people, a change in their ethics
or morals shows growth and enlightenment."

This course was not easy for the professors or for the students, who
struggled with the reflective nature of the pedagogy. As one professor
who taught the class after us said, "This is a difficult course because you have
to think about it after you have left it, when you go home at night. . . . It's a
course that everyone in our department should teach."

A similar struggle toward understanding is reflected in the words of one
of our youngest students, a suburban woman in her twenties:

> I have struggled to think in the manner that this course has forced me to. It is
> easier to see black and white than gray, but ethical thought doesn't permit
> this. A decision is only fair when all angles are explored and all voices heard,
> and even then someone will always question the decision that was made.
> However, I know that I can be at peace with myself if I have been ethical in my
> thought and decision-making processes.

The reflective nature of the ethics course and the discussion with peers,
in both small and large group settings, led many students to mention that
the ethics class had a positive effect on their doctoral cohort group. This
course was taught in the spring semester of the first year of the doctoral
cohort experience. What follow are samples of reflections from three very
different students who saw this growth:

> I can see the impetus for thought reshaping in our discussions in class. They
> are provoking and, most of all, mind-changing. I find that the course is also
> causing our cohort members to bond in a most desirable way. Our small group

discussions, though often side-tracked by extraneous banter, challenge us and cause us to divulge our innermost beliefs, feelings, and motivations. (African-American male, urban, mid-thirties)

[By] participating in our current class and experiencing the readings, I have felt a closeness to the people in our cohort that I did not have before. Perhaps it is enlightenment or there is less pressure and more cooperation than the other . . . classes which I have encountered. I like the concept of splitting into groups in order to share our moral beliefs . . . it promotes altruism, reasonable people. (White male, small-town, forties)

This course has greatly unified our cohort. In the fall, there were many instances when viewpoints were not respected and differences stood out. We were all very protective of our individual identities. However, on the night we sat in groups and worked on a common code of personal ethics, the aura of competition and individuality melted and made way for a new aura of acceptance. (White female, suburban, twenties)

In Conclusion

Throughout this chapter, we have stressed the importance of conversations between co-teachers, focusing on issues such as who they are and what and how they teach. Such conversations can lead to careful content analysis of what readings and resources are privileged in the classroom. They can also help identify what pedagogical approaches are employed to make certain that the content is delivered to all students. We feel that in-depth, thoughtful, and provocative discussions will help us assess what voices we tend to emphasize when we teach—the voice of justice, rights, law; the voice of critique and possibilities; the voice of care, concern, and connectedness; alternatively, a combination of these voices. It was also through this experience that we were able to recognize the need for an additional paradigm—the ethic of the profession.

References

America 2000: An education strategy. (1991). Washington, D.C.: U.S. Government Printing Office.

American Association of School Administrators. (1981). *Statement of Ethics for School Administrators.* Arlington, VA: Author.

American Association of University Women. (1992). *How Schools Shortchange Girls: A study of major findings on girls and education.* Washington, DC: Author.

American Association of University Women. (1995). *Achieving Gender Equity in the Classroom and the Campus: The next step.* Washington, DC: Author.

Anyon, J. (1980, winter). Social class and the hidden curriculum of work. *Journal of Education, 162*(1), 67–92.

Anyon, J. (2005). *Radical Possibilities: Public policy, urban education and a new social movement.* New York: Routledge.

Apple, M.W. (1986). *Teachers and Texts: A political economy of class and gender relations in education.* New York: Routledge.

Apple, M.W. (2000). *Official Knowledge: Democratic education in a conservative age* (2nd edn). New York: Routledge

Apple, M.W. (2001). *Educating the "Right" Way: Markets, standards, God, and inequality.* New York: RoutledgeFalmer.

Apple, M.W. (2003). *The State and the Politics of Knowledge.* New York: Routledge-Falmer.

Apple, M.W. (2004). *Ideology and Curriculum. 25th anniversary* (3rd edn). New York: Routledge.

Apple, M.W. (2006). *Educating the "Right" Way: Markets, standards, God, and inequality* (2nd edn). New York: Routledge.

Asbaugh, C.R. & Kasten, K.L. (1995). *Educational Leadership: Case studies for reflective practice* (2nd edn). White Plains, NY: Longman.

Associated Press. (2009). Columbine: 10 years later, p.1. Retrieved January 4, 2010 from http://www.msnbc.msn.com/id/30259632/.

Badaracco, J.L. (1997). *Defining Moments.* Cambridge, MA: Harvard University Press.

Bakhtin, M. (1981). *The Dialogic Imagination.* Austin, TX: University of Texas Press.

Banks, J.A. (2001). *Cultural Diversity and Education: Foundations, curriculum and teaching* (4th edn). Boston, MA: Allyn & Bacon.

Banks, J.A. & Banks, C.A.M. (2006). *Multicultural Education: Issues and perspectives* (6th edn). San Francisco, CA: Jossey-Bass.

Barth, R.J. (1990). *Improving Schools from Within: Teachers, parents, and principals can make the difference.* San Francisco, CA: Jossey-Bass.

Beauchamp, T.L. & Childress, J.F. (1984). Morality, ethics and ethical theories. In P. Sola (ed.), *Ethics, Education, and Administrative Decisions: A book of readings* (pp. 39–67). New York: Peter Lang.

Beck, L.G. (1994). *Reclaiming Educational Administration as a Caring Profession.* New York: Teachers College Press.

Beck, L.G. & Murphy, J. (1994a, April 6). *A Deeper Analysis: Examining courses devoted to ethics.* Paper presented at the annual meeting of the American Educational Research Association, New Orleans, LA.

Beck, L.G. & Murphy, J. (1994b). *Ethics in Educational Leadership Programs: An expanding role.* Thousand Oaks, CA: Corwin Press.

Beck, L.G., Murphy, J. & Associates (eds). (1997). *Ethics in Educational Leadership Programs: Emerging models.* Columbia, MO: University Council for Educational Administration.

Beckner, W. (2004). *Ethics for Educational Leaders.* Boston, MA: Pearson Education.

Begley, P.T. (ed.). (1999). *Values and Educational Leadership.* Albany, NY: State University of New York Press.

Begley, P.T. & Johansson, O. (1998, July). The values of school administration: Preferences, ethics, and conflicts. *Journal of School Leadership*, 9(4), 399–422.

Begley, P.T. & Johansson, O. (eds). (2003). *The Ethical Dimensions of School Leadership.* Boston, MA: Kluwer.

Belenky, M.F., Clinchy, B.M., Goldberger, N.R., & Tarule, J.M. (1986). *Women's Ways of Knowing.* New York: Basic Books.

Bennett, W.J. (1988). *Our Children and our Country: Improving America's schools and affirming the common culture.* New York: Simon & Schuster.

Bennett, W.J., Finn, C.E., & Cribb, J.T.E., Jr. (2000). *The Educated Child: A parent's guide from preschool through eighth grade.* New York: Simon & Schuster.

Bilchik, S. (1999). *Promising Strategies to Reduce Gun Violence Report.* United States Department of Justice, Washington, D.C.: Office of Juvenile Justice and Delinquency Prevention. Retrieved January 4, 2010 from http://www.ojjdp.ncjrs. gov/pubs/gun_violence/173950.pdf.

Blackburn, S. (2001). *Being Good: A short introduction to ethics.* Oxford: Oxford University Press.

Blackburn, S. (2006). Personal communications, February 1.

Bloom, A. (1987). *The Closing of the American Mind.* New York: Simon & Schuster.

Board of Education of Independent School District No. 92 of Pottawatomie County v. Earls, 536 U.S. 822 (2002).

Board of Education, Island Trees Union Free School District No. 26 v. Pico, 457 U.S. 853 (1981).

Bolman, L.G. & Deal, T.E. (1991). *Reframing Organizations: Artistry, choice, and leadership.* San Francisco, CA: Jossey-Bass.

Bourdieu, P. (1977). Cultural reproduction and social reproduction. In J. Karabel & A.H. Halsey (eds), *Power and Ideology in Education* (pp. 487–511). New York: Oxford University Press.

Bourdieu, P. (2001). *Masculine Domination.* Stanford, CA: Stanford University Press.

Bowles, S. & Gintis, H. (1988). *Democracy and Capitalism.* New York: Basic Books.

Boyer, E.L. (1990). *Scholarship Reconsidered: Priorities of the professoriate.* San Francisco, CA: Jossey-Bass.

Brown v. Board of Education, 347 U.S. 483 (1954).

Buber, M. (1965). Education. In M. Buber (ed.), *Between Man and Man* (pp. 83–103). New York: Macmillan.

Burant, T.J., Chubbuck, S.M., & Whipp, J.L. (2007). Reclaiming the moral in the dispositions debate. *Journal of Teacher Education, 58*(5), 397–411.

Cambron-McCabe, N.H. & Foster, W. (1994). A paradigm shift: Implications for the preparation of school leaders. In T. Mulkeen, N.H. Cambron-McCabe, & B. Anderson (eds), *Democratic Leadership: The changing context of administrative preparation* (pp. 49–60). Norwood, NJ: Ablex.

Campbell, E. (2000). Professional ethics in teaching: Towards the development of a code of practice. *Cambridge Journal of Education, 30*(2), 203–221.

Campbell, E. (2004). *The Ethical Teacher.* Maidenhead, UK: Open University Press.

Capper, C.A. (1993). Educational administration in a pluralistic society: A multi-paradigm approach. In C.A. Capper (ed.), *Educational Administration in a Pluralistic Society* (pp. 7–35). Albany, NY: State University of New York Press.

Carnoy, M. & Levin, H. (1985). *Schooling and Work in the Democratic State.* Palo Alto, CA: Stanford University Press.

Casella, R. (2003). Zero tolerance policy in schools: Rationale, consequences, and alternatives. *Teachers College Record, 105*, 872–892.

Center for Effective Discipline. (2010). U.S.: Corporal punishment and paddling statistics by state and race, states banning corporal punishment. Retrieved January 3, 2010 from http://www.stophitting.com/index.php?page=statesbanning.

Chen, G. (2008). Communities, students, schools, and school crime: A confirmatory study of crime in U.S. high schools. *Urban Education, 43*, 301–318.

Comer, J.P. (1988). Is "parenting" essential to good teaching? *NEA Today, 6*, 34–40.

Cooper, J.M. (1995). *Teachers' Problem Solving: A casebook of award-winning teaching cases.* Boston, MA: Allyn & Bacon.

Cornfield by Lewis v. Consolidated School District No. 230, 991 F.2d 1316 (7th Cir. 1993).

Crittenden, B. (1984). Morality, ethics and ethical theories. In P. Sola (ed.), *Ethics, Education, and Administrative Decisions: A book of readings* (pp. 15–38). New York: Peter Lang.

Cushner, K., McClelland, A., & Safford, P. (1992). *Human Diversity in Education: An integrative approach.* New York: McGraw-Hill.

Darling-Hammond, L. & Snyder, J. (1992). Reframing accountability: Creating learner-centered schools. In A. Lieberman (ed.), *The Changing Contexts of Teaching. Ninety-First Yearbook of the National Society for the Study of Education* (Pt. 1, pp.11–36). Chicago, IL: University of Chicago Press.

Delgado, R. (1995). *Critical Race Theory: The cutting edge.* Philadelphia, PA: Temple University Press.

DeMitchell, T.A. (1993). Private lives: Community control vs. professional autonomy. *West's Educational Law Quarterly, 2*(2), 218–226.

Dewey, J. (1902). *The School and Society.* Chicago, IL: University of Chicago Press.

Duke, D. & Grogan, M. (1997). The moral and ethical dimensions of leadership. In L. G. Beck, J. Murphy & Associates (eds), *Ethics in Educational Leadership Programs: Emerging models* (pp. 141–160). Columbia, MO: University Council for Educational Administration.

Fine, M. (1991). *Framing Dropouts.* Albany, NY: State University of New York Press.

Fishkin, J. (1983). *Justice, Equal Opportunity, and the Family*. New Haven, CT: Yale University Press.

Foster, W. (1986). *Paradigms and Promises: New approaches to educational administration*. Buffalo, NY: Prometheus Books.

Foucault, M. (1983). On the genealogy of ethics: An overview of work in progress. In H.L. Dreyfus & P. Rabinow (eds), *Michel Foucault: Beyond structuralism and hermeneutics* (2nd edn, pp. 229–252). Chicago, IL: University of Chicago Press.

Freire, P. (1970). *Pedagogy of the Oppressed* (trans. M.B. Ramos). New York: Continuum.

Freire, P. (1993). *Pedagogy of the City* (trans. D. Macedo). New York: Continuum.

Freire, P. (1998). *Pedagogy of Freedom: Ethics, democracy, and civic courage* (trans. P. Clarke). Lanham, MD: Rowman & Littlefield.

Fullan, M. (2003). *The Moral Imperative of School Leadership*. Thousand Oaks, CA: Corwin Press.

Furman, G.C. (2003). The 2002 UCEA presidential address: Toward a new scholarship of educational leadership. *UCEA Review, 45*(1), 1–6.

Furman, G.C. (2004). The ethic of community. *Journal of Educational Administration, 42*(2), 215–235.

Gay, G. (2000). *Culturally Responsive Teaching: Theory, research and practice*. New York: Teachers College Press.

Gay, G. (ed.). (2003). *Becoming Multicultural Educators: Personal journey toward professional agency*. San Francisco, CA: Jossey Bass.

Gilligan, C. (1982). *In a Different Voice*. Cambridge, MA: Harvard University Press.

Gilligan, C., Ward, J., & Taylor, J. (1988). *Mapping the Moral Domain: A contribution of women's thinking to psychology and education*. Cambridge, MA: Harvard University Graduate School of Education.

Ginsberg, A.E., Shapiro, J.P., & Brown, S.P. (2004). *Gender in Urban Education: Strategies for student achievement*. Portsmouth, NH: Heinemann.

Giroux, H.A. (1988). *Schooling and the Struggle for Public Life: Critical pedagogy in the modern age*. Minneapolis, MN: University of Minnesota Press.

Giroux, H.A. (ed.). (1991). *Postmodernism, Feminism, and Cultural Politics: Redrawing educational boundaries*. Albany, NY: State University of New York Press.

Giroux, H.A. (1992). *Border Crossings: Cultural workers and the politics of education*. New York: Routledge.

Giroux, H.A. (1994). Educational leadership and school administrators: Rethinking the meaning of democratic public culture. In T. Mulkeen, N.H. Cambron-McCabe, & B. Anderson (eds), *Democratic Leadership: The changing context of administrative preparation* (pp. 31–47). Norwood, NJ: Ablex.

Giroux, H.A. (2000). *Stealing Innocence: Youth, corporate power, and the poliltics of culture*. New York: St. Martin's Press.

Giroux, H.A. (2003). *The Abandoned Generation: Democracy beyond the culture of fear*. New York: Palgrave Macmillan.

Giroux, H.A. (2006). *America on the Edge: Henry Giroux on politics, education and culture*. New York: Palgrave Macmillan.

Giroux, H.A. & Aronowitz, S. (1985). *Education under Siege*. South Hadley, MA: Bergin & Garvey.

Glaser, J.W. (1994). *Three Realms of Ethics: Individual, institutional, societal*. Kansas City, MO: Sheed & Ward.

Goals 2000: Educate America Act. (1993). Washington, DC: U.S. Government Printing Office.

Gold, E. & Simon, E. (2004). *Public Accountability: School improvement efforts need the active involvement of communities to succeed.* XXIII(11), January 14, Reprint Department.

Goldberger, N., Tarule, J., Clinchy, B., & Belenky, M. (eds). (1996). *Knowledge, Difference and Power.* New York: Basic Books.

Gollnick, D.M. & Chinn, P.C. (1998). *Multicultural Education in a Pluralistic Society* (5th edn). Columbus, OH: Merrill.

Goodlad, J.I., Soder, R., & Sirotnik, K.A. (eds). (1990). *The Moral Dimension of Teaching.* San Francisco, CA: Jossey-Bass.

Gorman, K. & Pauken, P. (2003). The ethics of zero tolerance. *Journal of Educational Administration, 41*(1), 24–36.

Gratz v. Bollinger, 539 U.S. 244 (2003).

Greene, M. (1978). *Landscapes of Learning.* New York: Teachers College Press.

Greene, M. (1988). *The Dialectic of Freedom.* New York: Teachers College Press.

Greene, M. (ed.) (2000). *Releasing the Imagination: Essays on education, the arts and social change.* New York: John Wiley & Sons.

Greenfield, W.D. (1993). Articulating values and ethics in administrator preparation. In C.A. Capper (ed.), *Educational administration in a pluralistic society* (pp. 267–287). Albany, NY: State University of New York Press.

Greenfield, W.D. (2004). Moral leadership in schools. *Journal of Educational Administration, 42*(2), 174–196.

Greenwood, G.E. & Fillmer, H.T. (1997). *Professional Core Cases for Teacher Decision-making.* Upper Saddle River, NJ: Prentice Hall.

Grogan, M. (1996). *Voices of Women Aspiring to the Superintendency.* Albany, NY: State University of New York Press.

Gross, S.J. (1998). *Staying Centered: Curriculum leadership in a turbulent era.* Alexandria, VA: Association for Supervision and Curriculum Development.

Gross, S.J. (2004). *Promises Kept: Sustaining innovative curriculum leadership.* Alexandria, VA: Association of Supervision and Curriculum Development.

Gross, S.J. (2006). *Leadership Mentoring: Maintaining school improvement in turbulent times.* Lanham, MD: Rowman & Littlefield.

Gross, S.J. & Shapiro, J.P. (2002). Towards ethically responsible leadership in a new era of high stakes accountability. In G. Perrault & F. Lunenberg (eds), *The Changing World of School Administration* (pp. 256–266). Lanham, MD: Scarecrow Press.

Gross, S.J. & Shapiro, J.P. (2004). Using multiple ethical paradigms and turbulence theory in response to administrative dilemmas. *International Studies in Educational Administration, 32*(2), 47–62.

Gross, S.J., Shaw, K., & Shapiro, J.P. (2003). Deconstructing accountability through the lens of democratic philosophies: Toward a new analytic framework. *The Journal of Research for Educational Leadership, 1*(3), 5–27.

Grutter v. Bollinger, 539 U.S. 306 (2003).

Gun-free Schools Act of 1990, 18 U.S.C. 922 (q) (1)(A).

Gun-free Schools Act of 1994, 20 U.S.C. § 8921.

Guthrie, J.W. (1990). The evolution of educational management: Eroding myths and emerging models. In B. Mitchell & L. Cunningham (eds), *Educational Leadership and Changing Contexts of Families, Communities, and Schools. Eighty-ninth Yearbook of the National Society for the Study of Education* (pp. 210–231). Chicago, IL: University of Chicago Press.

Hansen, D.T. (2001). Teaching as a moral activitiy. In V. Richardson (ed.), *Handbook of Research on Teaching* (4th edn) (pp. 826–857). Washington, DC: American Educational Research Association.

Hersh, R.H., Paolitto, D.P., & Reimer, J. (1979). *Promoting Moral Growth: From Piaget to Kohlberg.* New York: Longman.

Hirsch, E.D. (1987). *Cultural Literacy.* Boston, MA: Houghton Mifflin.

Hirsch, E.D. (1996). *The Schools we Need and Why we Don't Have Them.* New York: Doubleday.

Hirst, P.H. (1974). *Moral Education in a Secular Society.* London: University of London Press.

Hodgkinson, H.L. (1992). *A Demographic Look at Tomorrow.* Washington, DC: Institute for Education Leadership.

Hoffman, N. (1981). *Woman's "True" Profession: Voices from the history of teaching.* Old Westbury, NY: Feminist Press.

Hostetler, K.D. (1997). *Ethical Judgment in Teaching.* Boston, MA: Allyn & Bacon.

Hutchings, P. (1998). Building on progress. *AAHE Bulletin, 50*(6), 10–11.

Hutchings, P. (ed.). (2000). *Opening Lines: Approaches to the scholarship of teaching and learning.* Menlo Park, CA: Carnegie Foundation for the Advancement of Teaching.

Hutchings, P. (ed.). (2002). *Ethics of Inquiry: Issues in the scholarship of teaching and learning.* Menlo Park, CA: Carnegie Foundation for the Advancement of Teaching.

Hyman, I.A. & Snook, P.A. (1999). *Dangerous Schools: What we can do about the physical and emotional abuse of our children.* San Francisco, CA: Jossey-Bass.

Jensen, A. (1969). How much can we boost IQ and scholastic achievement? *Harvard Educational Review, 39*(1), 1–123.

Kasten, K.L. (1995). *Educational Leadership: Case studies for reflective practice* (2nd edn). White Plains, NY: Longman.

Katz, M.S., Noddings, N., & Strike, K.A. (eds). (1999). *Justice and Caring: The search for common ground in education.* New York: Teachers College Press.

Kirschmann, R.E. (1996). *Educational Administration: A collection of case studies.* Englewood Cliffs, NJ: Prentice Hall.

Kohlberg, L. (1981). *The Philosophy of Moral Development: Moral stages and the idea of justice* (Vol. 1). San Francisco, CA: Harper & Row.

Lareau, A. (1987). Social class differences in family school relationships: The importance of cultural capital. *Sociology of Education, 60,* 73–85.

Lareau, A. (2003). *Unequal Childhoods: Class, race and family life.* Berkeley, CA: University of California Press.

Larson, C. & Murtadha, K. (2002). Leadership for social justice. In J. Murphy (ed.), *The Educational Leadership Challenge: Redefining leadership for the 21st century* (pp. 134–161). Chicago, IL: University of Chicago Press.

Lebacqz, K. (1985). *Professional Ethics: Power and paradox.* Nashville, TN: Abingdon.

Lehrer, J. (2009). *How we Decide.* Boston, MA: Houghton Mifflin Harcourt.

Levin, B. (1986). Educating youth for citizenship: The conflict between authority and individual rights in the public school. *Yale Law Journal, 95*(8), 1647–1680.

Lickel, B., Schmader, T., & Hamilton, D.L. (2003). A case for collective responsibility: Who else was to blame for the Columbine High School shootings? *Personality and Social Psychology Bulletin, 29*(2), 194–204.

Loewen, J. (1995). *Lies My Teacher Told Me.* New York: Touchstone.

Maher, F.A. & Tetreault, M.K.T. (1994). *The Feminist Classroom.* New York: Basic Books.

Marshall, C. (1995). Imagining leadership. *Educational Administration Quarterly, 31*(3), 484–492.

Marshall, C. & Gerstl-Pepin, C. (2005). *Re-framing Educational Politics for Social Justice.* Boston, MA: Allyn & Bacon.

Marshall, C. & Oliva, M. (2006). *Leadership for Social Justice: Making revolutions in education.* Boston, MA: Allyn & Bacon.

Martinez, S. (2009). A system gone berserk: How are zero-tolerance policies really affecting schools? *Preventing School Failure, 53*(4), 153–157.

McBroom v. Board of Education, District No. 205, 144 Ill. App. 3d 463, 98 Ill. 864, 494 N.E.2d 1191 (1986).

Merseth, K.K. (1997). *Case Studies in Educational Administration.* New York: Addison Wesley.

Mertz, N.T. (1997). Knowing and doing: Exploring the ethical life of educational leaders. In L.G. Beck, J. Murphy, & Associates (eds), *Ethics in Educational Leadership Programs: Emerging models* (pp. 77–94). Columbia, MO: University Council for Educational Administration.

Meyers, P.A. (1998). The "ethic of care" and the problem of power. *The Journal of Political Philosophy, 6*(2), 142–170.

Morholt, E., Brandwein, P.F., & Alexander, J. (1966). *A Source-book for the Biological Sciences* (2nd edn). New York: Harcourt, Brace & World.

Morrison v. Board of Education, 1 Cal. 3d 214, 82 Cal. Rptr. 175, 461 P.2d 375 (1969).

Murphy, J. (2005). Unpacking the foundations of ISLLC standards and addressing concerns in the academic community. *Educational Administration Quarterly, 41*(1), 154–191.

Murphy, J. (2006). *Preparing School Leaders: Defining a new research and action agenda.* Lanham, MA: Rowman & Littlefield.

Nash, R.J. (1996). *"Real World" Ethics: Frameworks for educators and human service professionals.* New York: Teachers College Press.

National Commission on Excellence in Education. (1983). *A Nation at Risk: The imperative for educational reform.* Washington, DC: U.S. Government Printing Office.

National Policy Board for Educational Administration (NPBEA). (1996). *Interstate School Leaders Licensure Consortium: Standards for school leaders.* Washington, DC: Council of Chief School Officers.

National Policy Board for Educational Administration (NPBEA). (2008). *Educational Leadership Policy Standards: ISLLC 2008.* Washington, DC: Council of Chief State School Officers Retrieved January 3, 2010, from http://www.ccsso.org/content/pdfs/elps_isllc2008pdf, pp. 1–5.

New Jersey v. T.L.O., 469 U.S. 325 (1985).

Nichols, S.L. & Berliner, D.C. (2007). *Collateral Damage: How high stakes testing corrupts America's schools.* Cambridge, MA: Harvard Education Press.

Nieto, S. (2007). *Affirming Diversity: The sociopolitical context of multicultural education* (5th edn), Boston, MA: Allyn & Bacon.

No Child Left Behind, 20 U.S.C. §1751(b) (1) (2002).

Noddings, N. (1984). *Caring: A feminine approach to ethics and moral education.* Berkeley, CA: University of California Press.

Noddings, N. (1992). *The Challenge to Care in Schools: An alternative approach to education.* New York: Teachers College Press.

Noddings, N. (2002). *Educating Moral People: A caring alternative to character education.* New York: Teachers College Press.

Noddings, N. (2003). *Caring: A feminine approach to ethics and moral education* (2nd edn). Berkeley, CA: University of California Press.

Noddings, N., Stengel, B.S., & Alan, R.T. (2006). *Moral Matters: Five ways to develop the moral life of schools.* New York: Teachers College Press.

Normore, A.H. (ed.). (2008). *Leadership for Social Justice: Promoting equity and excellence through inquiry and reflective practice.* Charlotte, NC: Information Age Publishing Inc.

O'Keefe, J. (1997). Preparing ethical leaders for equitable schools. In L.G. Beck, J. Murphy, & Associates (eds), *Ethics in Educational Leadership Programs: Emerging models* (pp. 161–187). Columbia, MO: University Council for Educational Administration.

Oakes, J. (1993). Tracking, inequality, and the rhetoric of reform: Why schools don't change. In S.H. Shapiro & D.E. Purpel (eds), *Critical Social Issues in American Education: Toward the 21st century* (pp. 85–102). White Plains, NY: Longman.

Olmstead v. United States, 277 U.S. 438 1928, p. 478.

Parker, L. & Shapiro, J.P. (1993). The context of educational administration and social class. In C.A. Capper (ed.), *Educational Administration in a Pluralistic Society* (pp. 36–65). Albany, NY: State University of New York Press.

Pennsylvania Code of Professional Practice and Conduct for Educators, 22 Pa.Code, §§ 235.1–235.11 (1992).

People v. Dukes, 580 N.Y.S.2d 850 (N.Y. Criminal Court 1992).

Peters, R.S. (1973). *Reason and Compassion.* London: Routledge & Kegan Paul.

Plessy v. Ferguson, 163 U.S. 537 (1896).

Purpel, D.E. (1989). *The Moral and Spiritual Crisis in Education: A curriculum for justice and compassion in education.* New York: Bergin & Garvey.

Purpel, D.E. (2004). *Reflections on the Moral and Spiritual Crisis in Education.* New York: Peter Lang.

Purpel, D.E. & Shapiro, S. (1995). *Beyond Liberation and Excellence: Reconstructing the public discourse on education.* Westport, CT: Bergin & Garvey.

Ravitch, D. (2003). *The Language Police: How pressure groups restrict what students learn.* New York: Knopf.

Ravitch, D. & Finn, C.E. (1987). *What Do Our 17-year-olds Know?* New York: Harper & Row.

Rebore, R. (2001). *The Ethics of Educational Leadership.* Upper Saddle River, NJ: Prentice Hall.

Roland Martin, J. (1993). Becoming educated: A journey of alienation or integration? In S.H. Shapiro & D.E. Purpel (eds), *Critical Social Issues in American Education: Toward the 21st century* (pp. 137–148). New York: Longman.

Safe and Drug-free Schools and Communities Act (SDFSCA) State and Local Grants Program. (1994). *Elementary and Secondary Education Act* (ESEA) 1994. Title IV, §§ 41114116, 20 U.S.C. 71117116.

Safford v. Redding, 129 S.Ct. 2633 (2009).

Sergiovanni, T.J. (1992). *Moral Leadership: Getting to the heart of school improvement.* San Francisco, CA: Jossey-Bass.

Sernak, K. (1998). *School Leadership: Balancing power with caring.* New York: Teachers College Press.

Sewell, T.E., DuCette, J.P., & Shapiro, J.P. (1998). Educational assessment and diversity. In N.M. Lambert & B.L. McCombs (eds), *How Students Learn: Reforming schools through learner-centered education* (pp. 311–338). Washington, DC: American Psychological Association.

Shapiro, H.S. (ed.). (2009). *Education and Hope in Troubled Times: Visions of change for our children's world.* New York: Routledge.

Shapiro, H.S. & Purpel, D.E. (eds). (1993). *Critical Social Issues in American Education: Toward the 21st century.* New York: Longman.

Shapiro, H.S. & Purpel, D.E. (eds). (2005). *Social Issues in American Education:*

Democracy and meaning in a globalized world (3rd edn). Mahwah, NJ: Lawrence
Erlbaum Associates.

Shapiro, J.P. (1979). Accountability: A contagious disease? *Forum for the Discussion of
New Trends in Education, 22*(1), 16–18.

Shapiro, J.P., Ginsberg, A.E., & Brown, S.P. (2003). The ethic of care in urban
schools: Family and community involvement. *Leading & Managing, 9*(2),
45–50.

Shapiro, J.P. & Gross, S.J. (2002, October). *Educational leadership in a time of turbulence:
Preparing for challenges by utilizing authentic ethical dilemmas.* Paper presented at the
7th Annual Values and Leadership Conference, Toronto, Ontario, Canada.

Shapiro, J.P. & Gross, S.J. (2008). *Ethical Educational Leadership in Turbulent Times:
(Re)solving moral dilemmas.* New York: Lawrence Erlbaum Associates (Taylor &
Francis Group).

Shapiro, J.P., Gross, S.J., & Shapiro, S.H. (2008, May). Ethical decisions in turbulent
times. *The School Administrator,* 18–21.

Shapiro, J.P. Sewell, T.E., & DuCette, J.P. (2001). *Reframing Diversity in Education.*
Lanham, MD: Rowman & Littlefield.

Shapiro, J.P., Sewell, T.E., DuCette, J.P., & Myrick, H. (1997, March). *Socio-cultural
and School Factors in Achievement: Lessons from tuition guarantee programs.* Paper
presented at the annual meeting of the American Educational Research
Association, Chicago.

Shapiro, J.P. & Smith-Rosenberg, C. (1989). The "other voices" in contemporary
ethical dilemmas: The value of the new scholarship on women in the teaching of
ethics. *Women's Studies International Forum, 12*(2), 199–211.

Shapiro, J.P. & Stefkovich, J.A. (1997). The ethics of justice, critique and care:
Preparing educational administrators to lead democratic and diverse schools. In
J. Murphy, L.G. Beck, & Associates (eds), *Ethics in Educational Administration:
Emerging models* (pp. 109–140). Columbia, MO: University Council for Educational
Administration.

Shapiro, J.P. & Stefkovich, J.A. (1998). Dealing with dilemmas in a morally polarized
era: The conflicting ethical codes of educational leaders. *Journal for a Just and
Caring Education, 4*(2), 117–141.

Shariff, S. (2009). *Confronting Cyber-bullying: What schools need to know to control
misconduct and avoid legal consequences.* London: Cambridge University Press,
pp. 2–3.

Shulman, L.S. (1997). The advancement of teaching. *AAHE Bulletin, 50*(1), 3–7.

Shulman, L.S. (1999). Taking learning seriously. *Change Magazine, 31*(4), 10–17.

Sleeter, C.E. & Grant, C.A. (2003). *Making Choices for Multicultural Education: Five
approaches to race, class, and gender* (4th edn). New York: Wiley.

Smith, C.D. (2009). Deconstructing the pipeline: Evaluating school-to-prison
pipeline equal protection cases through a structural racism framework. *Fordham
Urban Law Journal, 36*(4), 1009–1049.

Spillane, J., Halverson, R., & Diamond, J.B. (2001). Investigating school leadership
practice: A distributed perspective. *Educational Researcher, 30*(3), 23–28.

Starratt, R.J. (1991). Building an ethical school: A theory for practice in educational
leadership. *Educational Administration Quarterly, 27*(2), 185–202.

Starratt, R.J. (1994a). Afterword. In L.G. Beck & J. Murphy (eds), *Ethics in Educational
Leadership Programs: An expanding role* (pp. 100–103). Thousand Oaks, CA: Corwin
Press.

Starratt, R.J. (1994b). *Building an Ethical School: A practical response to the moral crisis in
schools.* London: Falmer Press.

Starratt, R.J. (1994c, April 6). *Preparing Administrators for Ethical Practice: State of the art.* Presentation at the annual meeting of the American Educational Research Association, New Orleans, LA.

Starratt, R.J. (2003). *Centering Educational Administration: Cultivating meaning, community, responsibility.* Mahwah, NJ: Lawrence Erlbaum Associates.

Starratt, R.J. (2004). *Ethical Leadership.* San Francisco, CA: Jossey-Bass.

Stefkovich, J.A. (2006). *Best Interests of the Student: Applying ethical constructs to legal cases in education.* Mahwah, NJ: Lawrence Erlbaum Associates.

Stefkovich, J.A., Crawford, E.R., & Murphy, M.P. (2009). Legal issues related to cyber-bullying. In S. Shariff & A. Churchill (eds), *Truths and Myths of Cyber-bullying: International perspectives on stakeholder responsibility and children's safety* (pp. 139–158). New York: Peter Lang.

Stefkovich, J.A. & Guba, G.J. (1998). School violence, school reform, and the fourth amendment in public schools. *International Journal of Educational Reform, 7*(3), 217–225.

Stefkovich, J.A. & O'Brien, G.M. (2004). Best interests of the student: An ethical model. *Journal of Educational Administration, 42*(2), 197–214.

Stefkovich, J.A., O'Brien, G.M., & Moore, J. (2002, October). *School Leaders' Ethical Decision Making and the "Best Interests of Students."* Paper presented at the 7th Annual Values and Leadership Conference, Toronto, Ontario, Canada.

Stefkovich, J.A. & Miller, J.A. (1999). Law enforcement officers in public schools: Student citizens in safe havens? *Brigham Young University Education and Law Journal,* winter, 25–69.

Stefkovich, J.A. & Shapiro, J.P. (1994). Personal and professional ethics for educational administrators. *Review Journal of Philosophy and Social Science, 20* (1&2), 157–186.

Strike, K.A. (1991). The moral role of schooling in liberal democratic society. In G. Grant (ed.), *Review of Research in Education* (pp. 413–483). Washington, DC: American Educational Research Association.

Strike, K.A. (2006). *Ethical Leadership in Schools: Creating community in an environment of accountability.* Thousand Oaks, CA: Corwin Press.

Strike, K.A., Haller, E.J., & Soltis, J.F. (1988). *The Ethics of School Administration.* New York: Teachers College Press.

Strike, K.A., Haller, E.J., & Soltis, J.F. (1998). *The Ethics of School Administration* (2nd edn). New York: Teachers College Press.

Strike, K.A. & Moss, P.A. (2007). *Ethics and College Student Life: A case study approach* (3rd edn). Upper Saddle River, NJ: Prentice Hall.

Strike, K. & Soltis, J.F. (1992). *The Ethics of Teaching* (2nd edn). New York: Teachers College Press.

Strike, K.A. & Ternasky, P.L. (eds). (1993). *Ethics for Professionals in Education: Perspectives for preparation and practice.* New York: Teachers College Press.

Tek Lum, W. (1987). *Chinese Hot Pot.* Honolulu, HI: Bamboo Ridge Press.

Texas Administrative Code, Title 19, § 177.1 (1998).

Tinker v. Des Moines Independent Community School District, 393 U.S. 503 (1969).

Torres, M.S. & Stefkovich, J.A. (2009). Demographics and police involvement: Implications for student civil liberties and just leadership. *Educational Administration Quarterly, 45*(3), 450–473.

Tyack, D.B. (1974). *The One-best System: A history of urban education.* Cambridge, MA: Harvard University Press.

U.S. Department of Education, America 2000: An education strategy. (1991). Washington, DC: U.S. Government Printing Office.

U.S. Department of Education, Goals 2000: Educate America Act. (1993). Washington, DC: U.S. Government Printing Office.

U.S. Department of Education, No Child Left Behind Act of 2001. Pub.L. No. 107–110, 115 Stat. 1425 (codified as amended at 20 U.S.C. 6301 et. seq.) (2002).

U.S. v. Lopez, 514 U.S. 549, 1995.

University Council for Educational Administration's Ethical Code Committee (2004–2009). Unpublished Document. Austin, TX: University Council for Educational Administration.

Utley, C.A. & Obiakor, F.E. (1995, July). *Scientific and Methodological Concerns in Research Perspectives for Multicultural Learners.* Paper presented at the Office of Special Education Project Direction Conference, Washington, D.C.

Vernonia School District 47J v. Acton, 515 U.S. 646 (1995).

Walker, K. (1995). The kids' best interests. *The Canadian School Executive, 15*(5), 2–8.

Walker, K. (1998). Jurisprudential and ethical perspectives on "the best interests of children." *Interchange, 29*(3), 283–304.

Warnick, B.R. (2009). Student speech rights and the special characteristics of the school environment. *Educational Researcher, 38*(3), 200–215.

Weis, L. & Fine, M. (1993). *Beyond Silenced Voices: Class, race, and gender in U.S. schools.* Albany, NY: State University of New York Press.

Weis, L. and Fine, M. (2005). *Beyond Silent Voices* (2nd edn). Albany, NY: State University of New York Press.

Welch, S. (1991). An ethic of solidarity and difference. In H. Giroux (ed.), *Postmodernism, Feminism, and Cultural Politics: Redrawing educational boundaries* (pp. 83–99). Albany, NY: State University of New York Press.

Williams by Williams v. Ellington, 936 F.2d. 881 (6th Cir. 1991).

Willower, D.J. (1999, October). *Work on Values in Educational Administration: Some observations.* Paper presented at the annual meeting of the University Council for Educational Administration Center for the Study of Leadership and Ethics, Charlottesville, VA.

Willower, D.J. & Licata, J.W. (1997). *Values and Valuation in the Practice of Education Administration.* Thousand Oaks, CA: Corwin Press.

Witherell, C. & Noddings, N. (1991). *Stories Lives Tell: Narrative and dialogue in education.* New York: Teachers College Press.

Wong, S.C. (1993). Promises, pitfalls, and principles of text selection in curricular diversification: The Asian-American case. In T. Perry & J.W. Fraser (eds), *Freedom's Plow: Teaching in the multicultural classroom* (pp. 109–120). New York: Routledge.

Young, I.M. (1990). *Justice and the Politics of Difference.* Princeton, NJ: Princeton University Press.

Youngs, B.B. (1989). The phoenix curriculum. *Educational Leadership, 46*(5), 23–24.

Yudof, M. G., Kirp, D. L., Levin, B., & Moran, R. F. (2002). *Educational Policy and the Law* (4th ed.). Belmont, CA: Wadsworth.

Zangwill, I. (1910). *The Melting Pot.* New York: Macmillan.

About the Contributors

Joan Poliner Shapiro is Professor of Educational Administration at Temple University's College of Education. Previously, she served as Associate Dean for Research and Development, and she was Chair of the Educational Leadership and Policy Studies Department at Temple. She has also been Co-director of the Women's Studies Program at the University of Pennsylvania, taught middle school and high school in the United States and United Kingdom, and supervised intern teachers. Most recently, she is the Vice President of Temple University's Faculty Senate and the Co-founder of an educational movement, called the New DEEL (Democratic Ethical Educational Leadership), with Steven Jay Gross. She holds a doctorate in educational administration from the University of Pennsylvania; in addition, she completed a postdoctoral year at the University of London's Institute of Education. Among her most recent honors are the Lindback Distinguished Teaching Award and the University Council for Educational Administration's Master Professor Award. In the area of scholarship, she has co-authored the following books: *Reframing Diversity in Education* with Trevor E. Sewell and Joseph P. DuCette (Rowman & Littlefield, 2001); *Gender in Urban Education: Strategies for student achievement* with Alice E. Ginsberg and Shirley P. Brown (Heinemann, 2004); and *Educational Ethical Leadership in Turbulent Times* with Steven Jay Gross (Erlbaum/ Routledge, 2008). She has also written many journal articles and book chapters focusing on accountability and gender issues in education and on ethical leadership.

Jacqueline A. Stefkovich is Professor of Education Law and Ethics at The Pennsylvania State University and Co-director of the University Council of Educational Administration's D.J. Willower Center on Leadership and Ethics. Previously, Dr. Stefkovich served as Associate Dean for Graduate Programs, Research, and Faculty Development, and also as Head of the Department of Education Policy Studies at Penn State. She holds a doctoral degree in Administration, Planning, and Social Policy from Harvard University's Graduate School of Education and a J.D. from the University of Pennsylvania Law School. She is licensed to practice law in Pennsylvania, New Jersey, and the District of Columbia. She has worked as a public school guidance counselor and teacher, a state-level administrator, and an educational consultant. Dr. Stefkovich's research interests focus on students' constitutional rights and on issues of ethics related to students' rights and school leadership. In addition to this book, she has authored or co-authored one monograph and three other books on these topics including: *Search and Seizure in the Public Schools* (Education Law Association, 2005) and *The Law and Education: Cases and materials* (Carolina Press, 2006) both with Lawrence Rossow, and *Ethics for School Business Officials* (Scarecrow Press, 2005) with William Hartman. Her most recent book, *The Best Interests of the Student: Applying ethical constructs to legal cases* (Routledge), was released in 2006. She has also written numerous book chapters and journal articles, the most recent focusing on school discipline equity issues, cyber bullying, and legal aspects of data-driven decision making.

Carly Ackley is Assistant Director of Admissions at Johns Hopkins University, Carey School of Business. She earned her Ph.D. in Educational Leadership from The Pennsylvania State University with her research focusing on Green School Leadership and her BS from the University of Tennessee in Child Development and Early Childhood Education. She has worked in both early childhood education and in higher education at the Smeal College of Business at Penn State. Dr. Ackley's research interests include green school practices and environment education, early childhood administration, and values and ethics in educational administration.

Aisha Al-Harthi graduated in 2007 from Penn State University's Adult Education Program in the Department of Learning and Performance Systems with a research interest in distance education and an emphasis on online-based learning. She is currently an Assistant Professor in the Department of Educational Foundations and Administration in the College of Education at Sultan Qaboos University, Oman.

Gregory Allen has been involved in education for 21 years as a music educator. He received his BA from Lincoln University and his MA from West Chester University. He is a doctoral candidate in the Department of Educational Leadership and Policy Studies at Temple University. Mr. Allen's research explores character through the perceptions and attitudes of ninth-grade urban high school students. He is convinced that secondary educators can help to cause paradigm shifts among troubled teenage youth regarding civility and sound moral character. He has also released an album of gospel-type songs called *Greg Allen & Friends/Live in Philadelphia!*

Kimberly D. Callahan is Assistant Principal at Upper Dublin High School, Maple Glen, Pennsylvania. She received her BS from Ursinus College and her Master's in Science Education and Ed.D. in Educational Administration from Temple University. Her dissertation consisted of an action research study of the integration between an academic high school and a technology career center in a suburban setting. Dr. Callahan has conducted several workshops on her primary research interest, the school-to-work system.

Joseph A. Castellucci is Principal of Lower Cape May Regional High School in Cape May, New Jersey. Prior to becoming a principal he was an assistant principal, and before that a high school social studies teacher. He received his Bachelor's degree from Penn State University and a Master's degree from Jersey City State College. He is pursuing his doctoral degree from Temple University where he is writing a doctoral dissertation about school change.

Lynn A. Cheddar is Assistant Principal at Saucon Valley Elementary School in Hellertown, Pennsylvania. After receiving a Master's in Education in Reading from Kutztown University, she is currently pursuing a doctorate in educational administration. She has worked as an Adjunct Professor at Cedar Crest College in Allentown and DeSales University in Center Valley, Pennsylvania. In addition, she conducts workshops and staff development at various educational conferences and in school districts in Pennsylvania.

Robert L. Crawford is a therapist in private practice and the founder of Connections Counseling and Consultation located in Woodbury, New Jersey. Dr. Crawford is a Licensed Professional Counselor and a Board Certified Expert in Traumatic Stress. In addition to serving as adjunct faculty, teaching psychology at Philadelphia University, Dr. Crawford is a consultant with the New Jersey Division of Mental Health, assisting in the development and coordination of disaster mental health counseling services in response to bioterrorism. He also advises the Diocese of Camden, New Jersey, in the clinical supervision of treatment for victims of clergy abuse. Dr. Crawford received his doctorate in educational administration from Temple University.

Addie Daniels-Lane serves as Principal of Patton J. Hill Elementary School in Trenton, New Jersey. She is an experienced educator who has held numerous positions in the field including vice principal, whole school reform facilitator, social studies teacher, and reading teacher. She received a BS degree from Seton Hall University. Graduate degrees include an MA in Counseling and an M.Ed. in Educational Leadership, both from the College of New Jersey. Ms. Daniels-Lane is pursuing a doctoral degree at Temple University, where her research has centered on understanding the impact of the No Child Left Behind, Highly Qualified Teacher mandates on the urban school.

Daniel L. Dukes is a doctoral student in the Educational Leadership Ed.D. program at The George Washington University in Washington, DC. He received his undergraduate degree from Texas Christian University and Master's degree from The University of Texas at Arlington. He is a former high school teacher, honors program coordinator, and high school principal (Model Secondary School for the Deaf). He has an extensive background in gifted and talented and deaf education programs. Mr. Dukes' research interests are in the area of ethical leadership, and his dissertation study focuses on academic integrity policies in public high schools.

Angela Duncan is an Assistant Professor of Education Theory and Policy Studies at Penn State University and serves as program coordinator for the Education and Public Policy undergraduate degree. Her areas of interest include the study of ethics and decision making, especially as it pertains to the differences between public, private, and boarding schools' governance. She has worked in administration at several different types of boarding school and serves as a consultant to the Durango Institute for Co-curricular Education. Dr. Duncan completed her undergraduate work in Music Education at Millikin University. She received her Master's degree from American University in Educational Leadership and Policy and her Ph.D. in Educational Leadership from Penn State.

James C. Dyson teaches eighth- and ninth-grade music in Swiftwater, Pennsylvania. He received a BS from West Chester University of Pennsylvania and an elementary education certification, Master's degree in secondary education, and elementary and secondary principal certifications from East Stroudsburg University. He completed his doctorate in educational administration from Temple University.

Patricia A.L. Ehrensal is Assistant Professor in Educational Administration and Policy Studies at The George Washington University, in Washington, DC. She received her Ed.D. from the Educational Leadership and Policy

Studies Department at Temple University. Her dissertation, *Talking about Drugs and Violence in Schools: Dominant elite national discourses in a comparative perspective*, deconstructed national discourses surrounding drugs and violence in schools in the United States and England. Dr. Ehrensal has published numerous book chapters and articles in peer-reviewed journals and has presented professional papers at conferences in the United States, England, Holland, and Denmark.

Susan C. Faircloth is an Associate Professor of Educational Leadership at Penn State University. Formerly, she served as Director of Policy Analysis and Research at the American Indian Higher Education Consortium (AIHEC), an organization representing Tribally Controlled Colleges and Universities. She is a graduate of Penn State's American Indian Leadership Program through which she earned a doctoral degree in Educational Administration. Her primary research interests include the role of the principal in the administration and supervision of special education programs and services, and the education of culturally and linguistically diverse students with disabilities, with an emphasis on American Indian and Alaskan Native students.

David M. Gates is a high school English Department chair and 30-year high school English teacher. For the past three years he was a Classrooms for the Future Coach. As an Adjunct Professor, Dr. Gates teaches graduate courses in educational administration and research design at Temple University and graduate courses for K-12 educators in the integration of technology and the internet into curriculum and pedagogy. Dr. Gates received his BS degree in secondary education from Indiana University of Pennsylvania and his Ed.M. and Ed.D. degrees from Temple University. His research interests include teacher evaluation, professional development, and the empowerment of K-12 students to meet the challenges of and be successful in the 21st Century.

Loree P. Guthrie recently retired as Assistant Superintendent at the Pocono Mountain School District in Swift Water, Pennsylvania. Prior to entering the field of administration she taught advanced placement senior English for 15 years. Dr. Guthrie was also involved in an educational partnership, housed within her district, for professional development as well as a transitions program for school-phobic children with East Stroudsburg University. She received her doctorate in Educational Administration from Temple University.

Kathrine J. Gutierrez is an Assistant Professor in the Department of Educational Leadership and Policy Studies in the Jeannine Rainbolt College of Education, University of Oklahoma, where she was the 2008 recipient of the College of Education Junior Faculty Award. Dr. Gutierrez holds a doctorate in Educational Leadership from Penn State University where she received the 2006 Donald J. Willower Dissertation Award in Educational Leadership. Her research interests include ethical and democratic leadership, curricular and instructional considerations for educational leadership preparation, organizational theory, and policy implications of legal school case decisions. She has presented her work in law and ethics at numerous national and international conferences.

Jane Harstad is Anishinabe from the Mille Lacs reservation in central Minnesota. She graduated with her Elementary Education degree and a concentration in American Indian Studies from the University of Minnesota, and taught elementary students for 11 years in St. Paul, Minnesota, before completing her Master's degree in Educational Leadership at Penn State University. Ms. Harstad is a graduate of the American Indian Leadership Program, and she is continuing with her doctoral degree at Penn State as well.

James K. Krause is a former Special Education Teacher and Administrator. He is currently an Associate Professor in the Department of Exceptionality Programs at Bloomsburg University of Pennsylvania, where he has been Department Chair for nine years. He also coordinates the Special Education Administration Certification Program. His research interests include inclusive practices for students with disabilities, special education administration, SE teacher education, program development, and attitudinal issues related to disabilities. He completed his doctoral degree in Educational Leadership and Policy Studies at Temple University.

Mary Beth Kurilko is known on Twitter as "girlmeetsweb" and is an Adjunct Communications Professor at Philadelphia University. From 2006 to 2009, she was Director of Web Communications at Temple University in Philadelphia. As Brand Manager and Editor-in-chief of Temple's web presence, she provided web marketing and communications direction across the university. Her prior position was as Associate Director of Undergraduate Admissions at Temple, where she managed the print and e-marketing campaigns for freshman recruitment. She earned her undergraduate and Master's degrees at Temple. Her graduate work in educational administration focused on standardized test score differentials in non-Asian minorities.

Kuan-Pei Lin is Assistant Professor in the Graduate Institute of Educational Administration at the National Pingtung University of Education in Taiwan. She completed her Ph.D. in Educational Leadership from Penn State University. She earned her MS in Counseling and Counselor Education from Indiana University. Her primary research interest is educational leadership and its application in Asian countries.

Hollie J. Mackey is Assistant Professor at the University of Oklahoma, and she is an enrolled member of the Northern Cheyenne tribe. She received her doctorate in Educational Leadership and was part of the American Indian Leadership Program at Penn State University. Her areas of interest include educational leadership, school discipline reform, ethics, educational law, school-university partnerships, multicultural education and equity. She has expertise conducting program evaluations and serving as a program coordinator for the Montana Office of the Commissioner of Higher Education. She has received a number of awards, including an Outstanding Graduate Assistant Teaching Award from Penn State.

Patricia A. Maloney is Assistant Superintendent at York Suburban School District in York Pennsylvania. She is a former classroom teacher, high school guidance counselor, assistant high school principal, and supervisor of student support services. She received her undergraduate and Master's degrees from Millersville University and her doctorate in Educational Administration from Temple University. Dr. Maloney's research interests are in the areas of alternative education and at-risk youth, and she has developed and implemented an alternative high school for at-risk students. Dr. Maloney has served as an Adjunct Professor at Temple University, teaching graduate courses in supervision and school violence. She also taught personnel administration for Temple.

Jeannette McGill-Harris has 15 years' experience in the field of education. She is currently Principal of Cadwalader Elementary School in Trenton, New Jersey. She is a former teacher, teacher trainer, and vice principal. She received her BS in elementary education from SUNY New Paltz College, her Master's from the University of Pittsburgh, and is currently enrolled as a doctoral student at Temple University.

Beatrice H. Mickey is Executive Administrator at the Cobbs Creek Environmental Education Center in Philadelphia. Formerly, she worked as an elementary, middle, and high school principal. She earned her Master's in English education and her doctorate in Educational Administration from Temple University. Dr. Mickey's area of expertise includes school organization, management, and instructional leadership. She has a broad teaching background with experience from the elementary school level, as a reading specialist, to the graduate level, as an Adjunct Professor of Education. Her research interests include instructional leadership at the secondary level, student-centered instructional practices, and the role of the teacher as a facilitator of learning.

G. Michaele O'Brien is an advanced doctoral student in educational leadership in the Department of Education Policy Studies at Penn State

University. She has co-authored numerous articles appearing in publications such as *Education and Urban Society, Illinois School Law Quarterly, School Business Affairs,* and *Education Law Reporter.* Ms. O'Brien is adjunct faculty in the Department of Educational Foundations at Millersville University, Pennsylvania.

Tamarah Pfeiffer is a member of the Dine' Nation and is Todichinii clan (Bitterwater) born for the Metal Hat people. She was an American Indian Leadership Fellow and earned her doctorate in Educational Administration from Penn State University. Ms. Pfeiffer earned her MS from Middlebury College (Breadford School of English) and her BA from the University of New Mexico in Secondary Education with an emphasis on English as a second language. She has been directly involved in Navajo education for the past 30 years as both a teacher and administrator. Her expertise as a teacher/action researcher has also brought her notable recognition with the Aga Khan Schools abroad.

Leon D. Poeske is Acting Administrative Director at Bucks County Technical School in Fairless Hills, Pennsylvania. He completed his doctoral dissertation at Temple University on the Secondary School Accreditation Process. Dr. Poeske taught mathematics for 11 years at the middle and high school levels and also served as a Peace Corps volunteer in West Africa.

Dipali Puri received her Ph.D. in Educational Leadership from Penn State University and is a Research Associate in the Department of Human Development and Family Studies at Penn State. She has taught an early field experience course for pre-service teachers who are freshmen and sophomores in both elementary and secondary education as well as a mid-level field experience course taken by juniors and seniors. She has also served as Editor/Project Director for the Pennsylvania School Study Council. Dr. Puri's research interests include teacher education, moral literacy, teacher leadership, action research, and pre-service teacher identity development.

Susan A. Rosano is a Teacher Coach in the School District of Philadelphia. Prior to this, she was a classroom teacher for 18 years. She received her BA in Elementary Education from Holy Family College. After receiving a Master's in Counseling from Liberty University, she enrolled in Temple University's doctoral program. She has administrative certification in Arizona, California, and Pennsylvania. She also has Pennsylvania teaching certificates in elementary education and middle years English. She is an American Federation of Teachers certified staff developer.

Jason Rosenbaum has been teaching in New York City public middle schools since 2000, where he has also served as a staff developer, curriculum designer, and grade team leader. He received an M.Ed. in Educational Leadership from Teachers College and an M.S.Ed. in Early Adolescent Education from Bank Street College of Education. In addition, he holds an MFA in theater from Columbia University and a BA from Middlebury College.

Elizabeth A. Santoro is an Elementary Principal for the North Penn School District in Montgomery County, Pennsylvania. She has been involved in elementary education for 25 years as a teacher and principal. She has worked in both the urban and suburban school settings over the span of her career. Ms. Santoro received her BS in Elementary Education from Chestnut Hill College, her Master's in Educational Administration from Villanova University, and her Superintendent's Letter of Eligibility from Arcadia University. She is pursuing her doctorate in Educational Administration at Temple University.

John A. Schlegel has been involved in education for over 30 years as a teacher and administrator. He received his BS in Secondary Education from Kutztown State College, his Master's in Guidance from Millersville State University, and his Ed.D. in Educational Administration from Temple University. Dr. Schlegel is Director of Secondary Education for the Cornwall-Lebanon School District in Pennsylvania.

Susan Hope Shapiro is Director of a child care center in New York City. Prior to this position, she was a teacher director at two other centers, and before that a teacher in a preschool classroom. Dr. Shapiro received her Bachelor's degree from the New School for Social Research, Eugene Lang College, and a Master's degree from Bank Street College of Education. She completed her doctoral degree at New York University in the Educational Leadership Program where she wrote a dissertation on the effects of 9/11/01 on early childhood directors. She has also served as an adjunct instructor at Pace University, and she has received external funding for diverse early childhood projects.

Spencer S. Stober is Director of the Ph.D. Program in Leadership and Associate Professor of Biology at Alvernia College in Reading, Pennsylvania, where he has been teaching genetics, general biology, and graduate courses in education since 1985. His research interests include ethical issues in genetic applications, and environmental education. He earned his doctorate in Educational Leadership and Policy Studies from Temple University. Dr. Stober also taught science for 12 years in the Governor Mifflin School District, Shillington, Pennsylvania.

David J. Traini had been in public education since 1978 prior to his retirement in 2007. He holds a Bachelor's degree in Philosophy from

Princeton University and a Master's degree in Educational Administration from Rowan University. He spent 11 years as a physical science teacher before joining the ranks of administration. He served as an administrator at the Cumberland Regional High School in Seabrook, New Jersey, one of the first schools in New Jersey to implement block scheduling. He currently teaches math and science at a small private school in North Carolina.

Monica N. Villafuerte has over 12 years of urban public school educational experience across a variety of disciplines including dance, mathematics, and world language education in New York City and New Jersey. She has taught elementary and middle school grades, working with at-risk, special needs, and multicultural students, including English-language learners. Ms. Villafuerte has extensive administrative experience having served as sixth-grade dean, school programmer, staff developer, and adult high school coordinator for approximately one-third of her tenure as an educator. She has a BS from New York University, an Ed.M. in Education Leadership from Columbia University, and an Ed.M. from Cambridge College.

William W. Watts has been an educator for the past 30 years and is a former athletic director. He is currently the Council Rock School District's Coordinator of Health and Physical Education and is actively involved in his School District's Student Assistance Program, Blue Ribbon Schools Program, and many other school organizations. Dr. Watts earned his BS in Health and Physical Education from the University of Pittsburgh, an MA in Educational Administration from Rider College, and his Ed.D. in Educational Administration and Policy Studies from Temple University. His dissertation study examined school violence.

Deborah Weaver retired as an elementary school principal in Elizabethtown, Pennsylvania. She received her BS from West Chester University, her M.Ed. degrees from both Penn State-Harrisburg and Shippensburg Universities, and her doctorate from Temple University. As a 33-year veteran in the field of education, her professional involvement has included classroom teaching at both the elementary and middle school levels, active participation in education-related organizations, and facilitation of workshops on curriculum, staff development, non-graded education, and aspiring school principals.

Christopher S. Weiler is a sixth-grade teacher at Doyle Elementary School in the Central Bucks School District in Doylestown Pennsylvania, where he has been teaching for nine years. Previously, he taught sixth grade in the Governor Mifflin School District in Shillington, Pennsylvania. He received his BA in Elementary Education from Lock Haven University, his

Master's degree in Educational Technology from Lehigh University, and his doctoral degree in Educational Administration from Temple University. Dr. Weiler's research interests include high stakes testing, the implementation of NCLB, including the impact of adequate yearly progress on leadership, and the use of turbulence theory and multiple ethical paradigms as an educational decision-making tool.

Lindy Zaretsky is Superintendent of Instructional Services and Leadership at Simcoe County District School Board in Ontario, Canada. She is a Sessional Instructor in Graduate Studies at Ryerson and York Universities in Toronto, the Ontario Institute of Studies in Education of the University of Toronto (OISE/UT), and Nipissing University in North Bay, Ontario. She received her Ph.D. in Educational Administration at the OISE/UT where she is a research associate. Dr. Zaretsky designs leadership development programs and sessions for educational institutions. Her research interests include action research and the school improvement process; special education and inclusive governance; social justice and training for leadership; parent advocacy, and dialogical and communal processes associated with partnerships in education.

Index

Note: Only authors and titles specifically cited in the narrative are included in the index.